Christian
Suffering

Christian Suffering

R. B. THIEME, JR.

R. B. Thieme, Jr. Bible Ministries
Houston, Texas

Financial Policy

No price is placed on any of our materials for two reasons. First, this is a grace ministry, dependent entirely upon the freewill offerings of believer-priests. To place a price on Bible doctrine is incompatible with grace. Second, people who are positive toward doctrine may be financially unable to purchase books or tapes. We do not wish to limit the positive volition of any believer.

Therefore, no price list for tapes or publications is furnished. No money is requested. When the Lord motivates a believer, that individual is free to give. When a believer, regardless of financial status, is positive toward doctrine, he has the privilege of receiving the teaching of the Word of God. This is grace.

This book is edited from the lectures and
unpublished notes of R. B. Thieme, Jr.

A catalog of available tapes and publications
will be provided upon request

R. B. Thieme, Jr., Bible Ministries
5139 West Alabama, Houston, Texas 77056

ISBN 1-55764-041-6

Contents

Chapter III   Divine Discipline

Chapter IV   Suffering for Blessing

Chapter V   Spiritual Self-Esteem

Chapter VI   Providential Preventive Suffering

Chapter VII   Spiritual Autonomy

Chapter VIII   Momentum Testing

Chapter IX   Spiritual Maturity

Chapter X   Evidence Testing

Epilogue   Suffering, Happiness, and the Essence of God

Appendix   Divine Judgment in Contrast to Divine Discipline

Preface

Before you begin your Bible study, be sure that, as a believer in the Lord Jesus Christ, you have named your known sins privately to God (1 John 1:9). You will then be in fellowship with God, under the control of the indwelling Holy Spirit, and ready to learn doctrine from the Word of God.

If you are an unbeliever, the issue is not naming your sins. The issue is faith in Christ:

> He that believeth on the Son hath everlasting life: and he that believeth not the Son shall not see life; but the wrath of God abideth on him. (John 3:36).

I
Suffering and Solutions

CATEGORIES OF CHRISTIAN SUFFERING AND STAGES OF SPIRITUAL GROWTH

THE BIBLE EXPLAINS SUFFERING and reveals powerful divine assets for coping with adversity. No believer in Jesus Christ needs to remain ignorant of the causes and solutions to any difficulty in his life. Suffering is not inexplicable. Every instance of suffering has a reason and an explanation.

Christian suffering can be understood most clearly in relation to the individual believer's spiritual growth. From this perspective, adversities may be classified into five categories. Two categories are typical of spiritual childhood; three characterize spiritual adulthood. The two categories of suffering in spiritual childhood are *punitive*. The three in spiritual adulthood are designed by God for *blessing*.

This study will examine the problems and divine solutions connected with self-induced misery, divine discipline, providential preventive suffering, momentum testing, and evidence testing. These five categories, which will be defined in due course, account for all suffering in the Christian life.

The correlation of *punitive suffering* with spiritual childhood and of *suffering for blessing* with spiritual adulthood is not a rigid law. A limited amount of suffering for blessing comes in spiritual childhood, and punitive suffering can hit

CATEGORIES OF CHRISTIAN SUFFERING	STAGES OF SPIRITUAL GROWTH
PUNITIVE	CHILDHOOD
1. SELF-INDUCED MISERY	
2. DIVINE DISCIPLINE	
FOR BLESSING	ADULTHOOD
3. PROVIDENTIAL PREVENTIVE SUFFERING	SPIRITUAL SELF-ESTEEM
4. MOMENTUM TESTING	SPIRITUAL AUTONOMY
5. EVIDENCE TESTING	SPIRITUAL MATURITY

FIVE CATEGORIES OF CHRISTIAN SUFFERING

the spiritually adult believer when he sins or makes bad decisions. The general pattern, however, gives us a basis for understanding the pressures in our lives.

Adversity plays a dominant role in the lives of adult human beings. Suffering is like a parent. What responsible parents do for their children, suffering does for adults. The discipline and restraints of childhood imposed by parents are replaced by the discipline and restraints of adult life enforced by suffering.

As a parent, a guardian, a referee ready to blow the whistle, an authority provided by God, suffering challenges us as believers to utilize the assets God has given us. Suffering depletes our human resources and confronts us with our total dependence on the grace of God. Suffering impresses upon us our need to conform to His plan.

Parents do more than discipline their children. Likewise, suffering is not merely a warning and a restraint but a teacher and motivator as well. Misfortune does not always come to injure, says a Latin maxim. Pain not only discourages us from going in the wrong direction, but it can also help to propel us in the right direction. The proper application of Bible doctrine under pressure produces spiritual growth. We see doctrine working. We experience the reality that God is "a very present help in trouble" (Ps. 46:1). As a result of using His provisions, our love for Him grows stronger, and we accelerate our spiritual advance.

Whether as a guardian or as a stimulus of spiritual growth, all suffering in the Christian life must be understood in relation to the plan of God. Suffering is designed for our good and for His glorification: He is glorified by sustaining and blessing us in *any* situation, whether prosperity or adversity. It is for His own glory, therefore, that amid the hardships and disasters of life God promises, "I will never desert you, nor will I ever forsake you" (Josh. 1:5; Heb. 13:5). He will "never let the righteous [any believer] be shaken [or totter or fall]" (Ps. 55:22). Rather than eliminating suffering from our lives, He gives us far greater benefits by walking with us "*through* the valley of the shadow of death" (Ps. 23:4).

Many principles in our study of suffering will apply to unbelievers as well as to believers, but we will concentrate on Christian suffering. We are studying the assets that God has graciously given to anyone who will believe in the Lord Jesus Christ. We are also identifying difficulties that arise when believers fail to utilize what God has given them.

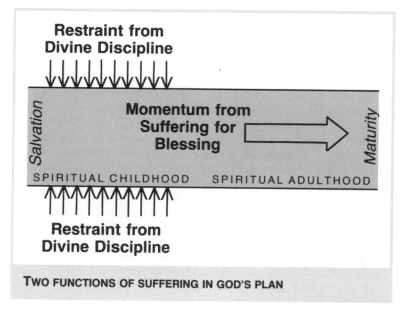

TWO FUNCTIONS OF SUFFERING IN GOD'S PLAN

DIVINE ASSETS: SPIRITUAL ROYALTY AND THE DIVINE DYNASPHERE

UNION WITH THE KING OF KINGS

Spiritual childhood begins at salvation. At the moment anyone first believes in Christ, God the Holy Spirit simultaneously accomplishes seven ministries in behalf of the new believer. One of these ministries is the baptism of the Spirit, in which the Holy Spirit instantaneously places the believer into permanent union with Jesus Christ.[1]

> For you are all sons of God through faith in Christ Jesus. For all of you who were baptized into Christ [the baptism of the Holy Spirit at salvation] have clothed yourselves with Christ. There is neither Jew nor Greek [no racial distinctions], there is neither slave nor free man [no social classes], there is neither male nor female [no sexual bias]; for you are all one in Christ [in union with Christ]. (Gal. 3:26-28, NASB)[2]

The Lord Jesus Christ is the "King of Kings and Lord of Lords" (Rev. 19:16). He holds the most exalted of all royal titles and is head of a new royal dynasty, the Church, to which we belong.[3] During the present era of history, the Church Age, every individual who believes in Christ as his Savior is adopted as an adult son and heir into the royal family of God (Rom. 8:15; Gal. 4:1-5; Eph. 1:4-5). Our adoption occurs at the first moment of faith in Christ, when we are placed in union with Christ (Gal. 3:26). We are royalty now and will be royalty forever. This is our eternal position; in our current experience, however, we must *learn* to think as royalty. We must *learn* to conduct ourselves as royalty.

In order to think and live as spiritual royalty, we need royal assets. Simultaneously with the baptism of the Spirit, therefore, God the Holy Spirit also places each new member of the royal family into a magnificent, invisible environment, a system of living that can be compared to a royal palace. Because the believer's very own invisible palace is a sphere of spiritual power, I have named it the *divine dynasphere*. In the function of the divine dynasphere, God has made available to each believer the exercise of divine omnipotence. The believer's utilization of divine omnipotence will be explained as our study proceeds.

The palace, or the divine dynasphere, is a teaching aid that clearly explains the tremendous assets and privileges that God has given to each Church Age believer. Living as royalty in the palace is a synonym for living the Christian way of life. Only in the palace can we use our spiritual assets, develop capacity

---

1. See Thieme, *The Integrity of God* (Houston: R. B. Thieme, Jr., Bible Ministries, 1979), pp. 105-12. Hereafter, cross references to my other books will be cited by title, date of publication (in the first reference), and page number only.

2. Unless indicated, Scripture references are my translations, representing more literally the original Hebrew or Greek text. References marked AV are quoted from the Authorized Version (King James); NASB, from the New American Standard Bible; and NIV, from the New International Version. Bracketed commentary reflects Bible class lectures (available on tape from R. B. Thieme, Jr., Bible Ministries, Houston) or correlates the quotation with the topic at hand.

3. See Thieme, *Christian Integrity* (1984), pp. 9-12.

for life, and live with wisdom, happiness, and graciousness as the spiritual aristocrats we are. Furthermore, the palace is the only sphere in which Christian growth can occur.

THE PROTOCOL PLAN OF GOD

Royalty lives by protocol. The Christian way of life can be called the *protocol plan of God* because the system—the divine dynasphere—for utilizing God's power is a system of protocol. God designed the Christian life; we must do things His way. Protocol is a rigid, long-established code prescribing complete deference to superior rank and strict adherence to due order of precedence and precisely correct procedure.[4] Each element in Webster's definition describes the plan of God for the believer's life.

1. LONG-ESTABLISHED CODE: *in eternity past* God created for each Church Age believer a rich portfolio of blessings, which glorifies God, who also designed the divine dynasphere as our means of taking distribution of those blessings (Eph. 1:3-4).

2. DEFERENCE TO SUPERIOR RANK: *sovereign and omnipotent God* holds infinitely superior rank.

3. DUE ORDER OF PRECEDENCE: the *highest priority* in our scale of values must be learning the Word of God, Bible doctrine, which teaches us *what* assets we possess and explains *how* to utilize them.

4. PRECISELY CORRECT PROCEDURE: only by adhering to *God's precise policies* for the royal family do we fulfill the conditions for receiving our blessings created in eternity past that glorify God.

Divine *grace* has created a royal way of life which divine *authority* commands the royal believer to execute. We are responsible for fulfilling the protocol plan of God, but God never issues an order for which He has not already provided the means of execution. To obey God's commands is to tap His resources.

THE GATES OF THE PALACE

The commands of God are like gates that open upon divine assets. The believer passes through these gates and uses his God-given assets by consistently

---

4. *Webster's Third New International Dictionary,* s.v. "protocol."

learning and obeying God's mandates, by following divine protocol. Obedience to divine authority puts the power of God into effect in the believer's life.

Although hundreds of divine mandates for the royal family are found in the New Testament, all of these commands can be classified into eight categories. I call these categories the gates of the believer's magnificent, invisible palace. The divine dynasphere consolidates God's mandates for the Christian life into one consistent, comprehensive system.

In *Christian Integrity* the divine dynasphere is developed in detail, but here a brief description of the eight gates will suffice, along with examples of divine mandates pertinent to each gate. This section of the book outlines the divine dynasphere; the next will fill in the outline, revealing the dynamics of the believer's palace when he faces suffering.

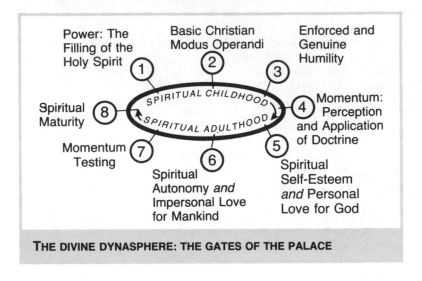

THE DIVINE DYNASPHERE: THE GATES OF THE PALACE

GATE 1, THE POWER GATE, is the silent, invisible, enabling ministry of the Holy Spirit. Omnipotent God the Holy Spirit sustains the believer, supplying the supernatural means of executing the supernatural Christian way of life.

Be filled with the Holy Spirit. (Eph. 5:18*b*)

Keep walking by means of the Spirit. (Gal. 5:16)

GATE 2, THE GATE OF BASIC CHRISTIAN *MODUS OPERANDI*, is the source of the believer's objectivity. In Gate 2, the most elementary systems of problem solving are available to the immature believer, which include the following:

The *Rebound Technique* is the grace means of restoring the believer to temporal fellowship with God after sin has broken that fellowship.[5] The believer initially enters Gate 1 at salvation, but he exits the divine dynasphere when he sins. He can reenter only through Gate 1. When the Christian follows the simple, grace mechanics of reentry, the Holy Spirit automatically resumes control of the believer's soul, restoring him to fellowship with God.

> If we acknowledge our sins [to God the Father], He is faithful and just so that He forgives us our sins and also cleanses us from all unrighteousness. (1 John 1:9)

Through the *Faith-Rest Drill* the believer mixes the promises of God with faith and thinks rationally to reach doctrinal conclusions (cf., Heb. 4:1-2).[6]

> In fact, we know that to those who love God, He works all things together for the good . . . To what conclusion are we forced, face to face with these things? If God [is] for us, who [can be] against us? (Rom. 8:28-31)

Hope is the believer's anticipation of promised blessings and his initial basis for motivation.[7]

> With reference to the hope, keep on rejoicing. (Rom. 12:12*a*)

GATE 3, THE GATE OF ENFORCED AND GENUINE HUMILITY, makes the believer teachable.

> Clothe yourselves with humility toward one another, for God is opposed to the proud, but gives grace to the humble. Humble yourselves, therefore, under the mighty hand of God, that He may exalt you at the proper time. (1 Pet. 5:5*b*-6, NASB)

GATE 4, THE MOMENTUM GATE, is designed for intake, metabolization, and application of Bible doctrine, which cause spiritual growth and personal love for God.

---

5. See Thieme, *The Plan of God* (1973).
6. See Thieme, *The Faith-Rest Life* (1961).
7. See *Integrity of God*, pp. 142-45, 165-84.

> Man shall not live on bread alone, but on every word that
> proceeds out of the mouth of God. (Matt. 4:4b, NASB)

GATE 5, THE GATE OF SPIRITUAL SELF-ESTEEM, is the entrance in-
to spiritual adulthood. Spiritual self-esteem is the strength of soul that comes
from personal love for God. Love for God is the spiritually adult Christian's
motivation in life. Spiritual self-esteem is also the beginning of sharing the happiness of God.

> For me, living is Christ, and dying is advantage. (Phil. 1:21)

> And you shall love the Lord your God with all your heart,
> and with all your soul, and with all your mind, and with all
> your strength. (Mark 12:30, NASB)

> Though you have not seen Him, you love Him, and even
> though you do not see Him now but believe in Him [Bible
> doctrine in the soul] you rejoice with an inexpressible and
> glorious happiness. (1 Pet. 1:8)

GATE 6, THE GATE OF SPIRITUAL AUTONOMY, is the stability of
spiritual adulthood, characterized by impersonal love for other people. Impersonal love is the functional virtue of the spiritually adult Christian toward all
mankind. Deriving its strength from the virtue of the believer himself rather than
being limited by questions of attractiveness or compatibility with others, impersonal love is the foundation for every correct mental attitude toward people.[8]

> You shall love your neighbor as yourself. (Mark 12:31b,
> NASB)

> Love your enemies and pray for those who persecute you.
> (Matt. 5:44b, NASB)

GATE 7, THE GATE OF MOMENTUM TESTING, involves suffering
which accelerates the believer's advance from spiritual autonomy to spiritual
maturity. Gate 7 is one of the categories of suffering for blessing.

> I press on toward the goal for the prize of that upward call
> from God in Christ Jesus, therefore, as many as are spiritual
> adults, let us keep on thinking this [the aggressive mental at-
> titude to continue advancing spiritually under pressure].
> (Phil. 3:14-15a)

---

8.   For a description of impersonal love, see pp. 83-87.

GATE 8, THE WINNER'S GATE, is the gate of spiritual maturity. This is the most advanced level of spiritual adulthood, in which God is glorified and the believer is blessed to the maximum under all circumstances, whether prosperity or adversity. The adult believer's inner happiness is stabilized and completely established in spiritual maturity.

> If you keep My mandates, you will reside in the sphere of My love [the divine dynasphere], just as I [the humanity of Christ] have fulfilled the mandates of My Father [who created the divine dynasphere] and I reside in the sphere of His love [during His first advent Christ lived in the proto-type of the divine dynasphere]. I have taught you these things that My happiness might be in you and that your hap-piness might be completed [spiritual maturity]. (John 15:10-11)

When the Holy Spirit placed us in the palace of the divine dynasphere, God the Father intended us to live there, not to get out of fellowship with Him through sin and move into the dungeon of Satan's counterfeit systems.[9]

We are spiritual royalty, however, regardless of where we live: our salva-tion is eternally secure. But we must reside in our palace to solve the problems of suffering and to grow spiritually. God's plan calls for us to handle suffering from inside the palace. Only in the palace is His omnipotence at our disposal for handling the problems of life.

CATALOG OF THE BELIEVER'S PROBLEM-SOLVING DEVICES

PROBLEM SOLVING IN SPIRITUAL CHILDHOOD

Each gate of the palace contains divine assets that may be used to solve par-ticular problems that cause or accompany suffering. What difficulties do these eight gates solve? To help the believer recall and utilize the grace of God in the midst of overwhelming pain, the divine provisions for problem solving are best described in highly objective language. The power and grace of God, therefore, will be presented in terms of "problem-solving devices." This terminology may sound harsh and mechanical, but there is a reason for it.

---

9. Satan's objective is to use mankind to prove his own superiority over God. The devil's multifaceted policy for achieving this goal is called the *cosmic system*. His diverse tactics express one strategy, which either encourages human arrogance or sponsors human an-tagonism to God. See *Christian Integrity*, pp. 158-70.

Under pressure the believer needs truth. If he is coddled, he may be in danger of intensifying his problem by slipping into self-pity. No one with integrity wants to feel sorry for himself. Furthermore, under stress the believer needs straight answers. He does not need a lot of beautiful language. His emotions are already highly charged, and emotionalism offers no hope of stabilizing him. Certainly the grace of God can be described in beautiful, poetic terms, but emotional stimulation will not solve the problem and might only complicate the Christian's suffering which already is difficult enough.

The purpose for the terminology I have chosen is to make absolutely clear to the suffering believer that God has provided real assets that both transcend his current misery and offer him effective help in time of need. The purpose is not to commiserate or to comfort him. This human dimension of the problem is not to be ignored, but that is not the focus of this book. This book is intended to *teach* and to present a system of orthodox doctrine with tremendous practical application.

Simple problem-solving devices are available for spiritual childhood in the first four gates of the divine dynasphere. More powerful problem-solving devices become effective in spiritual adulthood in the final four gates.

The Christian way of life is a supernatural way of life that demands a supernatural means of execution. The only power equivalent to the demand is the omnipotence of God. Therefore, Gate 1 is the invisible, behind-the-scenes ministry of God the Holy Spirit in the believer's life. The Holy Spirit administers Gate 1 entirely by Himself from His divine omnipotence. We contribute nothing. We merely ensure that we give Him control of our lives by using the rebound technique. Rebound is the believer's first responsibility in Gate 2.

Rebound, faith-rest, and hope are basic problem-solving devices found in Gate 2. *Rebound* allows the believer to reside consistently in his palace. It switches on the power of Gate 1. Because the spiritual child (indeed, every believer) is prone to leaving his palace (1 John 1:8, 10), he must quickly learn how to reenter. He exits the divine dynasphere by committing sin; he reenters by naming that sin to God (1 John 1:9). I call this divine provision the rebound technique because it causes the believer to bounce back after failure, restoring his fellowship with God, avoiding the trap of a guilt complex.[10]

The next problem-solving device in the Christian way of life is faith-rest, which enables the believer to control his own mental attitude. Emotion is a blessing, but it can also be a terrible cursing when it sweeps away reason. If emotion dominates thought in a crisis, the result can be disastrous. The spiritual child needs to know how to remain lucid when his emotions rise, how to think clearly under pressure. The accurate application of doctrine appropriate to a crisis

---

10.   See Thieme, *Rebound and Keep Moving* (1973).

demands a stabilized mentality. How does the distraught believer regain and maintain his self-control? The solution is the *faith-rest drill*. A confusing, complicated situation must first be reduced to utter simplicity by claiming stated promises of God (Heb. 4:1-3). Stabilized by divine promises, he can recall principles he has learned and eventually reach doctrinal conclusions. From the divine viewpoint he can then deal with the complexities of the situation.[11]

Another basic problem-solving device in Gate 2 is called "hope" in the Bible. Hope answers the question "Where am I going in life?" The believer learns pertinent doctrine about his own future blessings; his eager anticipation, or hope, of receiving those blessings motivates him to keep advancing in the protocol plan of God. Hope begins as a basic problem-solving device in Gate 2, but increases in strength as the believer grows spiritually. As a result, hope also becomes one of the key problem-solving devices of spiritual adulthood.

Arrogance is the believer's worst enemy. What is the immediate and long-term solution to the insidious, multifaceted problem of arrogance? In Gate 3, *enforced humility* is an immediate problem-solving device as the believer submits to the authority of God's system. Obedience to divine protocol means using perfect divine assets rather than trusting inferior human ability. As the believer learns more doctrine, he understands the reasons behind God's commands and sees how His commands reveal His matchless character. With a growing knowledge of Bible doctrine, enforced humility becomes *genuine humility,* the foundation for personal love for God.

The most critical issue in the believer's life is how does he solve the problem of ignorance? At salvation he knows nothing of God and His protocol plan. The solution in Gate 4 includes tremendous divine assets for learning, metabolizing, and applying the Mind of Christ (1 Cor. 2:16).[12]

The Bible draws an analogy between eating food and learning doctrine, which is the believer's spiritual food (Deut. 8:3; Matt. 4:4). Just as food must be metabolized to sustain the body, so doctrine must be metabolized before it is usable in spiritual growth, application, or problem solving. Someone may order a meal at a restaurant, and the food, if well presented, may be attractive to the eye. But the food nourishes him only when he eats it. Likewise, the believer learns doctrine academically, but doctrine benefits him only when he believes what he has learned. He must integrate the new doctrine he hears with the rest of the doctrine he knows for that new truth to contribute to his spiritual growth. To dispel his ignorance, the believer must establish a firm policy of learning Bible doctrine every day. He must always organize his day to accomplish his first priority, the assimilation of God's Word.

---

11. See *Christian Integrity,* pp. 102-9.
12. See *Integrity of God,* pp. 1-4.

PROBLEM SOLVING IN SPIRITUAL ADULTHOOD

Spiritual childhood continues from salvation until the believer reaches Gate 5, which is personal love for God. Spiritual adulthood extends from Gate 5 all the way to Gate 8, the winner's gate.

As the Christian moves into spiritual adulthood he finds solutions to many problems. How can he love God whom he cannot see? How can he have an objective yet positive attitude toward self, even though he knows his own flaws and weaknesses? How can he tolerate obnoxious, antagonistic people? How can he avoid being distracted by the people he loves?

These are problems in relationships, and the solutions lie in *virtue-love*. Virtue-love is the combination of Gates 5 and 6 of the divine dynasphere, which include personal love for God, spiritual self-esteem, spiritual autonomy, and impersonal love for all mankind. [13]

I express these biblical concepts in contemporary terminology to communicate the progression and the mechanics of spiritual adulthood. Gates 5 and 6 solve problems in relationships with God and with other people. *Toward God,* virtue-love derives its strength from God Himself, the object of the believer's personal love. Personal love for God naturally generates spiritual self-esteem and spiritual autonomy within the believer's own soul. The believer gains confidence concerning his eternal spiritual royalty, and that inner composure becomes the self-assured basis for kindness, thoughtfulness, and graciousness toward other people. *Toward others,* therefore, virtue-love is impersonal love for the entire human race. Impersonal love draws its strength not from the object of love but from the virtue of the believer himself, even when the object of love is totally incompatible or antagonistic toward him.

When the believer begins to acquire virtue-love, how does he coordinate his newly developed spiritual muscles? How do the first awkward expressions of virtue-love become the genuine poise of spiritual strength? The answer is suffering for blessing. Between Gates 5 and 6, and again after virtue-love is consolidated in Gate 6, God applies pressure to test the believer and to accelerate his advance. Gate 7 is a series of tests designed to propel him into spiritual maturity.

The mature believer is a winner in life. He has developed the capacity to receive the conveyance of "every spiritual blessing in heavenly places in Christ"(Eph. 1:3), all of which were tailor-made for him "before the foundation of the world" (Eph. 1:4). These fabulous blessings, now on deposit for each believer, are called "greater grace" (James 4:6). Conveyance of the believer's greater blessings glorifies God to the maximum. [14]

Now that the believer has reached maturity, he becomes aware of yet

---

13.   Virtue-love is described on pp. 90-93.

14.   The believer's special blessings on deposit in heaven may be compared to an escrow account. See pp. 136-39.

another problem. Having learned the doctrine of the angelic conflict, which explains the existence of the human race and the objective of human history, he knows that God's purpose is always to demonstrate His glory.[15] How is God glorified to the maximum? How does He express His glory in the life of a believer who already receives the magnificent blessings of maturity?

The answer is evidence testing. Evidence testing is Satan's cross-examination of a mature believer whom God has called to the stand as a witness for God's character, a demonstration of God's glory. Satan attempts to discredit each witness, but spiritual maturity gives the believer the strength to face the worst Satan can throw at him. When the believer uses divine assets under extreme duress, not only is God's perfection demonstrated to Satan, but the marvel of God's grace is also made dramatically clear to the mature believer himself. His occupation with the person of Christ sustains an inner happiness that is the greatest of all problem-solving devices (1 Pet. 1:6-8).

Whether enjoying prosperity or coping with adversity, the mature believer has access to all the problem-solving devices of the entire divine dynasphere. As he grows, he still uses all the problem-solving devices of spiritual childhood, but now they are reinforced with the strength of adulthood. Using the tremendous assets of his palace, he sustains his spiritual momentum throughout his life and handles suffering with such confidence that he becomes a maximum demonstration of God's perfect grace and integrity.

MENTAL ATTITUDE IN SUFFERING: THE PRINCIPLE OF THE OFFENSIVE

Besides the doctrines of the royal family and the palace, yet another concept must be understood in connection with suffering. The protocol plan of God is an aggressive plan. Its objective sharply focuses the believer's attention. The Christian's purpose in life is to know God, as He has revealed Himself in His Word. This goal is achieved by learning, metabolizing, and applying Bible doctrine, which not only causes the believer to personally love God but also creates true motivation in all realms of spiritual and temporal life.

Positive volition is more than a passive interest in God and His plan. The believer must take the offensive and employ divine assets to attain the goal that God has set for every believer.

No one stands still in the Christian life: if a believer does not advance, he retrogresses. This is emphatically true under pressure. Suffering never leaves the Christian the same as he was before; suffering can only make him better or worse. The believer who reacts to pain and pressure with arrogance—manifested in bitterness, vindictiveness, implacability, guilt, or self-pity—sets himself back

---

15. For an outline of the angelic conflict, see pp. 140-43.

in the Christian life. To advance, he must follow the example of Paul who repeatedly expresses the attitude of the offense: "I press on...reaching forward...I press on toward the goal of the upward call of God in Christ Jesus" (Phil. 3:12-14).

The offensive has always been an important principle in life. It is a military axiom that offensive action is the only means by which a victory is gained. Offensive action brings victory, while defensive action can only avoid defeat.

Just as the offensive increases the effectiveness of the military force adopting it, likewise taking the offensive in the spiritual life increases the believer's ability to handle any suffering he encounters. The offensive in the military also raises morale, permits concentration of effort, and allows freedom of action. Defensive action can be used to assist offensive action elsewhere, to gain time, to utilize terrain, or to compensate for weakness, but offensive action must be used where there is any reasonable chance for success.

There is always a "reasonable chance of success" in the Christian life. Taking our cue from the many biblical analogies drawn from military life (for example, Eph. 6:10-17 or Heb. 4:12), let us use the parallels between the Christian life and a military operation as a means of anticipating where our study of suffering will carry us.

The believer has an objective in life, which is to know and love God. This personal objective implies that the believer must attain spiritual maturity, in which status his life glorifies God to the maximum. How does he reach his assigned objective? He goes on the offensive *by metabolizing Bible doctrine while consistently living in the divine dynasphere.* Doctrine gives him spiritual momentum. From doctrine he develops capacity to love God; he attains spiritual self-esteem. Spiritual self-esteem is a remarkable achievement, which we will study in detail. It is the giant step into spiritual adulthood, the first major intermediate objective along the route of advance to maturity.

Because spiritual self-esteem can easily become arrogance, God strengthens the believer's spiritual self-esteem with providential preventive suffering. This is the first category of Christian suffering designed for blessing. When strengthened, spiritual self-esteem becomes spiritual autonomy, which is a base of further operations. The believer continues his advance to spiritual maturity through the valley of momentum testing, which is yet another category of Christian suffering for blessing. Upon reaching spiritual maturity, the believer is in a position to face the challenge of evidence testing and to glorify God to the maximum.

Suffering plays a major role in the believer's advance. His personal determination to achieve maturity by obeying God's mandates makes him equal to any suffering in life. Mental alertness and a readiness to use the assets God has provided are the attitudes of the spiritual winner.

II
The Law of
Volitional Responsibility

SELF-INDUCED MISERY

BY FAR THE MOST PREVALENT CATEGORY of human suffering is self-induced misery. People in general and believers in particular cause themselves tremendous anguish, both within their own souls and in the overt circumstances they create. The law of volitional responsibility recognizes that a believer's decisions have natural and logical consequences. When he makes bad decisions, suffering will naturally result. In nearly every instance of Christian suffering, therefore, part or all of the problem can be traced back logically to the choices of the one who suffers.

Before God created the human race, He decreed that man would have free will. By divine decree, our decisions (or indecisions) have real repercussions for which we are responsible. Just as there are scientific laws in which science observes the faithfulness of Jesus Christ who "uphold[s] all things by the word of His power" (Heb. 1:3 cf. Col. 1:16), so also there are laws of human consequence in which each individual's thoughts, decisions, and actions establish the trends in his life.

Every human being has free will. We make decisions constantly. Some of those decisions are good, others bad. You probably discovered in early youth that when you chose to take certain actions you were punished, but when you chose to take others you avoided punishment and perhaps enjoyed some measure of blessing. This principle also holds true of the spiritual life. When we follow divine protocol we are blessed; when we violate protocol we suffer. The obvious conclusion is that we must learn God's system and abide by it.

The implication of the law of volitional responsibility is that every human being must take the responsibility for his own decisions and actions. If properly reared, a person understands that he never blames others for his unhappiness. He acknowledges any mistakes or wrong decisions he has made regarding relationships, activities, motives, and functions in life and fulfills the obligations he has incurred. If he suffers from causes beyond his control, he does not allow the pain to tyrannize his soul. Rather than poison himself with bitterness and self-pity, he makes the most of his present options and opportunities through good decisions compatible with the protocol plan of God.

The law of volitional responsibility is clearly taught in Scripture.

> Be not deceived; God cannot be mocked. Whatever a man sows, this he will also reap. (Gal. 6:7)

Sowing and reaping can be beneficial or detrimental. In Galatians 6:7 they illustrate the law of volitional responsibility, warning the believer not to ignore or violate the protocol plan of God. The seeds a farmer plants will invariably produce their own species of plant and fruit. Likewise, the sins a person commits sprout and follow a natural pattern of growth.

Tracing the results of a particular sin is not the point of this verse. Just as no two seeds are exactly alike and just as they are affected by nearly infinite combinations of soil and weather, a believer's sins produce suffering in keeping with all the variables of his life. The harvest of suffering will differ from one person to another even if they seem to commit the same sins. But anyone who thinks he will escape the consequences of his own decisions deceives himself. He assumes that God has not sovereignly decreed man to have free will. If man's decisions had no effect, he would not be free. However, man *is* free. Bad decisions *have* bad effects.

Arrogance is self-deception. An inflated opinion of self is the believer's great enemy, an illusion which will relentlessly undermine his life and happiness. Most suffering in life is caused by arrogance. In contrast to Bible doctrine, which orients the believer to reality, arrogance is divorcement from reality. The divine decrees guarantee that the consequences of man's decisions occur in reality, and because the arrogant believer's perception and thought are divorced from reality, his suffering will seem to come out of nowhere. The natural results of his decisions often will take him by surprise. Situations for which he himself is responsible will shock and disappoint him, will confound his expectations, will dash his misplaced hopes.

In arrogance and ignorance the believer will falsely blame his misfortunes on other people, environment, childhood trauma, bad luck, the devil, or even God. Because he is out of touch with reality, he is ultimately illogical in his thinking. Blaming others is rationalization; everyone is responsible for his own decisions.

VOLITION AS THE SOURCE OF SIN, HUMAN GOOD, AND EVIL

Volition, which is a component of the human soul, is the source of personal sins and human good and is also a source of evil.

PERSONAL SIN is an act of volition contrary to the will and standards of God. *Personal sin* is distinguished from *Adam's original sin,* which caused the fall of the entire human race, and distinct also from the *old sin nature,* which is the genetic legacy of Adam's sin in the body of each of his descendants.[16] Personal sin is one manifestation of man's fallen state.

The old sin nature is a source of temptation, but volition is the source of every personal sin. Personal sin results from volition's saying yes to temptation, whether or not the individual knows he is transgressing God's will. The presence of the old sin nature is no excuse for committing personal sins, nor is ignorance. God has given us assets with the power to overcome these handicaps. Personal sins are classified as (1) *mental attitude sins,* like arrogance and jealousy, (2) *verbal sins,* such as gossip, maligning, and lying, and (3) *overt sins,* like murder, theft, and fornication.

HUMAN GOOD is man's relative righteousness, which can never meet the standards of God's absolute righteousness. Certain categories of human good are legitimate between people, but when offered to God, man's "righteousnesses are like filthy rags" (Isa. 64:6). Religion vainly seeks to earn the approbation of God through the "dead works" of human good (Heb. 6:1; 9:14), whereas Christianity, which is not a religion, is a personal relationship with God based not on human good but on perfect divine righteousness. At the moment of salvation, God imputes His own righteousness to every believer (Gen. 15:6; Rom. 3:22; 4:3) and declares each believer justified, vindicated, acceptable to the absolute standards of God (Rom. 3:19-30).

EVIL is a self-destructive way of thinking that is hostile to the will of God. Evil is Satan's multifaceted policy as ruler of the world, a policy of guaranteed misery which many Christians execute.[17]

---

16. See *Integrity of God,* pp. 57-77.
17. The cosmic system is Satan's evil policy toward mankind. See *Christian Integrity,* pp. 158-70.

SINS OF IGNORANCE AND ERRORS IN JUDGMENT

Sin, human good, and evil are absolutely excluded from the plan of God for the believer's life. But since believers still have their old sin natures after salvation (1 John 1:8, 10), and since many believers fail to learn what constitutes sin, human good, and evil or how to deal with them, Christians will inevitably commit these violations of divine protocol.

Suffering under the law of volitional responsibility will afflict the believer who does not know he is involved in sin, human good, or evil. Because volition operates in ignorance as well as in cognizance, whether or not a believer knew a particular thought or act was wrong, he nonetheless chose to commit it. He did it because he wanted to do it. Consequently, he must take responsibility for that decision and for any resultant suffering. He is foolish if he remains oblivious to the correlation between his decisions and his misery.

No one has an excuse for practicing sin, human good, or evil. Free will is always the cause. Even in psychosis people use their volition. Indeed, psychosis is primarily volitional. In fact, many psychotic individuals have exceedingly strong wills. Very few people are born psychotic; most mental illness is acquired through arrogance, self-centeredness, selfishness, self-righteousness, and the practice of making thousands of subjective wrong decisions over an extended period of time. In deliberate rebelliousness, in ignorance, or in psychosis, suffering piles on top of suffering—for which the individual bears responsibility.

Not all suffering under the law of volitional responsibility arises from sin, human good, or evil. Occasionally, our suffering originates from nothing more than poor judgment. The very fact that we are imperfect means that our judgment will be flawed from time to time. No matter how smart we are, someone can always deceive us. Despite wisdom and objectivity, we all have areas of subjectivity and sentimentality that can distort our thinking. Intelligence is no protection. Experience affords little help. Advice from friends or warnings from experts will never keep us from doing the foolish things we set our minds on doing. A great deal of suffering arises from errors in human judgment.

Violations of the divine laws of establishment guarantee suffering to both believer and unbeliever under the principle of volitional responsibility.[18] The Scriptures describe in detail operational laws for the entire human race within the framework of national entities. The sanctity of life and property, of privacy and freedom, must be respected or suffering will result. If a believer commits murder, for example, he has not only committed a sin against God but he has violated the laws of establishment concerning the sanctity of human life. He

---

18. See Thieme, *Divine Establishment* (1976).

should therefore suffer capital punishment because he made the criminal decision to commit murder (Rom. 13:1-4).

The Christian way of life is more demanding than the establishment life of the unbeliever. The believer's life has a divine purpose; the unbeliever's life does not—except to become a believer. Hence, the Christian suffers from violations of establishment principles, as would any unbeliever, but he also suffers when he ignores the mandates of God's protocol plan. He is commanded to reside and function in the palace, the divine dynasphere, under the enabling power of God the Holy Spirit, but if he ''quenches'' or ''grieves'' the Holy Spirit through sin (Eph. 4:30; 1 Thess. 5:19), he cuts himself off from God's purpose for his life and enters the dungeon of Satan's system. All suffering from the cosmic system is classified under the law of volitional responsibility, but the believer in the cosmic system suffers more severely than does the unbeliever in the cosmic system.

WHEN BIBLE DOCTRINE WILL NOT WORK

God desires every member of the royal family to solve the problems of adversity—and prosperity—through his own doctrinal thinking. God wants every believer to learn and metabolize Bible doctrine and to utilize, in his own experience, the fabulous problem-solving devices of the protocol plan. No one can execute the protocol plan of God through the doctrine in someone else's soul. Although human relationships can be supportive and encouraging to a limited degree, ultimately each believer must advance alone. In fact, the doctrine in his soul becomes the basis for perpetuating his relationships with others. He cannot lean on anyone else for the strength he must possess within himself.

There is an exception to this principle, however. Persistent negative volition to doctrine causes the believer to cross a barrier from which he cannot return without professional medical help. Two categories of believers fall under this description. The Christian whose negative volition takes the form of *immoral* degeneracy reaches a hopeless situation which might be illustrated by incurable venereal diseases. Of course not all victims of such diseases illustrate this point, but for the purpose of example, believers who become involved in promiscuity, drug abuse, or homosexuality crystalize their negative volition until they cannot recover. Bible doctrine cannot cure fatal diseases, and obviously a physically dead believer cannot apply doctrine in this life. Immoral degenerates must rely on medicine in order to regain or maintain a level of physical health in which they can return to the perception, metabolization, and application of doctrine.

Likewise, the believers involved in *moral* degeneracy can also pass the point of no return. Self-righteous Christians can become so enmeshed in arrogance that their divorcement from reality becomes some form of psychosis. A psychotic believer cannot apply doctrine. He needs psychiatric help, not doctrine. Again, the solution lies in medicine rather than in the Word of God. In many cases today, psychiatry can help restore a person to a degree of normality from which he can again benefit from the teaching of doctrine.

In both moral and immoral degeneracy, believers pass the point of no return through hundreds and thousands of decisions. Their own volition is responsible for the fact that now they must seek help from medicine before they can utilize the magnificent doctrinal resources made available by the grace of God.

The protocol plan of God does not function on neglect by the immoral degenerate or on the human dynamics of the moral degenerate. The plan of God operates on the omnipotence of God for the believer who fulfills divine protocol. Therefore, the powerful problem-solving devices of the Christian way of life are not panaceas that make suffering magically disappear from the lives of moral or immoral degenerates. The law of volitional responsibility eventually carries degenerate believers beyond the reach of Bible doctrine. Doctrine as the solution to the problems of life is for the believer who is executing the protocol plan of God through residence, function, and momentum inside the divine dynasphere.

COLLECTIVE SUFFERING

The law of volitional responsibility not only explains individual suffering but also accounts for the collective suffering that man brings upon himself. A corporation may go bankrupt through the bad decisions of a few company officers and government officials. Suffering from their decisions touches many other people.

With so many individuals operating in the world, each with free will, a certain amount of suffering inevitably overflows into one's life from the decisions of others. Volition is still the cause. If not created by one's own volition, suffering results from someone else's volition. The innocent suffer with the guilty, but innocent or guilty, each believer must apply the solutions available in the divine dynasphere through his own good decisions. If he personally fails to use divine assets and problem-solving devices, the blame for his misery can fall only upon the believer himself.

Ultimately there are no innocent parties; man by nature is a flawed and imperfect creature. Since the fall of Adam, no one is naturally great; nobility of soul is a rare achievement. Evidence of this biblical principle is found in the tremendous amount of suffering in the world today, suffering that has been rampant through thousands of years of human history. In every generation, there is always a plethora of suffering. Each individual (excluding the humanity of Christ) is identified with Adam in his fall; each is genetically related to fallen Adam. Because of Adam's deliberate decision to sin in the Garden, we are born with genetic and environmental handicaps to which we add our own volitional flaws from personal sin and poor judgment, creating our own suffering under the law of volitional responsibility.

Human weakness, ignorance, and arrogance weave a tapestry of inevitable suffering for many people. However, we are not doomed by our handicaps to lives of misery and despair. A principle of grace is far more powerful than is the unavoidable law of volitional responsibility: while man manufactures his own problems and resultant suffering, God manufactures solutions and blessings in the midst of suffering.

FORGIVENESS AND RESPONSIBILITY

All personal sins were judged at the cross (1 Pet. 2:24; 2 Cor. 5:21).[19] The Gospel of salvation is the supreme illustration of the doctrine that divine sovereignty and human free will coexist by divine decree.

In grace God the Father, who is the author of the divine plan, took direct, unilateral action and solved the sin problem. He imputed all the sins of mankind to Christ on the cross and judged Him as our substitute (1 Pet. 2:24). Jesus Christ died for the sins of every member of the human race, paying in full, once and for all, the penalty demanded by the absolute righteousness of God (1 Pet. 3:18). That is why the Scripture says "*whoever* believes may in Him have eternal life" (John 3:15).

One nonmeritorious act of positive volition to believe in Christ appropriates the work of eternal, omnipotent, sovereign God. This is grace (Eph. 2:8-9). Through God's perfectly meritorious work and man's nonmeritorious faith, God totally removes the barrier between fallen man and Himself, reconciling the believer to Himself forever.

Even though sins were judged on the cross, and we have eternal salvation through faith in Jesus Christ, our daily living on earth involves the natural repercussions of our sins. Sin has temporal consequences toward God, toward self, and toward other people. In relation to God, the sin caused by negative volition removes the believer from temporal fellowship with God in the palace of the divine dynasphere. When we rebound, the sin is always forgiven and we are restored to fellowship with God. Admitting, naming, citing our sins privately to the Father is our responsibility toward God (1 John 1:9), which is our *first* obligation after committing a sin.

What is our responsibility toward self? In relation to self, the danger lies in allowing the sin that God has now forgiven to kindle a mental attitude reaction.

---

19.   Although not judged at the cross, human good and evil were rejected (reserved for future judgment), and errors in human discernment did not enter into the exclusive work of God. See *Integrity of God,* pp. 105-12.

Like a chain smoker who lights his next cigarette on the butt of the last one, the chain sinner ignites a mental attitude sin on a sin that rebound has taken away.

For example, when a believer guilty of hatred confesses his sin to God, God forgives him and forgets the sin. If the believer then fails to forget what God Himself has forgotten, the old hatred can lead to further sins of bitterness and revenge. Likewise, fornication is a sin that, even though totally forgiven by God, may cause the devastating sin of guilt. Or, in erroneous zeal to make up for a sin for which Christ was already judged on the cross, a believer may enter into self-righteous, crusader arrogance which once again ejects him from the divine dynasphere. An essential part of rebound, therefore, is the *isolation of sin,* which cuts off the destructive consequences of sin in our own experience.[20]

We must never allow one sin to become the cause of another and another in a subjective chain reaction. After perfect God has forgiven us, a guilt complex or self-pity or a "root of bitterness springing up" must be classified as nothing but a devastating mental attitude sin, a prime cause of self-induced misery (Heb. 12:15). By understanding and applying the powerful doctrines that underlie the simplicity of the rebound technique, we are able to prevent the now-forgiven sin from igniting another sin.[21]

We are responsible to rebound and move on in our Christian lives rather than be enslaved to past sins by bitterness or a guilt complex. Any suffering that our sinning brings about is converted by rebound from cursing to blessing. Although we may be the cause of our own pain, our situation has now become an opportunity to utilize divine assets, to see God's provisions in action, to grow in grace.

Since we are responsible for all of our decisions, what is our obligation to people who have been hurt by our sinning? What is our responsibility to those harmed by our bad judgment? Although our sins are forgiven and we are restored to fellowship with God, although we have avoided chain sinning and have proceeded to apply doctrine in our own lives, our sins may continue to have injurious effects on other people. Rebound and the isolation of sin are marvelous problem-solving devices supplied by the grace of God, but they give us no excuse for irresponsibility toward others. Rebound is a license for spiritual growth, never a license for sin. Nor does God's grace in rebound ever justify a believer's flip attitude toward the freedom, privacy, property, or feelings of others.

Here we sail into dangerous waters where we must "rightly divide the Word of truth" (2 Tim. 2:15). To be right with man does *not* mean that we are right with God. *Unbelievers* can have honorable relationships with other people, proving that human relationships are not at the heart of the Christian way of life. What the unbeliever can do is not the Christian life.

In the protocol plan of God, relationship with God comes first and has a positive impact on relationships with people. A right relationship with God leads

20. See Thieme, *Isolation of Sin* (1976).
21. See *Christian Integrity,* pp. 32-35.

to a right relationship with man. The believer's most important function after committing a sin is to restore his fellowship with God inside the divine dynasphere where he is filled with the Spirit and thereby perpetuates his spiritual growth.

Much less important, but still part of the believer's volitional responsibility, is the fulfillment of his obligations to other people. Every situation is different; each believer must apply doctrine for himself. There is no pat solution by which the Christian resolves his human relationships, but certain biblical principles must guide his thinking and application.

Responsibility to people we have harmed lies between two extremes that we must avoid. We must not be insensitive, nor should we allow ourselves to be enslaved by anyone's implacability. In other words, we are not to ignore the just cause of anyone who suffers because of our decisions, but neither should we be motivated by fear or a guilt complex. Between these two erroneous extremes lies our responsibility.

If the suffering we cause can be alleviated, we should go to the extent that justice, sensitivity, and common sense dictate in easing the situation. Often the problem is complex. Usually both parties in any dispute are guilty in some degree. Some "solutions" would only aggravate the problem. We should be thoughtful and generous and should walk the extra mile (Matt. 5:41), but when nothing more can be done, we must leave the situation in the Lord's hands for solution as we press on in our Christian lives (2 Sam. 12:13). No matter whose volition originally causes the suffering, each person is ultimately responsible for applying Bible doctrine in his own life.

Above all else, the believer lives his life as unto the Lord, not as unto people. This is not to be construed as ignoring the human dimension of the problem, but the believer's application of the law of volitional responsibility does not mortgage his future to pay for his past failures. Instead, the protocol plan of God demands the virtues of humility, personal love for God, and impersonal love toward other people. Bad decisions make suffering inevitable, and when a believer commits a sin, he must take responsibility for its consequences toward God, self, and others.

THE LIMITED EXAMPLE OF ESTABLISHMENT COURAGE

In the devil's world a certain amount of suffering is unavoidable, but *self-induced misery* can always be avoided. The key is found in the application of truth resident in the soul. All truth is ultimately based on the absolute person of God, and all human integrity is loyalty to some category of truth. Truth exists in three categories:

1. DIVINE LAWS OF ESTABLISHMENT for believers and unbelievers alike,

2. THE GOSPEL OF SALVATION for unbelievers,

3. BIBLE DOCTRINE for believers only.

When inculcated with truth, the human soul can triumph over terrible adversity. This point is dramatically illustrated by the establishment-oriented unbeliever. Although he has limited resources of truth, he displays admirable stability and courage under stress. If the unbeliever can handle suffering with the restricted power of establishment truth, then far greater are the believer's dynamics as he utilizes Bible doctrine and the omnipotence available in the divine dynasphere to meet the challenges of life.

The effectiveness of divine establishment as a limited source of strength dramatically reveals the superior power of doctrine. American prisoners of war in North Vietnam provide a notable example of unbelievers and believers whose inner strength was derived from establishment principles. These men were sustained by a code of establishment concepts through years of bestial, crippling torture. Rear Admiral James B. Stockdale, (Ret.), the senior American prisoner of war, was awarded the Medal of Honor for his "valiant leadership and extraordinary courage" as the leader of prisoner resistance.[22] He confirms that even under extreme suffering, the law of volitional responsibility remains operational, and he describes the prisoners' ability to avoid self-destructive mental attitude sins.

> There are a lot of things [a torturer] can't do with torture. Aristotle said that compulsion and free will can coexist, and he was right. . . . A man about to undergo torture must have burned into his mind the fact that he can be hemmed in only within a very narrow window and that he need not volunteer information. . .
>
> To keep your integrity, your dignity, your soul, you have to retain responsibility for your actions, to deal with guilt. ("Yes, I lost the bubble, I might have done better, but I didn't.") You need to look squarely at what you did and measure its limited gravity in the light of the overall truth of the total situation, then use the guilt, such as it is, as a cleansing fire to purge the fault, as a goad for future resolve, and above all not be consumed by it. But you have to do all this

---

22. U.S. Congress, Senate, *Medal of Honor Recipients, 1863-1978,* 96th cong., 1st sess., 14 February 1979, p. 928.

yourself. To say that guilt doesn't exist or that it was the work of "evil spirits" or "brainwashers" is self-delusion. . . . What is indispensable to avoiding the web of fear and guilt is the ability to stand isolated, without friends and surrounded by entreaters, and quite uncharitably say "no," without the crutch of anger, without embarrassment, with finality and with commitment to the consequences. . . .

Young Americans in Hanoi learned fast. They made no deals. They learned that "meeting them halfway" was the road to degradation. My hypothetical young prison mate soon learned that impulses, working against the grain, are very important in political prisons, that one learns to enjoy fighting city hall, to enjoy giving the enemy upside-down logic problems, that one soon finds himself taking his lumps with pride and not merely liking but loving that tapping guy next door, the man he never sees, the man he bares his soul to after each torture session, until he realizes he is thereby expiating all residual guilt. Then he realizes he can't be hurt and can't be had as long as he tells the truth and clings to that forgiving band of brothers who are becoming his country, his family.[23]

American prisoners of war applied establishment truths concerning personal freedom and responsibility as well as humility, honesty, and mutual respect. They avoided torturing themselves with mental attitude sins. Moreover, free from self-induced misery, they learned to actually enjoy the challenges of their unspeakable situation. Their success did not stem from mere stubbornness, which can be a counterfeit of integrity. Anger, fear, guilt, vengeance, implacability, or insecurity may motivate unyielding tenacity. This pseudo-strength may appear admirable and may even achieve a degree of success, but the inner result of such false motivation is only wear and tear on the soul. In particular, fear is a tremendous drain of mental and physical energy.

God is the source of establishment truth, but the protocol plan of God both includes and exceeds divine establishment. If the true application of establishment principles creates genuine strength of soul, the application of Bible doctrine has far greater dynamics. The part is always less than the whole. The advancing believer understands that "the overall truth of the total situation" includes the magnificent grace of God, His divine omnipotence, and the problem-solving devices of His protocol plan.

---

23. James Bond Stockdale, "Dignity and Honor in Vietnam," *Wall Street Journal*, April 16, 1982.

Free volition causes suffering under the law of volitional responsibility, but the existence of free will also strips away every excuse for self-induced misery. The believer's own negative volition is his only hindrance to advancement in the protocol plan of God. Far surpassing establishment truth, fabulous equal privileges and equal opportunities are granted by God to every believer for the fulfillment of His plan, purpose, and design. There is no excuse for failing to perceive, metabolize, and apply Bible doctrine in the power of the divine dynasphere.

MAKING GOOD DECISIONS, FOLLOWING DIVINE PROTOCOL

The believer is responsible for most of his own suffering, but what is the solution? He must reverse the trend. Rather than make bad decisions, the believer must begin to make *good* decisions, which also have logical repercussions—in *good* results. The believer who obeys the mandates of God frees the omnipotence of God to advance and bless him. This means that he must *learn* Bible doctrine. Only the believer who understands and properly uses the problem-solving devices available to him in the palace of the divine dynasphere fulfills his destiny in the plan of God.

Divine protocol is precise. "God is not a God of confusion" or sloppiness (1 Cor. 14:33). The believer is free to express his individual volition within the boundaries established by the plan of God. God's plan must be accurately understood and applied. The believer who distorts God's plan by overemphasizing isolated elements rather than living by the entire system of protocol is not solving his problems; he is compounding them.

The rebound prayer, for example, is the means of reentering the divine dynasphere and of restoring the ministry of God the Holy Spirit in the believer's life. But even a precisely accurate rebound prayer generally does not cause pain to instantly, magically cease. In reaction to pain, prayer is often taken out of its protocol context and falsely applied to suffering. Prayer is a weapon for the strong, not a crutch for the weak.[24] Prayer has many wonderful applications within the rules God has laid down, but no amount of prayer will reverse the natural results of bad decisions.

When a believer prays for himself or asks others to pray for him because he is hurting from bad decisions, he may be hoping prayer will achieve what it was never designed to accomplish. If he merely wishes his suffering to end, he wants God to suspend the law of volitional responsibility, change His entire plan for the human race, and somehow miraculously make the pain go away. The source of

---

24. See Thieme, *Prayer* (1975).

the suffering is the wrong decisions the believer himself has made—regarding business, or personal relationships, or when facing temptation or sin. There are divine solutions to suffering, which we are studying, but imploring God for relief is not one of them. In fact, the removal of suffering might deny the believer a special blessing available to him only through the suffering.

The protocol plan of God establishes the correct procedure to use; the believer must learn and obey the system God has established. The ignorance and confusion of believers who have never learned the protocol of the Christian life can only intensify their suffering.

III
Divine Discipline

AN EXPRESSION OF GOD'S GRACE

WE HAVE SEEN THAT MOST CHRISTIAN SUFFERING arises from the believer's own thoughts, decisions, and actions. One bad decision follows another until his life is unbearable. He makes a shamble of his present experience and destroys his future options. No one can devastate a person's life as he can himself.

At some point in this self-destructive process, God intervenes with divine discipline. God will not stand by while members of the royal family sink into degeneracy; He takes stern measures to alert them to their dire situation and to encourage them to rebound and reenter the palace. In His perfect wisdom God knows when to warn each believer. Our heavenly Father knows the most effective way to confront us with the fact that we are totally dependent on His grace.

All divine discipline is administered in grace. The Christian under discipline may doubt that God is treating him in grace, but he could not imagine how much more he would hurt if God were *not* acting in grace. God severely punishes believers but not because He likes to see us squirm. He is perfect. He is just. We are His children, the royal family of God, and He punishes us for our benefit.

By definition, divine discipline is the sum total of punitive action taken by the justice of God in grace to correct, to punish, to encourage, to train, to motivate the believer's free will toward the protocol plan of God. Divine discipline is for believers only (Heb. 12:8) and occurs only in this life, not in eternity (Rev. 21:4).

Divine discipline is a warning that the believer is outside the boundaries of God's plan. Just as a football game is played inside the boundaries of the playing field, so the plan of God must be executed within the bounds of divine protocol (2 John 9). Just as the referee blows a whistle when the ballcarrier steps out of bounds, so God blows a whistle on us and administers divine discipline when we live outside the divine dynasphere.

DISCIPLINE AS PARENTAL TRAINING IN HEBREWS 12

When a believer cuts off his fellowship with God through sin and remains in the cosmic system, God in His grace must deal with him as a child. Bible doctrine has been ignored; God must get the believer's attention through pain.

> And so you yourselves have forgotten a principle of doctrine which teaches you as sons: My son [God addresses believers as His children], do not make light of corrective discipline from the Lord nor be fainting when you are reprimanded by Him. (Heb.12:5)

Hebrews 12:5 encourages us by explaining that divine discipline is tailored to each believer. God treats us as individuals. Discipline is neither too lenient ("do not make light") nor too severe ("nor be fainting") but is administered for maximum effectiveness in every believer's life.

> For whom the Lord loves He disciplines, and He punishes every son whom He welcomes home. (Heb. 12:6)

Divine discipline from the Lord is part of parental training in the royal family of God. The premise in comparing divine discipline with child rearing in the home is that, except for the humanity of Jesus Christ, there is no such thing as a perfect child. Some children are unquestionably better behaved and more responsive to instruction than others, but every child needs training so that eventually he will be able to function in adult society. Parents try to instill authority orientation in their children, and anyone who leaves home without authority orientation makes himself a monster who will manufacture misery for himself and others under the law of volitional responsibility.

On the spiritual side of the analogy, there is no such thing as sinless perfection in this life, again with the exception of Christ's impeccable humanity. As long as any believer lives in his mortal body, in which the old sin nature resides, he will continue to sin. As he matures spiritually, he will sin less frequently and perhaps will commit different categories of sin, but periodically he will succumb to temptation and enter the cosmic system.

> If we [believers] say we have no sin [no sin nature], we are deceiving ourselves, and the truth is not in us . . . . If we say that we have not sinned [do not commit personal sins], we make Him a liar, and His Word is not in us. (1 John 1:8, 10)

If the believer remains in the cosmic system, his thinking loses touch with the reality of God's protocol plan. Under prolonged cosmic influence, his arrogance becomes antagonism toward God; he multiplies his own unhappiness and incurs divine discipline. Like parental training, divine discipline is designed to inculcate humility, which is orientation to reality and authority. Only the humble believer is teachable (Ps. 25:8-9); he desires to understand how he fits in the overall scheme of God's grace. Only with humility can anyone be objective and responsive to the authority of Bible doctrine.

Although self-evaluation when accompanied by arrogance rapidly slips into subjectivity, we have the responsibility to analyze our lives. We should be first to recognize our own weaknesses. If we do not, divine discipline enforces humility on us, teaching us to see ourselves as we really are in relation to God and His marvelous plan. The very fact that we receive discipline from God tells us we are divorced from reality and that God is bringing us back to grace-oriented objectivity. From that solid footing we can rebound and resume our spiritual growth.

> Because of corrective discipline, endure. (Heb. 12:7a)

This is a command to endure suffering *inside* the divine dynasphere. In other words, rebound! And after rebound, keep applying doctrine!

Hebrews 12 continues with an explanation of divine discipline in terms of parents and children. The entire passage should be cited (with exposition) as documentation of God's magnificent purpose in disciplining His own.

> As a result, God will deal with you as sons, for what one is a son [royal family] whom the Father has not disciplined? But if you are without discipline, of which all [believers] have become participants, then you are bastards [unbelievers] and not sons.
>
> Another point: We had our human parents for corrective discipline, and we respected them. Therefore, to a greater degree you will become subordinate to the Father of our spirits and continue living [in the divine dynasphere]. For

they [human parents] on the one hand, disciplined us for a short time [during our childhood] according to what seemed best to them, but He [God] on the other hand disciplines us for our profit in order that we might receive a share of His holiness [blessing from the justice of God].

So, on the one hand, all discipline while in progress appears to be an occasion not for happiness but sorrow; afterwards [after recovery by rebound], on the other hand, sorrow pays back with interest a prosperous gain from virtue [resumption of momentum inside the divine dynasphere] to those who are taught by it [discipline teaching the humble believer].

Therefore, restore to power [rebound, or restore to the divine dynasphere] the listless hands and the disabled knees [illustrations of how the believer can suffer]. Be making straight tracks by means of your feet [momentum in the divine dynasphere] in order that the cripple [the believer in the cosmic system] may not be put out of joint [permanently] but rather be healed [restored through rebound]. (Heb. 12:7*b*-13)

CATEGORIES OF DIVINE DISCIPLINE

God is never arbitrary in administering discipline: His punishment is always appropriate to the individual in question. From His perfect divine justice, all discipline not only fits the violation but also matches the believer's receptivity. Hence, there are three categories of divine discipline:

1. WARNING DISCIPLINE

2. INTENSIVE DISCIPLINE

3. DYING DISCIPLINE

When the believer does not use rebound, these three categories of discipline are progressive. Mild discipline gives way to more and more severe discipline if the believer fails to respond.

The believer who refuses to live in the divine dynasphere receives warning discipline, added to the misery he has already created for himself under the law of volitional responsibility. He has isolated himself from fellowship with God; he has shut Christ out of his thoughts.

> Behold, I [Christ] stand at the door and I keep knocking.
> (Rev. 3:20a)

That knock at the door is warning discipline. As a general rule, warning discipline is in itself less severe than the believer's self-induced misery. However, the combination of warning discipline and self-induced misery adds up to a significant shock. Because he has not yet declined into the later stages of negative volition, this believer is still sensitive to the truth. He can still profit from this degree of discipline so that God does not have to proceed to the next stage of punitive suffering. He can still hear the knocking on the door. God can catch his attention with relatively mild suffering.

If the believer ignores or rejects divine warnings, he eventually requires intensive discipline. By habitual obstinance he has dulled his sensitivity to truth; warning discipline is no longer sufficient. God still has a marvelous plan for blessing this cosmic believer, but God's plan can be executed only in the power of the divine dynasphere. God continues to support him with logistical grace, keeping him alive so that he might return to his palace. Where there is life there is hope, and God fans the feeble flame of hope by continuing to discipline the believer even after he has insulted and blasphemed God by choosing to remain in Satan's cosmic system.

Stiffer divine discipline is required to jolt the habitually rebellious believer into objectivity. Intensive discipline alone is worse than self-induced misery: when these two categories of suffering are combined, the total pain from God and from self is extremely severe. This adds up to unbearable suffering for the believer who persists in the cosmic system.

God is exceedingly patient with His children. He extends to the believer every possible opportunity to fulfill His protocol plan. But with each rejection of God's gracious appeal to return to the divine dynasphere, the Christian renders himself less capable of making a positive decision. "Hardness of heart," or scar tissue of the soul, eventually locks his volition in negative (Heb. 4:7; 6:6). Having passed the point of no return, he arrives at the third and final stage of divine discipline, the sin unto death (1 John 5:16).

Dying discipline, or the sin unto death, is a horrible departure from time into eternity. The Christian involved has no inner resources for meeting death. In ignorance of doctrine, death becomes a terrifying plunge into the unknown.

God's work of salvation can never be canceled; even the most hardened, self-righteous Christian is immediately "absent from the body and...at home face to face with the Lord" when removed from life on earth (2 Cor. 5:8). Such a recalcitrant believer will enjoy complete happiness in heaven (Rev. 21:4), but he receives no eternal rewards with which to glorify the Lord Jesus Christ forever (1 Cor. 3:15). This cosmic believer is a loser in life; his tailor-made blessings for time and eternity are never delivered to him but remain permanently on deposit in heaven as a memorial to his lost opportunity and to God's magnificent, irrevocable bounty (Eph. 1:3; 1 Pet. 1:4).

BELIEVERS WHO SERVE SATAN

Not every Christian with locked-in negative volition is removed immediately from this life. God may keep a believer alive for a long time in the intensive stage of divine discipline. Representing many different personalities, attitudes, and styles of living, and taking many different human approaches to life, cosmic Christians who periodically receive intensive discipline serve Satan as cosmic evangelists. Satan uses these negative believers to distract positive believers from the protocol plan of God. Cosmic Christians draw other believers into the pseudo-strength and superficial attractions of the cosmic system (Rev. 2:2).

With great finesse God may employ these eternally saved "enemies of the cross" (Phil. 3:18) as agents of momentum testing in the lives of growing believers. Specifically, Christians suffering intensive divine discipline may administer the people test, the thought test, the system test, or the disaster test to spiritually adult believers.[25]

Besides "enemies of the cross of Christ" (Phil. 3:18), other biblical terms for cosmic *believers* include "enemies of God" (James 4:4), "haters of God" (John 15:23), "anti-Christs" (1 John 2:18, 22; 4:3; 2 John 7), "hostile toward God" (Rom. 8:7), "men of the flesh" (1 Cor. 3:1-3), "double-minded" (James 4:8), "agents of the devil" (1 John 3:8), and "disciples of the devil" (1 John 3:10). All these phrases refer to eternally saved believers, not to unbelievers.

Cosmic believers are like aggressors in army field exercises. Often troops who have only a few weeks remaining in the service will be issued weapons and blank ammunition in order to play the role of the enemy against soldiers who are being trained. The aggressors and the men in training are members of the same army, but the only troops benefiting from the simulated combat are those being tested, not the aggressors. Likewise, the only reason God sustains the lives of some negative believers is to use them to train others. These "enemies of God" (James 4:4) are still members of the royal family; their eternal life is secure. But the only role they can play in the glorification of Christ is to be a test for positive believers. Because of their own failures to execute the protocol plan of God, they become merely a means of building strength in someone else. Obviously, this is not a Christian's highest calling.

These cosmic Christians on the verge of maximum discipline may be sweet, sincere, and highly legalistic individuals who have distorted Christianity into a

---

25. These are categories of momentum testing in Gate 7 of the divine dynasphere. See pp. 97-112.

religion of human good works. They may be *moral* degenerates rather than *immoral* degenerates. The growing believer who can see through their facade, discerning the evil of self-righteousness, yet avoiding condescension himself, accelerates his growth in the divine dynasphere. God's genius is wonderfully displayed as He permits a negative Christian in Satan's system to ambush a positive Christian in the divine dynasphere. The believer who is going in the wrong direction inadvertently contributes to the maturity of the believer advancing in the right direction (Ps. 76:10a).

LEARNING THE HARD WAY

Divine discipline may incidentally help someone besides the one being punished, but primarily discipline is a teacher, a private tutor of the one in pain. Through suffering, God confronts the believer with his ignorance of Bible doctrine.

Believers who fail to learn doctrine will suffer all their lives until they are removed by the sin unto death. They may be negative at different points in the learning process, which involves reception, retention, and recall of doctrine. Those who refuse to listen to Bible teaching (no reception) will live out their days in a welter of ignorance, self-induced misery, and divine discipline. They will be unhappy and will never understand why.

Other believers who do listen to doctrine, even those who listen consistently, may reject true information they do not like to hear (reception, but no retention). The points of doctrine they resist must be learned another way, the hard way, through divine discipline. Divine discipline is suffering, but not for its own sake; divine discipline is teaching. Where the believer has reception and retention but no recall of doctrine for application, divine discipline solves the problem by forcing the believer to concentrate on doctrine in a humanly hopeless situation. God must teach—and all of us must learn—a certain number of lessons through suffering.

We have a choice: learn the easy way through Bible teaching, or learn the hard way through suffering. These are the two systems of learning in the Church Age. Instruction from one's pastor is God's unlimited means of communication (depending on how diligently the pastor studies). In contrast, discipline from God is a limited means of communication. The academically prepared, orthodox pastor who teaches the Word of God line by line, verse by verse, can cover the whole realm of divine truth, resulting in spiritual momentum and maturity in his listeners. Discipline, however, can only motivate the believer to return to the plan of God and resume learning doctrine under his pastor. Divine discipline has a limited objective, to alert the believer that he is out of bounds and to motivate his recovery through rebound. Concentrating in Bible class may be difficult from time to time, but it is not nearly as painful nor as limited as receiving discipline directly from God.

Discipline reminds us that we never get away with anything. God never overlooks any member of His royal family. No believer is ever ignored by the grace of God. Sooner or later God will provide sufficient punishment to remind the believer of what is really important in life.

FURTHER BIBLICAL DOCUMENTATION OF DIVINE DISCIPLINE

God takes punitive action in order to teach and train us. Divine discipline motivates us to *learn* so that the renewing of our minds with Bible doctrine becomes a way of life. We may learn the hard way from time to time, but we learn nonetheless.

> Those whom I love [believers, who possess God's imputed righteousness] I reprimand [warning discipline to the cosmic believer] and I punish [intensive discipline]; therefore, be zealous [motivation from divine discipline] and change your mind [rebound]. (Rev. 3:19)

In context, the well-known challenge of Revelation 3:20 deals with warning discipline, not with salvation.

> Behold [Now hear this!] I stand at the door [opportunity for rebound] and I keep knocking. If anyone [*believer* living in the cosmic system, addressed as "beloved" in verse 19] hears My voice and opens the door [rebound], I will enter face to face with him [recovery of residence in the divine dynasphere], and I will dine with him and he with Me [fellowship with God, the grace provision of Bible doctrine as spiritual food necessary for growth]. (Rev. 3:20)

The Church Age believer always belongs to Christ's royal priesthood, even when he lives in the cosmic system. He always has the right to approach the throne of grace with rebound and be restored to his palace (Heb. 4:16). Discipline alerts the cosmic believer to the fact that something is wrong with his life. The Lord graciously keeps knocking, giving the believer continuing opportunities to rebound. Failure to respond after hearing God's warnings results in intensive discipline.

> Behold, he [cosmic believer] shall have labor pains of vanity
> [warning discipline] because he has become pregnant with
> frustration [wrong decisions causing self-induced misery],
> therefore he has given birth to a life of deceit. (Ps. 7:14)

Arrogance in any of its myriad forms is a "life of deceit." The arrogant believer denies the results of his own bad decisions and ignores the warning discipline that God adds to his self-induced misery. If he is a *moral* degenerate, he practices sin and evil behind a facade of respectability. Preoccupied with his own righteousness and zealous to convert others to his brand of human good, he refuses to believe that he causes most of his own trouble or that God is trying to get his attention through suffering. If he is an *immoral* degenerate, his sins will be more blatant. He may blame circumstances or environment for his behavior. He may claim to be no worse than others by fallaciously comparing his few strengths against their weaknesses. He may look upon his sins as isolated exceptions rather than as the consistent trend of his life.

Both moral and immoral degeneracy attempt to justify self, but both are equally abhorrent to God. The only way God can break through the "life of deceit" is with pain that strikes the degenerate believer in his particular area of sensitivity. God "makes war against the arrogant" (Prov. 3:34; James 4:6; 1 Pet. 5:5), attacking arrogance where the discipline will hurt most and be most effective. The believer who remains adamant in his arrogance loses all sensitivity to God's appeals and eventually incurs maximum discipline which removes him from this life.

> Therefore, because you are lukewarm [a cosmic believer],
> in fact neither hot [an advancing believer] nor cold [an
> unbeliever], I am about to vomit you out of My mouth [the
> sin unto death]. (Rev. 3:16)

Addressed to the local church in Laodicea, Revelation 3:16 uses the notorious Laodicean water supply to illustrate the malaise of cosmic involvement. While neighboring Hierapolis was renowned for its hot springs and nearby Colossae enjoyed cold springs, Laodicea had neither. Its piped water was lukewarm by the time it arrived and had an offensive mineral smell. The Laodicean believers perfectly understood the startling, anthropomorphic image of God vomiting.

Lukewarm water illustrates the cosmic believer's lack of capacity for life. As a result of the law of volitional responsibility, life begins to turn sour, growing noxious under progressive stages of divine discipline. If bad decisions are not remedied by good decisions—to rebound and execute the protocol plan of God—the believer will sink into the cosmic system until God unceremoniously expels him from this life.

He [a negative believer] dug a grave [bad decisions resulting in cosmic involvement] and explored it [perpetuating his misery], therefore he has fallen into a ditch which he himself has constructed [self-induced misery]. His frustration shall return on his own head; his violent oppression of others shall descend on the crown of his head. (Ps. 7:15-16)

All three stages of divine discipline are illustrated in Paul's description of certain Corinthian believers who came to the communion service drunk.

For this reason [believers partaking of the Eucharist while outside the divine dynasphere] many are weak [warning discipline] and sick [intensive discipline] and a number of believers sleep [dying discipline], but if we would judge ourselves [rebound] we should not be judged. (1 Cor. 11:30-31)

When the believer rebounds, his discipline may cease, diminish, or continue at the same intensity. Whatever suffering remains after rebound is designed for blessing rather than for cursing. Restored to his palace, the believer is now in position to apply the divine assets he has attained and to benefit from using God's resources under pressure.

Behold, happy is the man whom God reproves. Therefore, do not despise the discipline of El-Shaddai [the "many-breasted God," a divine title emphasizing God's logistical grace], for He inflicts pain [warning discipline] and He bandages the wound. He wounds [intensive discipline] and His hands heal. (Job 5:17-18)

In contrast with most Christian suffering, which is self-inflicted, the purpose of discipline is healing. God is like a physician who must cause pain to set a fracture or to perform life-saving surgery. We hurt ourselves when we ignore the law of volitional responsibility and continue to live in the dungeon of the cosmic system; God must hurt us more to bring us back to health and strength. He gives only what contributes most to our blessing and happiness: in discipline God gives us exactly what our cosmic status requires.

DISCIPLINE AND ETERNAL SECURITY

The God of logistical grace disciplines His children, but never does He abandon us. Even in the pressure of intensive discipline, the "many-breasted God" faithfully supplies all the logistical grace we need to sustain our lives. Discipline never implies that God forsakes us.

Divine discipline never means loss of salvation. Once anyone believes in Christ, that believer's salvation cannot be canceled by anything he thinks, says, or does. Salvation is the irreversible work of God. Only human arrogance could presume that a failure by man could undo the permanent work of God. Christ on the cross paid for all man's sins, including the sin of arrogance, so that no human sin, no human decision, no human absurdity can destroy the believer's eternal relationship with God.

Even renunciation of faith does not affect the believer's eternal status as a member of the royal family of God.

> Faithful is the Word:
> For if we died with Him [at the moment of faith in Christ,
>   the baptism of the Holy Spirit identifies us with Christ
>   in His death],
> We shall also live with Him [eternal salvation is now an
>   unconditional fact].
> If we persevere [in the palace during our Christian lives
>   on earth],
> We will rule with Him [as an eternal reward].
> If we deny Him [refuse to use divine assets],
> He will deny us [eternal rewards].
> If we are faithless [spend our lives in the cosmic system],
> He remains faithful [we are eternally saved];
> He cannot deny Himself. (2 Tim. 2:11-13)

At the moment of salvation God imputes His absolute righteousness to every believer and declares him righteous or justified (Rom. 3:21-28). If God excluded from eternal salvation anyone who possesses God's own righteousness, He would have to deny Himself and contradict His own pronouncement of justification. Our salvation is as strong as the essence of God.

When God provided salvation, He knew in His omniscience that believers would be easily distracted. He is not shocked when a Christian ignores his own royal birthright. We may be appalled by the unfaithfulness of members of the royal family, but the sins that shock us have already been judged on the cross. God is not forced to change His plan because man periodically demonstrates the foolishness which God always knew he would exhibit. God's plan is greater than human sin and failure. His grace is immutable. He is not thrown off balance by every shadow of turning in a believer's life (James 1:17). Divine discipline, no matter how severe, never cancels salvation. Instead, God is training His children to obey His protocol plan.

THE PROTECTIVE ROLE OF DISCIPLINE

TRIPLE COMPOUND DIVINE DISCIPLINE

Two specific categories of divine discipline will serve to illustrate how God administers punishment. First, His treatment of individuals is demonstrated in triple compound divine discipline; second, His punishment of families, groups, and nations is illustrated by the four-generation curse. These two examples will show how divine discipline not only punishes the guilty but also protects mankind from self-destruction. If negative volition were unrestrained, the human race could not survive. The freedom which the believer exercises under the law of volitional responsibility is guarded by the authority of divine discipline.

Verbal sins such as gossip, judging, and maligning warrant harsh divine discipline because they destroy the privacy of their victims. Privacy is an essential component of freedom. Living his own life before the Lord would become difficult for a believer if he were vilified and his personal business were constantly criticized. Sins of the tongue violate the sanctity of human freedom, and if a believer actually were living in the cosmic system, maligning him would only interfere with his recovery (Rom. 14:10-14).

God has protected individual privacy through the divine laws of establishment and has doubled the guarantee to each Church Age believer by adding the privacy of the priesthood. At salvation, God appoints each Christian to the royal priesthood of Christ (Heb. 5:6, 10; 1 Pet. 2:5, 9; Rev. 1:6; 5:10; 20:6).[26] Every member of the royal family is his own priest, representing himself before God; each royal priest is answerable to God alone for his spiritual life.

Because God has so thoroughly guarded the believer's privacy, He obviously will not permit the unrestrained practice of sins that directly attack privacy. In fact, He administers triple compound divine discipline to believers habitually guilty of sins of the tongue.

Triple compound divine discipline deals first with the believer's decision to commit mental attitude sins. There is always a motive behind verbal sins, and that motivation may be arrogance, jealousy, bitterness, hatred, vindictiveness, implacability, self-pity, or a guilt complex, any of which is liable for divine discipline. Mental attitude sins motivate the believer to exalt self and put down someone else. In other words, after deciding to indulge in mental attitude sins,

---

26. See *Integrity of God,* p. 95, and *Christian Integrity,* pp. 94-96.

the believer makes the additional bad decision to convert his mental sins into verbal sins, which incur a second liability to divine discipline. One of the most foolish actions a believer can take is to become involved in verbal sinning.

> Judge not that you be not judged [divine discipline].
> (Matt. 7:1)

Judging is a general term for verbal sins directed against another person. In judging, someone states or implies something derogatory about someone else. Whether or not the accusation is true is of no consequence. Even if the information were accurate, and accuracy is difficult to establish, there is no excuse for repeating gossip. And to merely hint at someone's sins or failures is just as wrong as actually declaring them.

Judging violates the principle of grace. God has granted each believer-priest the right to conduct his own life before the Lord. In particular, all believers, in every stage of spiritual growth, have an equal right to assemble in the local church to hear the teaching of Bible doctrine. When other members of the congregation assume God's prerogative by judging a believer, they interfere with his spiritual momentum. He cannot concentrate on Bible doctrine and apply it to his own life if he is thrown on the defensive by the wagging tongues of other Christians. Therefore, according to the principle of grace, and in light of God's desire for each believer's spiritual advance, gossip incurs a triple liability, which we will classify as triple compound divine discipline. The slanderer is liable for:

1. The MENTAL ATTITUDE SINS that motivate him,

2. The VERBAL SIN itself, and

3. The SINS HE MENTIONS in the slander.

Different Christians will enjoy different activities, will represent a wide variety of tastes in dress and deportment, will hold diverse opinions on numerous topics. Certain characteristics in any believer will be offensive to other Christians. These qualities are expressions of personality and background rather than targets for malignant criticism. Each believer-priest's responsibility is to grow in grace and live his own life as unto the Lord, not to supervise the lives of his fellow Christians and coerce them into his own mold of spirituality.

> For God sees not as man sees, for man looks at the outward appearance, but the Lord looks at the heart. (1 Sam. 16:7*b*, NASB)

Obviously exceptions to the principle of privacy exist. Parents have the right and responsibility to regulate the lives of their minor children who live at home. Because a pastor is responsible to protect members of his congregation from invasions of privacy, he must be alert to discourage gossip. Likewise, a supervisor who evaluates his subordinates is not committing a sin when, as part of his professional responsibilities, he truthfully reports an employee's weaknesses and failings. If that supervisor, however, spreads his reports to people who have no professional need to know, he too is guilty of judging.

Anyone who engages in judging is actually guilty of two sins: the verbal sin itself and the mental sin that motivated him to gossip or malign his victim. Each of these sins calls for divine discipline; suffering is already compounded. But that is not the end of discipline for sins of the tongue. Yet another administration of punishment is added, based on the sins that are mentioned in gossip.

> For in the way you judge, you will be judged, and by what measure you measure to others, it will be measured back to you. (Matt. 7:2)

The maligner is liable for the discipline that would have gone to the one he maligns. If the victim is actually guilty of sins, God has already been dealing with him, either through the law of volitional responsibility or through divine discipline. But as soon as his sins are made a subject of gossip, all the discipline is transferred over to the one who has maligned him. If the victim of gossip is not guilty of sin, he is blessed while his antagonist receives discipline appropriate to the sins mentioned in gossip.

This adds up to triple liability and triple compound discipline. The maligner is punished for mental attitude sins, for verbal sins, and for the sins he mentions in judging his victim. Triple compound divine discipline is extremely harsh. It is a kind of poetic justice that gives believers a marvelous incentive to avoid the sin of gossip. Every believer should develop a conscious habit of keeping his mouth shut when tempted to run someone down or make innuendos against someone he cannot stand.

The ability to control one's tongue always accompanies spiritual growth.

> If anyone does not stumble in what he says, he is a perfect [mature] man, able to bridle the whole body as well. (James 3:2*b*)

DISCIPLINE IN HISTORICAL PERSPECTIVE

SATAN, MAN, AND GOD

Up to this point we have concentrated on suffering caused by individual believers. A staggering amount of human misery, however, seems to originate beyond any believer's personal responsibility, afflicting thousands of people throughout wide geographical areas. How do mass historical disasters such as wars, famines, epidemics, and economic depressions fit into the biblical doctrine of suffering? The answer to this critical question will provide the frame of reference necessary for understanding the four-generation curse, which will be our second example of how God administers discipline.

Widespread historical suffering always involves three sources: Satan, man, and God. Satan rules the world (John 12:31; 14:30; 16:11; Eph. 2:1-8; 1 John 2:13-14). Even in his fallen state, Satan is still the most powerful creature (apart from the resurrected humanity of Christ) ever to come from the hand of God. The devil is an extraordinary genius of unparalleled executive ability. The cosmic system is his brilliant strategy and policy for ruling his kingdom.

Satan's ambition is to prove himself equal with God (Isa. 14:14), but no creature stands independent of the Creator. Satan will never be God's equal in any sense of the term. Arrogance always causes a person to overestimate his abilities—indeed, Satan's lust for success and power has produced only misery. In the phrase of L. S. Chafer, much of the world's suffering is caused by the devil's "inability to execute all that he has designed."[27] Satan's arrogance, his cosmic system, his frustration, violence, and ultimate incompetence create an environment of misery on earth. Suffering is a fact of life in the devil's world, and man makes himself the willing victim of Satan through freewill decisions that place him in the cosmic system.

If Satan cannot succeed independently of God, obviously man cannot. In fact, when man lives outside the plan of God, he is far from independent; instead, he becomes a slave in the devil's self-destructive cosmic system. Angelic and human rejection of God's plan causes only self-induced misery and would destroy the human race if Jesus Christ did not retain control over human history.

Jesus Christ controls human history despite Satan's reign over the world (Ps. 2; John 5:22; Rev. 1:5, 18). Our Lord exercises control through direct and indirect action. He *directly* intervenes by providentially controlling the variables of history that lie beyond the scope of human volition, variables like climate, weather, and natural disasters. He *indirectly* controls world affairs through the agency of human volition, when man freely complies with truth and utilizes available divine omnipotence. Truth is revealed in the divine laws of

---

27. *Systematic Theology,* 8 vols. (Dallas: Dallas Seminary Press, 1947), 2:100.

of establishment, the Gospel, and Bible doctrine. Divine omnipotence is available in the divine dynasphere.

With perfect justice Jesus Christ administers either blessing or cursing. He blesses believers and unbelievers who adhere to the divine laws of establishment. He delivers far greater blessings to believers who execute the protocol plan of God and achieve spiritual maturity. Blessings to the mature believer overflow to the friends, relatives, and associates who live and work in his periphery. These people are blessed either directly by God or indirectly through the mature believer. The mature believer, therefore, has tremendous, invisible impact because individuals and organizations receive blessing by their association with him.

God is glorified by blessing mature believers. Consistent with God's eternal purpose, Jesus Christ lovingly watches over mature believers (Ps. 1:6; 33:18-22; 34:15-19; 66:7), directing the course of history for their advantage (Rom. 8:28). They may not know one another, but God knows each of them. They are the hub, the pivot on which turns the prosperity of the organizations to which they belong—families, social and service groups, professional associations, corporations, local churches, geographical areas, towns, cities, or nations. Our Lord blesses the human race through the royal family, specifically through spiritually mature members of the royal family.

Conversely, Jesus Christ disciplines believers and judges unbelievers who reject truth and violate His plan.[28] Just as there is a principle of blessing by association, there is also cursing by association. Self-induced misery by itself makes the cosmic Christian a pariah, obnoxious to everyone he meets. Added to the law of volitional responsibility, divine discipline to this cosmic believer also affects people in his periphery and organizations to which he belongs (Jonah 1:4-16). Cursing by association expands to become collective divine discipline against the cosmic believer's nation. In addition to satanic rebellion and human disobedience, therefore, the third source of suffering on a historical scale is divine retribution.

COLLECTIVE DISCIPLINE AND THE CLIENT NATION TO GOD

Although church and state must always remain separate, all categories of truth—establishment, the Gospel, and Bible doctrine—are consistent with one another as well as coherent within themselves. Through the divine laws of establishment, God has divided mankind into nations (Gen. 11:9; Acts 17:26), and along these national lines flow certain spiritual blessings (Gen. 22:18). Among

---

28.   See Appendix, "Divine Judgment in Contrast to Divine Discipline," p. 181.

the nations of the earth, *client nations* are used by Jesus Christ as a conduit of blessing to mankind.

A client nation is one whose government protects the freedom, privacy, and property of its citizens and, while maintaining the separation of church and state, does not hinder the presentation of the Gospel and Bible doctrine within its borders. From within the client nation, nongovernmental organizations such as local churches or mission boards initiate and support biblically orthodox missionary work in foreign countries. Evangelism, Bible teaching, and foreign missions indicate the spiritual vigor of the client nation.

Adherence to the divine laws of establishment also makes the client nation a haven for Jews, a refuge from anti-Semitic persecution in other parts of the world (Gen. 12:3). The Jews suffer horribly as a prime satanic target in the angelic conflict because God created them as His special instrument for blessing mankind (Gen. 12:1-3; 22:18) and because His unconditional covenants to Israel hinge on the historical survival of the Jews (Ps. 89:28-37). Israel was God's original and unique client nation; the Jews are His eternal chosen people (2 Sam. 7:10-16). If all Jews could be destroyed, reasons Satan, then God could not keep His word to them. Divine integrity would thus be compromised, and Satan would win his case in the angelic conflict. However, Christ the Messiah will fulfill all unconditional covenants to the Jews when He restores Israel to client-nation status at His second advent and rules forever as King of the Jews (Isa. 5:26; 11:11-13; Zech. 10:6-12).

Because Israel is under divine discipline during the Church Age, God currently blesses mankind through a succession of Gentile client nations during "the times of the Gentiles" (Luke 21:24).[29] The Roman Empire under the Antonine Caesars (A.D. 96-192) was the first Gentile client nation. Since that time, many other client nations have risen and fallen, including the Frankish kingdom of Charlemagne in the eighth century and Great Britain of the eighteenth and nineteenth centuries. The United States of America is a client nation today.

In the client nations of the Church Age, blessing by association within the believer's personal periphery expands to become the royal family's invisible historical impact. Never before the Church Age has God granted to each individual believer the privilege of utilizing divine omnipotence and of having a powerful, invisible impact on history. In Israel a few mature believers used only a fraction of the divine assets we possess and had a significant influence on national and world history. Certain principles of historical impact did exist in the Age of Israel. Even in Israel the believers were the "salt of the earth," the preservative and seasoning of the land (Matt. 5:13), also called the "remnant according to the election of grace" (Rom. 9:27; 11:5). That principle still applies:

---

29.   The "times of the Gentiles" extend from the destruction of the Jewish state in A.D. 70 until Christ will restore Israel at His second advent. See Thieme, *Dispensations* (1974).

as go the believers, so goes the client nation (Ps. 33:10-19). But now, each member of the royal family is also a "new [spiritual] species" (2 Cor. 5:17) with a new system of protocol and power that gives him far greater potential for making an impact on history than had any believer of the Jewish Age.

The mature Church Age believer has invisible influence in at least three realms:

1. BLESSING BY ASSOCIATION in his personal periphery,

2. HISTORICAL IMPACT in his nation, and

3. INTERNATIONAL IMPACT as he supports missionary activity to non-client nations.

Unheralded in the annals of human history, Christians in relatively small numbers anonymously determine the uptrends and downtrends of civilization. Jesus Christ prospers His client nation when its believers advance in the divine dynasphere; He disciplines the nation when believers live habitually in the cosmic system. Usually a nation will begin to decline under the weight of its own degeneracy. If enough believers ignore the increasingly severe stages of individual discipline and remain in the cosmic system, the nation's spiritual pivot shrinks and the nation itself must receive collective divine discipline. As an application of this doctrine, your primary duty to your country is to advance to spiritual maturity in the divine dynasphere.

Divine retribution against the client nation intensifies through five cycles of discipline, which include social disintegration, economic collapse, and political chaos (Lev. 26:14, 18, 21, 23, 27). The fifth cycle destroys the nation's sovereignty through the horrors of military conquest, reducing the vanquished populace to poverty, barbarism, and slavery (Deut. 28:49-67).

> My people are destroyed for lack of knowledge [of Bible doctrine]. Because you [believers] have rejected knowledge, I [God] also will reject you [the Northern Kingdom of Israel] from being My priest [client nation]. Since you have forgotten the law of your God, I also will forget your children [loss of client-nation privileges and blessings]. (Hosea 4:6, NASB)

COLLECTIVE DISCIPLINE AND INDIVIDUAL BELIEVERS

How do the five cycles of national discipline, which devastate wide areas and whole populations, affect individual Christians?

Blessing and cursing by association differ in one key respect. Blessing by association frequently benefits people who personally reject Christ and the protocol plan of God. This often explains why "the wicked prosper" (Jer. 12:1-2); they receive blessing by association despite their own indifference to God as the source of their prosperity.

Cursing by association, however, does not destroy the advancing or mature believers who may live or work in the periphery of cosmic believers. The law of culpability states that no one suffers divine discipline apart from his own negative volition.[30] The positive impact of growing believers offsets the negative influence of cosmic believers. When the pivot is too small to balance the spin-off of negative Christians, however, God must administer divine discipline.

In a magnificent display of perfect timing and omnipotence in the control of history, the disasters that God sends upon cosmic believers are coterminous with suffering for blessing for growing believers. The sweep of collective suffering across the face of contemporary history administers to some believers the various categories of suffering for blessing and to other Christians all three categories of divine discipline. The same historical event may bring blessing on one hand but warning discipline, intensive discipline, or dying discipline on the other hand. No one is ever lost in the shuffle; God never forsakes any believer (Ps. 37:25). God always has you personally in mind.

The mature or growing believer is never deprived of blessings by downtrends in history (Ps. 23:4-5; Jer. 39:10-18).[31] Since Jesus Christ controls history in this Church Age, all the negative forces of international economics and politics cannot obstruct the timely delivery of blessings to even one mature Christian (Rom. 8:38-39). War, economic depression, and religious persecution never hinder divine omnipotence (Job 5:19-27). While the world seems to be collapsing around the protocol believer, he enjoys a stimulating life of blessing and total confidence in God. Just as God built a wall of fire around Jerusalem when she stood vulnerable in the midst of her enemies (Zech. 2:5), the divine dynasphere protects the growing believer from the destructiveness of mass suffering.

The cosmic believer is caught up in the same historical disasters that besiege the advancing believer. This negative believer, however, is a cause of collective divine discipline and lacks the inner resources of Bible doctrine needed to meet the crisis. He has no inner dynamics because he has failed to utilize God's power system. Instead of suffering for blessing, his pain is divine discipline, whether warning or intensive.

---

30. See pp. 48-50.

31. Tape-recorded lessons on David, Daniel, and the Book of Revelation present the doctrine of historical trends. See p. iv.

Some believers, shocked into objectivity by historical trauma, recover from the cosmic system. Others persist in their personal degeneration. For them the collective suffering of the nation serves as the instrument of the sin unto death. Christians will be among the victims of nearly any historical catastrophe.

Suffering in itself does not conclusively indicate whether God is blessing a believer, or disciplining him, or permitting him to create self-induced misery. Therefore, each Christian must apply doctrine for himself and determine his own status before the Lord. No believer has a right to judge, malign, or gossip about another believer in personal suffering and historical disasters.

THE FOUR-GENERATION CURSE AS COLLECTIVE DISCIPLINE

In contrast to triple compound discipline for gossip, which deals with individuals, the four-generation curse is an illustration of divine discipline related to historical trends. We usually think of collective discipline as punitive action in a particular geographical area, but the four-generation curse deals with a group of people defined not only as they extend over a geographical area but also as they extend over a period of time. God is never arbitrary. In the administration of perfect divine justice, God considers every facet of every situation, including the factor of time and the manner in which one person is influenced by others.

God first declared the four-generation curse in the Ten Commandments.

> You shall not make for yourself an idol or form anything in heaven above or on earth beneath or in the waters below. You shall not bow down to them or worship them; for I, the Lord your God, am a jealous God punishing the children for the sins of their fathers to the third and fourth generation of those who hate Me. (Ex. 20:4-5, NASB)

How can a God of grace, justice, and love "visit the iniquity of the fathers on the children and on the third and the fourth generations of those who hate [Him]" (Deut. 5:9; Num. 14:18)? God is never unfair to anyone. A villainous ancestry does not prejudice God against any individual. Instead, as we shall see, the divine policy of a four-generation curse punishes the guilty while protecting the innocent and guaranteeing the freedom of each individual to express his positive or negative volition.

God treats every individual as a person, yet He does not fail to deal with destructive collective trends that intensify from one generation to the next. As an essential part of giving mankind free will, God allows human volition enough free rein to be genuinely free. Patterns of sin which are habitually repeated become ingrained characteristics of a family, group, or nation. Children learn sins and evils from their parents and perpetuate family trends. Rather than instantly disciplining man, God permits negative volition to run its course.

Many possible categories and combinations of "wickedness, rebellion, and sin" are allowed to form and harden for three or four generations as expressions of human freedom (Ex. 34:6). But when negative volition runs so rampant as to threaten His plan, God "does not leave the guilty unpunished" (Ex. 34:7). After a period of grace before judgment, extending over these three or four generations, He administers collective discipline to the family, group, or nation.

To protect the human race from self-destruction, God administers collective discipline that grows progressively severe from one generation to the next. In the third or fourth generation, He sends a catastrophe to dissipate or eliminate the trend. This form of discipline allows evil patterns to develop in the course of human history but destroys them before they can jeopardize the plan of God. God permits no trend of present history to hinder the positive volition of subsequent generations.

Under this system of collective discipline, each generation is disciplined for the same sins because those sins are committed by each generation. The sons commit the sins of the father. "Those who hate [God]" (Ex. 20:5; Deut. 5:10) are disciplined because they themselves reside perpetually in the cosmic system and establish patterns of evil in their lives. But no one suffers under the four-generation curse except by his own volition. At any point the curse may be broken by believers who execute the protocol plan of God, refusing to follow the evil pattern of their progenitors.

> Fathers shall not be put to death for their children, nor children be put to death for their fathers; each is to die for his own sin. (Deut. 24:16)

The sins of the father have to be repeated in the next generation for culpability to be established and for punitive action to be administered from God. Otherwise, a different law applies: the law of grace.

> Know therefore that the Lord your God is God. He is the faithful God, keeping His covenant of grace to a thousand generations of those who love Him and keep His mandates. (Deut.7:9)

After first announcing the four-generation curse, God immediately promised that obedience to His plan will always break the curse.

> But showing love to thousands who love Me and keep My commandments. (Ex. 20:6)

No one suffers under the four-generation curse apart from his own culpability. Despite historical trends, God's grace is always operative on the earth. Indeed, the curse upon a family or nation can be broken in any generation when individuals believe in Christ and form a pivot of mature believers by fulfilling the plan of God.

> The Lord is good [divine essence is perfect] and His love endures forever. His faithfulness continues through all generations. (Ps. 110:4)

God's motivation in delaying historical discipline is illustrated by His patience toward mankind prior to the Last Judgment at the end of human history.

> The Lord is not slow about His promise [to judge mankind], as some count slowness, but is patient toward you, not wishing for any to perish but for all to come to a change of mind [about Christ as Savior, for unbelievers, or about the protocol plan of God, for believers]. (2 Pet. 3:9)

The four-generation curse furnishes a principle that helps us interpret human history from the divine viewpoint: historical disasters are often divine discipline sent to break up destructive trends and to give the next generation opportunity to fulfill the plan of God. Proverbs 30:11-14 documents four generations of increasing degeneracy, beginning with disrespect for parental authority and culminating in "a generation whose teeth are [like] swords... to devour the afflicted." God protects the human race from the self-destruction of such rampant arrogance.

The principle of the four-generation curse, which the Bible presents in the context of the ancient world, sheds light on upheavals in modern history. The French Revolution, for example, was a conflagration of evil trends that had crystallized in the long reign of Louis XIV. The Sun King, as he was called, destroyed the pivot of mature believers in France by revoking the Edict of Nantes and, furthermore, reduced the French aristocracy to sycophantic courtiers. The disappearance of a spiritual pivot and the absence of a vigorous aristocracy destabilized every level of society. As a result, unrestrained middle-class jealousy incited lower-class violence. Ultimately, French society was destroyed in the Reign of Terror, and a new order was established under Napoleon. The Russian Revolution also vented evils that had built up for many years before overt violence broke out.

What does the four-generation curse teach us? First, it warns us that rejection of God's plan can become the accepted, ingrained tradition of a family or nation. A little neglect, a little compromise, a little arrogance soon becomes a way of life. Second, this system of divine discipline advises us that opposition to God leads to terrible suffering personally and to disaster for the nation. Third, the four-generation curse reveals God's marvelous grace. He patiently applies discipline to each rebellious generation but will never permit evil trends to destroy the options of future generations. Because of God's grace, exhibited in collective divine discipline, the human race cannot destroy itself.

The doctrine of the four-generation curse encourages the believer to utilize divine assets in his own life because this category of discipline emphasizes his invisible impact on history. Believers can either perpetuate the four-generation curse or break the pattern of discipline. The privileges and opportunities of the royal family imply tremendous responsibility. If a Christian fails to live and grow in his palace, he contributes to divine discipline against his entire nation.

THE SOLUTION TO THE FOUR-GENERATION CURSE

The four-generation curse never implies that *guilt* passes from parents to children but that parents who oppose God's plan will *influence* their children to follow the same pattern of opposition. Children are influenced by their parents and tend to repeat their parents' sins.

The fuse on historical disaster burns for three or four generations as children perpetuate the sins of their parents. Toward the end of this period, God initiates the cycles of discipline against the nation to warn believers to return to the protocol plan of God and break the curse.

At any time, a generation can respond with positive volition to the Gospel and Bible doctrine, heading off national catastrophe. A biblical example of an eleventh-hour recovery is the Assyrian Empire's response to Jonah's message (Jonah 3:10). Another example is the spiritual recovery of the second generation of Jews in the Exodus. Had they continued in the rebellion of the first generation, collective divine discipline would have intensified. In reality, their positive volition broke the curse that already had prevented their fathers from entering the promised land.

In modern history the United States is rapidly approaching historical disaster—economically, militarily, socially, spiritually. The one factor that stands between our nation and maximum divine discipline is the positive volition of believers. Only divine grace can avert the horrible suffering of the four-generation curse, but God will bless this nation only if there is a strong pivot of mature believers to be the recipients of His grace benefits.

The solution to the four-generation curse requires severe punishment of criminal youths (Deut. 21:18-21) but emphasizes instructing children in the laws of establishment and Bible doctrine.

You will inculcate these doctrines of Mine in your hearts and minds, tie them as notes on your hands, and as training aids tie them around your foreheads. Teach them to your children, talking about them when you sit down at home, when you travel, before you go to bed, and when you wake up. Write these on the doorframes of your houses and on your gates so that your days and the days of your children may be many in the land that the Lord has promised to give to your ancestors [promises made to Abraham, Isaac, and Jacob], as long as the heavens remain above the earth. (Deut. 11:18-21)

The perpetuation of the client nation to God always involves training the next generation. Rather than be a negative influence, parents must be a positive influence by teaching divine establishment, the Gospel, and Bible doctrine to their children. Parents should bring blessing by association to their children rather than lead them to disaster under the four-generation curse.

SUMMARY OF PUNITIVE SUFFERING AND PREVIEW OF SUFFERING FOR BLESSING

In concluding our study of punitive suffering and in approaching the subject of suffering for blessing, we can draw a series of contrasts.

In disciplinary suffering, which is deserved, the issue is *sin* and wrong decisions from a position of weakness. In the adult believer's undeserved suffering, the issue is *blessing* and momentum because of right decisions from a position of strength. Spiritual momentum from metabolized Bible doctrine results in still greater blessing.

The believer's status under divine discipline is *cosmic involvement,* which is described by a variety of terms: worldliness, carnality, apostasy, reversionism. Under suffering for blessing, the believer's status is always residence in the palace of the *divine dynasphere.* There is a tremendous difference between living in a palace and wasting away in a dungeon.

Under discipline the suffering is *unbearable.* The promise that "no temptation has overtaken you . . . beyond what you are able" to bear (1 Cor. 10:13a), describes testing, not divine discipline. Testing is designed to exercise and strengthen the believer's spiritual muscles, but discipline must be severe enough to shock the believer, to get his attention. He must learn from the suffering that human resources are inadequate; he must hurt unbearably so that he is forced to consider the divine solution. Under testing, suffering for blessing is always

	DIVINE DISCIPLINE	SUFFERING FOR BLESSING
ISSUE	Sin	Blessing
STATUS	Cosmic System	Divine Dynasphere
INTENSITY	Unbearable	Bearable
VIEWPOINT	Arrogance	Humility
SOLUTION	Rebound	Advanced Problem-Solving Devices
INTENDED RESULT	Cursing Turned to Blessing	Accelerated Growth

DIVINE DISCIPLINE IN CONTRAST TO SUFFERING FOR BLESSING

bearable. The believer under testing is using the assets of the divine dynasphere which constitute "the way of escape...that [he] may be able to endure it" (1 Cor. 10:13*b*).

The believer's viewpoint when he incurs divine discipline is *arrogance* and subjectivity. In suffering for blessing, his viewpoint is *humility* and objectivity.

The solution to divine discipline is the *rebound technique,* which is the Christian's most basic problem-solving device. The solution to suffering for blessing involves *more advanced systems of problem solving.*[32]

The result of divine discipline, when the believer uses rebound, is that *cursing is turned to blessing.* The suffering ends, is diminished, or continues at the same intensity, but in any case the purpose now is blessing instead of punishment. God's solutions are always designed for blessing. The result of suffering for blessing is that the Christian gains multiple benefits from the *acceleration of spiritual growth:* enlarged capacities and the greater blessings of spiritual maturity.

There are five categories of Christian suffering, but all five categories are designed for the believer's personal benefit. We have just covered the first two; the last three are the subject of the remainder of this book.

---

32. See pp. 9-13.

FOR PUNISHMENT:
1. Self-Induced Misery
2. Divine Discipline

FOR BLESSING:
3. Providential Preventive Suffering
4. Momentum Testing
5. Evidence Testing

When the believer remains outside the divine dynasphere, which is tantamount to being out of fellowship with God, he reaps punitive suffering from his own bad decisions or as a result of divine discipline. This suffering is still beneficial to him because it can make him face the reality of his dependence on God's grace, bringing him to the point of rebound and recovery. Punitive suffering can show him that his scale of values is wrong and that he must correct his priorities.

But when the believer resides inside the divine dynasphere and suffers through no fault of his own, the benefit is even greater. The purpose now is not to take a negative believer and motivate recovery but to take a growing believer and accelerate his growth. In contrast to punitive suffering, which is beneficial on a limited scale, suffering for blessing is designed by God to accelerate the believer's growth through the stages of spiritual adulthood that lead to spiritual maturity.

IV
Suffering for Blessing

SUFFERING AND GROWTH IN
SPIRITUAL ADULTHOOD

THE PROTOCOL PLAN OF GOD includes two systems of spiritual growth. *Gradual growth* comes through the perception and metabolization of Bible doctrine. God commands every believer to operate consistently under this system throughout his life on earth (Matt. 4:4; Eph. 4:11-13; 2 John 4-6). The second system, *accelerated growth*, occurs when metabolized doctrine is tested under pressure. After attaining spiritual adulthood, further growth *requires* periodic suffering. This suffering for the purpose of blessing draws upon the believer's reservoir of doctrine, exercising and increasing his inner strength. Bible doctrine is spiritual nourishment; suffering for blessing is spiritual exercise.

In spiritual childhood, most suffering is self-induced misery or divine discipline. The only pain that can be construed as suffering for blessing in the life of the spiritual child is the suffering that continues after rebound. In spiritual childhood suffering for blessing is like a teacher, but in spiritual adulthood suffering for blessing is more like a demanding college professor.

By definition, suffering for blessing is the undeserved pain, hardship, or difficulty that God periodically sends into the life of the spiritually adult believer for the purpose of accelerating spiritual growth and demonstrating the total sufficiency of His grace.

Suffering for blessing by its very connotation is not intended to hurt the believer or to make him miserable but to advance him. For the adult believer undeserved suffering is strictly a matter of blessing. Indeed, only God can bless with suffering; suffering caused by self is harmful.

God does not administer suffering for blessing until the believer is qualified to handle it. That is why suffering for blessing is reserved for spiritual adulthood. Nor does God send suffering for blessing until the believer has capacity to appreciate God as its source and to be grateful for the problem-solving devices that He has provided in the palace of the divine dynasphere. Again, this explains why God can periodically give suffering for blessing only to spiritually adult believers. But God never gives the believer more suffering than he can bear.

> No testing has overtaken you but such as is common to man-kind; but God is faithful, who will not permit you to be tested beyond what you are able [to bear], but with the testing will also provide a solution [a way out], that you may be able to endure it. (1 Cor. 10:13)

In God's protocol plan, strength precedes suffering for blessing. God provides the means of dealing with a situation before He applies the pressure so that suffering for blessing never overloads any believer. Only by his own bad decisions can the believer create more suffering for himself than he can bear. Only the believer himself can decide to live outside his palace. Only he can refuse to learn Bible doctrine so that he has no spiritual resources to draw upon.

When pressure crushes a believer, the cause of defeat is always his own volition, never the sovereignty of God. Suffering for blessing is always bearable. Unbearable suffering under the law of volitional responsibility, with divine discipline added on, is designed to awaken the believer to his dependence on God's protocol system.

Obedience to divine protocol prepares believers for suffering. All problems of suffering are resolved in the mechanics of the protocol plan of God, and all solutions stem from Bible doctrine. Consistent residence and function in the divine dynasphere arms the believer for the pressures of his life.

THE PATTERN OF MOMENTUM IN SPIRITUAL ADULTHOOD

The final three categories of suffering in the Christian way of life are reserved for spiritual adults. We will devote an entire chapter to each category.

1. *Providential preventive suffering* keeps the believer from distorting his new-found spiritual self-esteem into arrogance. At the same time providential preventive suffering converts spiritual self-esteem into spiritual autonomy.

2. *Momentum testing* accelerates the believer's spiritual momentum, carrying him from spiritual autonomy into spiritual maturity.

3. *Evidence testing* demonstrates the efficacy of God's grace in the life of the spiritually mature believer.

These three categories of undeserved suffering are specialized provisions of God's grace. Their purpose is the continued spiritual growth of a believer who has faithfully adhered to divine protocol over many years. Sadly, in any generation relatively few Christians obey divine mandates and utilize His marvelous grace assets. Few ever reach spiritual adulthood. Easily distracted from their true destiny as members of the royal family of God, most believers lack the consistency, the humility, the positive volition to stick with the protocol plan.

Not many believers will ever face suffering for blessing. Hardly any will enjoy the benefits of experiencing God's grace in action under extreme duress. Personal and historical disasters rarely find believers prepared to enjoy God's provisions. Instead, self-induced misery and divine discipline are by far the most common forms of Christian suffering. If you have not learned a great deal of Bible doctrine, you have no right to assume that the pressures in your life are suffering for blessing. If, however, you have inculcated your soul with God's thinking, you can anticipate a challenging, stimulating life of special grace from God—in adversity and in prosperity.

In spiritual adulthood, the believer's spiritual momentum follows a definite pattern:

1. Consistent perception and metabolization of Bible doctrine inside the divine dynasphere results in the believer's giant step into personal love for God and spiritual self-esteem.

2. When tested under providential preventive suffering, spiritual self-esteem becomes spiritual autonomy.

3. By successfully passing the momentum tests, spiritual autonomy becomes spiritual maturity.

4. When spiritual maturity stands up under evidence testing, God is glorified to the maximum in the historic angelic conflict.

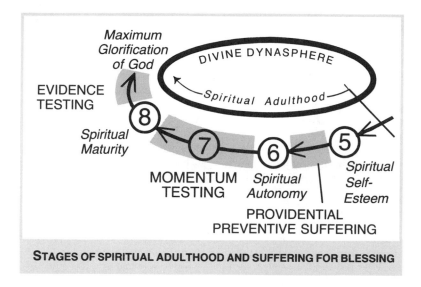

STAGES OF SPIRITUAL ADULTHOOD AND SUFFERING FOR BLESSING

Paul describes this pattern of momentum in his second epistle to the Corinthians.

> Then He [God] assured me: My grace [has been and still] is sufficient for you; for the power is achieved with weakness...for when I am weak, then I am powerful. (2 Cor. 12:9-10)

We will examine this passage more thoroughly when we focus on providential preventive suffering. Here we need to note only the *pattern* of the adult believer's continued progress.

"The power is achieved with weakness" states that suffering is necessary for spiritual advance. The Greek noun *dunamis,* "power," refers to God's omnipotence as utilized by the believer in the advance through spiritual adulthood: spiritual self-esteem, spiritual autonomy, and spiritual maturity. The adult believer has power because he consistently lives inside the divine dynasphere. The verb *teleo,* which is ambiguously translated "made perfect" in the King James Version, means "to finish, to accomplish, to fulfill, to achieve," the latter best agreeing with the context in verse 9.

How is power achieved? How does the believer advance through the final gates of his palace? The Greek preposition *en* plus *astheneia*—in the instrumental case of manner—indicates the manner in which the action of the verb is carried out: "with weakness."

"Weakness" refers to the progressive phases of suffering for blessing. Weakness here is not failure or sin but *helplessness*. Suffering for blessing puts the spiritually adult believer in a situation he cannot resolve with human resources. He is helpless and must totally depend on divine assets that he has acquired by metabolizing Bible doctrine in his soul. The suffering itself does not advance the believer; his utilization of God's power in suffering is what advances him.

Power and weakness exist together at the same time: the adult believer uses the strength of spiritual self-esteem to move through his weakness in providential preventive suffering. He uses the strength of spiritual autonomy to go through his weakness in momentum testing. And he uses the strength of spiritual maturity to move through his weakness in evidence testing. He not only exercises the power inherent in each stage of spiritual adulthood to meet the test, but when he succeeds in passing each test, he "achieves the power" of the next stage of spiritual adulthood. With each test he passes, he moves up.

What degree of strength is required to endure providential preventive suffering? Spiritual self-esteem. What power is required to pass momentum testing? Spiritual autonomy. And what is needed to pass evidence testing? Spiritual maturity.

As a result of dealing with the undeserved suffering that God sends, the believer's strength increases so that he is able to cope with the next increment of suffering when it comes. In His perfect wisdom God gives each believer the unique sequence of blessing and suffering, of prosperity and adversity, necessary to bring him to maximum glorification of God.

V
Spiritual Self-Esteem

THE FLAW IN HUMAN SELF-ESTEEM

BEFORE GOD ADMINISTERS SUFFERING FOR BLESSING, the believer must have the inner strength necessary to endure and profit from the test. In other words, the believer must have spiritual self-esteem. God will not send suffering for blessing until first the believer is confident in his relationship with God and in his own ability to use the assets that God has given him. His soul must be inculcated with Bible doctrine so that he loves God and lives by his own doctrinal thinking (Rom. 14:22).

For believer and unbeliever alike, a person's attitude toward self affects his entire outlook on life. An important branch of psychology emphasizes the key role of self-esteem.

> Of all the judgments we pass in life, none is as important as the one we pass on ourselves; for that judgment touches the very center of our existence.
>
> We stand in the midst of an almost infinite network of relationships: to other people, to things, to the universe. And yet, at three o'clock in the morning, when we are alone with ourselves, we are aware that the most intimate and powerful of all relationships and the one we can never escape is the relationship to ourselves. No significant aspect

of our thinking, motivation, feelings, or behavior is unaffected by our self-evaluation.[33]

This psychologist has made an accurate observation. He recognizes man's genuine need to regard himself in a positive light. Although self-esteem solves many problems in life, human self-esteem ultimately has a fatal flaw.

> The heart of man is more deceitful than all else and is desperately sick; who can understand it? (Jer. 17:9, NASB)

The problem is that man is rarely worthy of his own esteem. Since the fall of Adam, the human race has been inherently depraved. Man is born spiritually dead, utterly isolated from his Creator, totally incapable of a relationship with God (Eph. 2:1). Man proves his depravity by the personal sins he commits and by the human good and evil he practices. Man is commonly arrogant, greedy, self-centered, superficial, cowardly, petty, devious, self-righteous, cruel, violent. Only by a concerted effort of the will can he even partly control his old sin nature (1 John 1:8). Human nobility of soul is a rare and transitory achievement.

Unbelievers who follow the divine laws of establishment have a legitimate basis for human self-esteem. They live by true principle. Their integrity gives them cause for self-respect. From strength of character, they may also achieve a degree of success in a profession, in marriage, in family life, in relationships with others. Such men and women of genuine self-esteem are exceptional, however, and even these few are far from perfect. Part of their virtue is their humility; they know that their self-esteem is measured by a temporal, relative standard. They honestly face the reality of their own weaknesses and failings.

In contrast to the exceptional individuals with establishment virtue, the great majority of the human race lacks self-esteem. Regard for self is nearly always some form of arrogance. Most people deceive themselves with intellectual rationalizations or psychological delusions concerning their own importance.

Man feels the need for a positive self-image, yet he falls short of his own relative standards, to say nothing of totally failing by God's absolute standards. The very self which man desires to esteem is weak and prone to evil. Man's best intentions and greatest achievements are undercut by ignorance, handicaps, distractions, and temptations. Human self-esteem is an elusive and flimsy substitute for what man really needs and what God in His grace has provided: *spiritual self-esteem.* Spiritual self-esteem is based on who and what God is, not

---

33.   Nathaniel Branden, *Honoring the Self* (Los Angeles: Jeremy P. Tarcher, Inc., 1983), p. 1.

on who and what man is. It stands on God's absolute integrity, not on man's unstable character.

THE SUPERIORITY OF SPIRITUAL SELF-ESTEEM

Spiritual self-esteem belongs to the protocol plan of God. The Christian achieves spiritual self-esteem by faithfully learning and applying Bible doctrine, by advancing step by step within God's protocol system until he reaches Gate 5, personal love for God. Spiritual self-esteem is an inevitable result of personal love for God. The believer's self-confidence is not derived from self but from knowing that he has a unique relationship with the God of the universe.

Believers of the royal family of God have greater cause for spiritual self-esteem than do believers of any other dispensation. God displays His glory in the Church as never before and as never again in human history. His objective is to show "the riches of His grace which He has lavished upon us" (Eph. 1:7-8) and to demonstrate "what is the surpassing greatness of His power toward us who believe" (Eph. 1:19). Even a partial list of the advantages granted to every Church Age believer will demonstrate the superiority of spiritual self-esteem over human self-esteem.

As Church Age believers we are a "new [spiritual] species" in union with Christ (2 Cor. 5:17). By the baptism of the Holy Spirit at the moment of salvation, we are "created in Christ Jesus" for the purpose of utilizing divine power, not human power (Eph. 2:10). God has made available to us the exercise of divine omnipotence for the execution of His plan (Acts 1:8; 1 Cor. 2:4; 2 Cor. 4:7; Eph. 1:19-20; Col. 1:10-12; 2 Tim. 1:7). Never before the Church Age did God extend this privilege to every believer. Only partial utilization of God's omnipotence was made available to a few believers of previous dispensations.

We are instructed to "walk in newness of life" (Rom. 6:4; Eph. 2:10; 4:24) because the new spiritual species is designed to utilize total availability of the omnipotence of all three Members of the Trinity. The omnipotence of God the Father created for every Church Age believer a portfolio of invisible assets which includes the divine dynasphere (Eph. 1:3). The omnipotence of God the Son sustains the universe and perpetuates human history (Heb. 1:3). The omnipotence of God the Holy Spirit provides the function of the divine dynasphere (Acts 1:8).

Furthermore, our bodies are indwelt by all three Members of the Trinity. *God the Father* indwells us for the glorification of His protocol plan which He designed in eternity past for each Church Age believer (John 14:23; Eph. 1:3, 6, 12; 4:6; 2 John 9). *God the Holy Spirit* indwells us to create a temple for the indwelling of Christ as the Shekinah Glory,[34] to be a downpayment of our royal inheritance, and to empower us in the execution of the Father's plan (Rom. 8:11; 1 Cor. 3:16; 6:19-20; 2 Cor. 6:16; Eph. 1:14). *God the Son* indwells us for a number of reasons:

1. As a sign or badge of the royal family (John 14:20),

2. As a guarantee of the availability of divine power in time (2 Cor. 13:4-6; Rom. 8:10),

3. As a guarantee of life after death in the presence of God forever (Col. 1:27),

4. As the depositary of special blessings for time and eternity (Eph. 1:3) and as the escrow officer who will deliver these blessings to the believer when he reaches spiritual adulthood and when he appears before the Judgment Seat of Christ (1 Cor. 3:13-14; 2 Cor. 5:10),[35]

5. As motivation for continued momentum when facing the three categories of suffering for blessing: providential preventive suffering, momentum testing, and evidence testing (Gal. 2:20),

6. As the basis for assigning highest priority to relationship with God over relationships with people, and to the use of divine power over the exercise of human power (1 John 2:24),

7. As the basis for the glorification of Christ, the Shekinah Glory, in the unique life of the Church Age believer (John 17:22-23, 26).

Never before the Church Age did *any* Member of the Trinity indwell *any* believer. But every Church Age believer is permanently indwelt by the entire Trinity. As a consequence, many other advantages also belong to us. For worship and privacy in our unique relationship with God, we have been inducted into the highest of all priestly orders. Every Church Age believer belongs to the royal priesthood of our great high priest, Jesus Christ (Heb. 4:14; Rev. 1:6). In

---

34.   As a guarantee of blessing to Israel, the glory of God dwelt in the Tabernacle and later in the Temple (Ex. 25:22; Lev., 16:2; 26:11; Isa. 60:2). Because Jesus Christ is the God of Israel (John 1:11, 14), this residing or *Shekinah* Glory was the presence of the second Person of the Trinity in His client nation, Israel. In the Church Age, the believer's body is the temple of the Shekinah Glory (John 16:13-14; 17:22; Col. 1:27).

35.   See pp. 136-39.

addition, each of us has been granted a royal warrant from God to be Christ's ambassador in Satan's kingdom (2 Cor. 5:20). We represent Christ on earth and have an invisible impact on history. Furthermore, each Church Age believer possesses his own royal palace, the divine dynasphere, the prototype of which was designed exclusively for the humanity of Christ (John 15:10). We are heirs of God, joint heirs with Jesus Christ (Rom. 8:17). We will accompany our Lord and glorify Him forever (Eph. 2:6-7).

Even this partial delineation of our royal assets shows that our status is unique. There are no ordinary Christians. Each "ordinary" Christian has a position and a function far superior to anything available to the greatest believers of previous dispensations.

Our extraordinary status is revealed to us through our consistent, faithful, lifelong intake of Bible doctrine. Doctrine teaches us who we are in the plan of God. Doctrine orients us to God's will, plan, and purpose for our lives and emphasizes the attainment of spiritual self-esteem, spiritual autonomy, and spiritual maturity. Advance in the protocol plan of God manifests the spiritual royalty to which God has elevated us. God has given us a basis for spiritual self-esteem totally related to grace, unspoiled by human weaknesses of any kind.

THE SOURCE OF SPIRITUAL SELF-ESTEEM

Personal love for God precedes spiritual self-esteem and becomes the source of this initial stage of spiritual adulthood. Who is this infinite and eternal Person who has granted us so exalted a position in Christ? What is the character of our majestic God?[36]

God reveals Himself to us in His Word. He has "exalted [His] word above [His] name" (Ps. 138:2). His essence is reflected on every page of Scripture: in every doctrinal dissertation, in every biblical illustration and application, in every passage of historical narrative, in every line of biblical poetry.

To be "transformed by the renewing of [his] mind" (Rom. 12:2), the believer must learn every biblical doctrine his pastor teaches. Even if its relevance is not obvious at the moment, every doctrine contributes a vital facet to the Christian's understanding of God's essence and personality. The Bible was not designed merely to provide solutions for a believer's current problems; the Bible's purpose is to reveal the magnificent and multifaceted character of God.

> How precious . . . are Thy thoughts to me, O God! How vast
> is the sum of them! (Ps. 139:17, NASB)

---

36. See *Integrity of God*, app. A, "The Doctrine of Divine Essence," pp. 231-56.

To learn God's essence is a marvelous, lifelong endeavor for which we have been given powerful assets related to the divine dynasphere. This greatest of all enterprises demands right priorities and the self-discipline for faithful intake, metabolization, and application of Bible doctrine. To understand God's attributes is to love Him. This constitutes the very purpose of our lives.

In spiritual childhood the believer does not have the capacity or capability to love God. Much sincerity, emotionalism, and sentimentality is misconstrued as love for God. In reality, to *love* God, the believer must *know* God. This requires cognition of Bible doctrine.

God is invisible. The incarnate Lord Jesus Christ is the visible "exact representation of His [invisible] essence" (Heb.1:3), but the resurrected humanity of Christ is now absent from the earth. How does the believer love someone whom he has never seen (1 Pet. 1:8)?

Love is based on perception. We come to know and love God through His Word. In fact, Bible doctrine is the Mind of Christ (1 Cor. 2:16). Doctrine reveals to us God's attributes, His wisdom, His love for us, His brilliant system of protocol. We love God when our souls are inculcated with doctrine so that we think His thoughts, share His viewpoint, and appreciate His perfect integrity and matchless grace. Learning doctrine takes time; love for God does not come overnight. But after years of faithfully learning the Word of God, the day will come when the believer will wake up and realize that Jesus Christ is his best friend. That will be the giant step from spiritual childhood into spiritual adulthood. That will also be the beginning of spiritual self-esteem.

THE PATTERN FOR SPIRITUAL SELF-ESTEEM

The believer's spiritual self-esteem is patterned after two precedents:

1. DIVINE SELF-ESTEEM and,

2. the SPIRITUAL SELF-ESTEEM OF THE HUMANITY OF CHRIST residing in the prototype divine dynasphere.

God can personally love only that which is perfect. Because He is absolute righteousness, God loves Himself. He is totally worthy of His own demanding, uncompromising love. Within the essence of God, therefore, we discover the ultimate pattern for spiritual self-esteem: His perfect love is directed toward His own perfect righteousness. God has total self-esteem and has found a way to make spiritual self-esteem available to the Church Age believer.

The humanity of Christ is the pattern for spiritual self-esteem for the royal family of God. The divine dynasphere was originally designed for our Lord's humanity, a gift from God the Father given on the first Christmas.[37] Throughout His first advent the humanity of Jesus Christ resided and functioned constantly inside the prototype divine dynasphere. Though tempted far beyond anything we have ever known, He never departed from the Father's plan; He never stepped out of the divine dynasphere.

From early childhood, the humanity of Jesus Christ learned Bible doctrine and lived by the doctrine in His soul. From His youth He "kept increasing in wisdom [Bible doctrine] and stature, and in favor with God and man" (Luke 2:52, NASB). This pattern continued throughout our Lord's first advent. Doctrine was first priority in His life (Matt. 4:4; Luke 11:28; John 7:15-16; 8:25-27). His final words on the cross were not only a quotation of Scripture, but the Scripture He quoted was a tribute to the Father as "God of doctrine" (Luke 23:46, cf. Ps. 31:5).[38] In the humanity of Christ, doctrine produced personal love for God, which inevitably resulted in spiritual self-esteem.

When we study evidence testing, we will examine our Lord's spiritual self-esteem as it developed through spiritual autonomy into spiritual maturity. We will see that He set the precedent for our spiritual self-esteem.

KNOWING HOW TO LIVE AND HOW TO DIE

The believer with spiritual self-esteem is dependent on God but not inordinately dependent on other people. The independence in his soul contributes to his capacity for meaningful personal relationships. Every Christian lives in a world of people. A few people will love him, others will tolerate him, some will despise him. For the vast majority, he will always remain a total stranger. Although surrounded by people, each believer must do many things for himself. He must think his own thoughts, establish his own priorities, make his own decisions, suffer his own pain, and eventually do his own dying.

The critical importance of spiritual self-esteem is dramatically seen in the fact that no one can die another person's death. Friends may stand by and perhaps lend comfort, but when the time for death comes, each one goes it alone. Nor can anyone bear another's pain, feel another's emotions, or think another's thoughts. Always there is a place for sensitivity, compassion, and encouragement from one person to another, but ultimately the most basic activities of life require spiritual self-esteem of each individual believer.

One of the greatest achievements in life is the ability to equate living and dying. Life on earth includes the period in which an individual knows that he is

---

37. See *Christian Integrity,* pp. 9-12.
38. See Thieme, *The Blood of Christ* (1979), pp. 13-14.

dying; dying is part of living. Only by facing the reality of death with doctrinal objectivity can any believer face life from the divine viewpoint (Phil. 1:20-21). And only through suffering for blessing and attaining the stages of spiritual adulthood can the believer equate living and dying and thereby benefit from suffering.

Every believer must *learn* how to live and *learn* how to die. Being alive does not imply that a person has the slightest idea of *how* to live, of how to fulfill the potential that human life affords. Nor does being a member of the royal family of God mean that a believer knows how to conduct himself as a spiritual aristocrat. A Christian does not necessarily know the first thing about the Christian way of life and the mechanics of executing God's will, purpose, and plan for the Church Age. Certainly possessing eternal life does not guarantee that he knows how to pass from time into eternity with confidence and poise.

After salvation we must learn Bible doctrine to know how to live and die in prosperity or adversity, in pleasure or pain, in the company of others or alone. Even learning Bible doctrine is something each believer must do for himself— under the teaching ministry of his pastor-teacher. Every Christian must make his own decisions to give doctrine first priority in his life, to assemble where the Word of God is taught, to be filled with the Holy Spirit while he listens, to concentrate on the pastor's message, to believe the truth, to properly apply the doctrine he understands. This is what the Bible means when admonishing us to "cherish [guard, or keep] understanding."

> He who gets wisdom loves his own soul;
> He who cherishes understanding will prosper. (Prov. 19:8)

To "get wisdom" and to "cherish understanding" describe the believer's faithfulness in consistently learning and applying doctrine over a long period of time. At all stages of spiritual growth, he requires daily nourishment from doctrine.

To "love [one's] own soul" is a description of spiritual self-esteem. This legitimate love for self, combined with "prosper[ity]," reveals the pattern of growth in spiritual adulthood. The believer grows spiritually by "get[ting] wisdom" and enters spiritual adulthood when he attains spiritual self-esteem. As spiritual self-esteem is stabilized, strengthened, and tested under the pressure of suffering for blessing, he advances stage by stage to spiritual maturity. He "prosper[s]" all along the way.

This is how the Christian learns to live and die for himself. When the Mind of Christ has been inculcated and metabolized into the soul of the believer, that individual acquires spiritual self-esteem. Inside the divine dynasphere the virtues of the humanity of Jesus Christ are formed in him (Rom. 13:14; Gal. 4:19;

1 Pet. 2:9*b*), including our Lord's great personal love for the Father (John 15:10). From his own love for God and divine viewpoint thinking, the believer then has the contentment, stability, composure, and all the other characteristics of spiritual self-esteem with which to face the challenges of living and dying.

> Yea, though I walk through the valley of the shadow of death,
> I will fear no evil; for thou art with me. (Ps. 23:4*a*, AV)

THE CHARACTERISTICS OF SPIRITUAL SELF-ESTEEM

Spiritual self-esteem can be explained categorically as having fourteen characteristics.

1. THE BEGINNING OF CONTENTMENT. Contentment, or capacity for happiness in one's present circumstances, begins in spiritual self-esteem, grows stronger in spiritual autonomy, and reaches a peak in spiritual maturity (2 Cor. 12:10; 1 Tim. 6:6-8; Heb. 13:5). In spiritual adulthood, sharing the happiness of God is the Christian's greatest and most effective problem-solving device (Phil. 4:11).

2. MENTAL STABILITY. A stabilized mentality comes from the correct and accurate application of Bible doctrine in adversity and in prosperity (Phil. 4:12-13).

3. COMPOSURE MARKED BY SELF-ASSURANCE. Self-assurance is characteristic of the believer who can correctly and accurately apply doctrine to life and who has experienced the efficacy of doctrine in his own life (James 1:22-25).

4. GRACE ORIENTATION TO LIFE. The believer with spiritual self-esteem appreciates the extension of God's grace toward him without distorting that grace policy into antinomian license (Rom. 6:1). Furthermore, he demonstrates a gracious attitude toward other people without distorting toleration into compromise of integrity (Rom. 12:10).

5. DOCTRINAL ORIENTATION TO REALITY. Spiritual self-esteem orients the believer to reality by maintaining his humility, by avoiding inordinate ambition and competition, by developing spiritual common sense, spiritual independence, and a sense of humor (Rom. 12:3; Phil. 2:3-4).

6. GOOD DECISIONS FROM A POSITION OF STRENGTH. The divine dynasphere is the position of strength in which good decisions are possible, based on divine viewpoint thinking—in Gate 4—and motivation from personal love for God—in Gate 5 (Eph. 6:10; Phil. 2:2; Col. 1:11).

7. THE BEGINNING OF PERSONAL CONTROL OF ONE'S LIFE. Spiritual independence is based on maximum use of one's royal priesthood, by which the believer represents himself before God. His perspective in life is focused on God rather than on people (Col. 2:7; Heb. 12:2-3).

8. THE USE OF SPIRITUAL SELF-ESTEEM AS A PROBLEM-SOLVING DEVICE. Spiritual self-esteem solves the problems of inadequacy, fear, emotional disturbance, lack of personality identity, and uncertainty concerning one's niche in life (2 Tim. 1:7). Furthermore, the believer with spiritual self-esteem solves his own problems from the doctrine he knows rather than running here and there for counseling and spiritual advice. He views difficulties as opportunities to utilize the doctrine in his soul (2 Tim. 2:3-4).

9. THE BEGINNING OF A PERSONAL SENSE OF DESTINY. The believer's personal sense of destiny becomes stronger as he progresses through the three stages of spiritual adulthood. The meaning, purpose, and definition of his life become clear as he resolves his relationships with God, self, and people.

10. POST-SALVATION EPISTEMOLOGICAL REHABILITATION. Epistemology is the study of knowledge itself, addressing the question of how man knows what he knows. After salvation the believer must concentrate on a new source of truth, Bible doctrine, under the teaching ministry of an academically prepared, theologically orthodox, Spirit-filled pastor. The believer must acquire a new doctrinal frame of reference through learning and metabolizing the Word of God by faith, for "the righteous [believer with imputed divine righteousness] shall live by faith" (Rom. 1:17). Post-salvation epistemological rehabilitation is a term that encompasses all the Bible doctrine the believer has learned between salvation and spiritual adulthood. This renovation of thought includes everything from understanding spirituality and how to execute the protocol plan of God, to appreciating one's portfolio of invisible assets, to mastering the subject of this book, Christian suffering. Metabolized doctrine has "transformed [the spiritually adult believer] by the renewing of [his] mind" (Rom. 12:2).

11. COMMAND OF SELF. Fulfilling the responsibilities that accompany independence, the believer exercises self-control, self-restraint, poise, and self-

regulation (Prov. 19:11; 1 Cor. 14:33; 2 Tim. 2:10). Command of self facilitates good communication with other people, which is mandatory in all successful relationships.

12. A NEW ATTITUDE TOWARD LIFE. Personal love for God gives the believer a dynamic attitude, viewpoint, and perspective on life. His thoughts and priorities change as his focus on Christ motivates him in everything he does (John 15:10-17).

13. QUALIFICATION FOR PROVIDENTIAL PREVENTIVE SUFFERING. Spiritual self-esteem gives the believer the ability to handle suffering for blessing. The characteristics of spiritual self-esteem qualify him to pass the test of providential preventive suffering and advance him into the next stage of spiritual adulthood, which is spiritual autonomy (1 Pet. 4:12-16).

14. ATTAINMENT OF THE FIRST PHASE OF THE UNIQUE LIFE. God has designed a unique life for the Church Age believer, part of which is experienced and part of which is not (Rom. 8:10). The nonexperiential aspect of the unique life includes the indwelling of all three Members of the Trinity. This is the Church Age believer's permanent status, not his progressive experience. The experiential aspect of the unique life is the glorification of Christ in the body of the believer (Eph. 5:1; 1 Cor. 6:20).

A distinction must be made between the permanent, unchanging, unfelt indwelling of Christ as the Shekinah Glory and the Christian experience of Christ being glorified in our bodies (Phil. 1:20-21). A distinction also must be made between the permanent, unchanging, unfelt *indwelling* of the Holy Spirit and His invisible, behind-the-scenes *function* in the divine dynasphere through which He glorifies Christ in our bodies (John 16:13-14).

Each stage of spiritual adulthood brings a new experiential glorification of Christ. This progressive experience begins with spiritual self-esteem, which is described by the phrase "Christ...formed in you" (Gal. 4:19). In spiritual autonomy, which is the next stage of Christian growth, the glorification of Christ in the unique life of the royal family will be described as "Christ [being] at home in your heart" (Eph. 3:16-17). In spiritual maturity, the final stage of spiritual adulthood, the unique life will be expressed as "Christ [being] glorified in [your] body" (Phil. 1:20-21).

DESCRIPTION OF SPIRITUAL SELF-ESTEEM

Spiritual self-esteem is the assertion of Bible doctrine resident in the soul; it is living by one's own thinking from that doctrine; it is making application of metabolized doctrine under all circumstances, including suffering for blessing.

The Christian who gains spiritual self-esteem has crossed the dividing line between spiritual childhood and spiritual adulthood, between spiritual dependence and spiritual independence, between punitive suffering and suffering for blessing. Spiritual self-esteem is the giant step in the believer's life, the first stage of spiritual adulthood.

The believer with spiritual self-esteem thinks and applies Bible doctrine to life, motivated by his personal love for God. He understands enough doctrine to think independently, having the courage of his own perceptions and doctrinal applications rather than being erroneously influenced by others. Furthermore, instead of arrogantly exaggerating his strengths or his weaknesses, he orients to the biblical reality of who and what he is as a member of the royal family of God and at the same time never loses sight of who and what God is. He accepts his human limitations while emphasizing the equal privileges and opportunities that God gives to every Church Age believer. He utilizes available divine assets; he exploits his options.

When a believer has attained spiritual self-esteem, he does not feel threatened by others. He refuses to be manipulated through guilt or fear by those who would impose erroneous, legalistic standards on him. If he is guilty of sin, human good, or evil, he assumes the responsibility for his own decisions, good or bad, and resolves his problems according to divine protocol.[39] He understands his right as a member of the royal family of God to live in the privacy of his own priesthood. His life does not belong to other people but to God. God's logistical grace sustains him, not so he can live up to the expectations of others, but so he can adhere to divine mandates in the protocol plan of God. Spiritual self-esteem enables the believer to exploit all the problem-solving devices in the divine dynasphere. With spiritual self-esteem he can begin to enjoy happiness and tranquillity of mind in every category of suffering for blessing.

The Christian with spiritual self-esteem knows he belongs to a winning plan. He understands what God accomplished for him in eternity past. He knows at the present time how to thrive in God's protocol system. He has learned that a fabulous eternal future awaits him after death. God's protocol plan gives his life meaning, purpose, and definition. He advances in the certainty that logistical grace will support his life and empower his indomitable will to triumph over any handicaps or weaknesses he may possess. Spiritual adulthood and continuing spiritual growth *are* the believer's triumph over his handicaps, genetic and acquired.

With spiritual self-esteem the believer persists in learning and applying Bible doctrine because he loves God and is sure of His promised blessings in time and eternity (Heb. 6:18). Personal love for God is the highest motivation

---

39. See pp. 21-23.

in life. The believer with spiritual self-esteem confidently persists in the plan of God without needing flattery or fanfare, without relying on recognition, encouragement, counsel, inspiration, or bullying from other believers. He leans on no one but God. Rather than borrow motivation and fortitude from the soul of someone else, he uses the doctrine in his own soul. He has nothing to prove to anyone. He fears no one. He does not crave the approval of people or overreact to their indifference, disapproval, or rejection. Nor does he slavishly imitate the personality or demeanor of others. He is content with his own personality; he has identified his own niche in life.

Spiritual self-esteem makes the believer intellectually independent, but it does not make him a boor. Many positive Christians go through the awkward, sophomoric stage of being overconfident religious zealots, bursting with answers, eagerly imposing their ideas on other people. Such arrogance is not spiritual self-esteem. Spiritual self-esteem makes the believer a good listener; his genuine humility in Gate 3 of the divine dynasphere makes him teachable. He appreciates the graciousness of other people and recognizes legitimate authorities, including the authority of the pastor who teaches Bible doctrine. Spiritual independence means the believer flourishes *within* God's structures of human and spiritual authority, not outside His protocol system as a rebel, a crusader, or a self-styled free spirit.

Although modern psychology cannot provide spiritual self-esteem, it can accurately describe the lack of spiritual and human self-esteem.

> . . . The two most striking characteristics of men and women who seek psychotherapy are a deficiency of self-esteem and a condition of self-alienation. In some crucial ways they do not feel appropriate to life and its requirements, and they lack adequate contact with the world within, with their needs, wants, feelings, thoughts, values and potentialities. Thus diminished in consciousness, they are estranged from their proper human estate. Large areas of the self lie undiscovered, unexpressed, unlived. They are sleepwalkers through their own existence.[40]

The believer wakes up to reality by learning Bible doctrine in the power of the divine dynasphere. In studying the two punitive categories of Christian suffering, we noted that if a member of the royal family of God fails to wake up through perception and application of Bible doctrine, he will be shaken by self-induced misery and divine discipline.

---

40. Nathaniel Branden, *Honoring the Self* (Los Angeles: Jeremy P. Tarcher, Inc., 1983), p. 4.

VI
Providential Preventive Suffering
PAUL'S THORN IN THE FLESH

AS THE FIRST CATEGORY of suffering for blessing, providential preventive suffering performs a dual function. Its offensive role is to accelerate the believer's spiritual momentum beyond spiritual self-esteem into spiritual autonomy; its defensive role is to prevent him from falling victim to arrogance.

Spiritual self-esteem is probably the most vulnerable stage of the Christian life. As the believer begins to think for himself and live by the doctrine in his own soul, he may distort his new-found independence. He may assume that his strength comes from self rather than from God's Word and the divine dynasphere. As he flexes his new spiritual muscles and enjoys the results of spiritual growth, he may forget that God is the source of his growth.

God in His grace does not wait for the believer to fail. Rather than picking up the pieces, God provides the means of keeping the believer from falling apart. In grace God takes preventive action by sending suffering for blessing. Providential preventive suffering reminds the believer of his dependence on the protocol plan of God and forces him to use divine assets under circumstances that human ability cannot resolve.

As an unbeliever, Paul was aware of his own genius. With concentration and self-discipline he exploited his tremendous human assets. As a young man he excelled academically in a rigorous education. He then channeled his unusual nervous energy and extraordinary intellectual powers to rise within the religious and political establishment in Judea. Human dynamics enabled him to advance rapidly within an evil system.

Paul was a man of action who was also at home in the realm of ideas. He was a master of both Jewish theology and Greek philosophy. The application of his human genius was the zealous persecution of Christians. He had relished the success that his human abilities had achieved; he was ambitious for further promotion. After believing in Christ, Paul had to learn dependence on divine rather than human power, but he never lost his strong personality or his brilliant intellect. Hence, when he reached spiritual self-esteem, he was in danger of corrupting his own spiritual advance. He might have assumed that his own mental prowess enabled him to comprehend the deep things of Bible doctrine, when in fact metabolized doctrine resided in his soul only because of God's grace system of perception. To protect Paul from his natural vulnerability to arrogance, God sent providential preventive suffering, which Paul called his "thorn in the flesh."

> And for this reason, lest I should become arrogant because
> of the extraordinary quality of revelations, I was given a
> thorn in the flesh, an angel from Satan that he might torment
> me, lest I should become arrogant. (2 Cor. 12:7)

Paul was chosen by God to serve as the apostle to the Gentiles, the principal spokesman for the doctrines of the royal family of God. These "mystery" doctrines had never been revealed prior to the Church Age.[41] Because of God's sovereign decision to use him in this special way, Paul had a unique ministry, and the divine revelations given to him exceeded those of any other apostle. Peter acknowledged Paul's superior comprehension of doctrine, recognizing that Paul's "epistles contain some things that are hard to understand, which ignorant and unstable people distort" (2 Pet. 3:15-16).

God gave Paul the unparalleled blessing of teaching and recording Church Age doctrine, but Paul was also given another blessing called a "thorn in the flesh." Doctrine orients the believer to reality; arrogance divorces him from reality. Arrogance must be prevented because it neutralizes the effectiveness of doctrine in the believer's life. Doctrine provides spiritual self-esteem; arrogance is self-alienation. Arrogance is the insidious enemy of the spiritual life, the very attitude that corrupted Lucifer, who was originally the greatest of all the angels.[42] Paul's ministry might have been destroyed by arrogance, but the thorn in the flesh was given to him to preserve him in a period of grave danger.

Bible scholars have speculated on the nature of Paul's thorn in the flesh, but Paul deliberately omits the details to emphasize the principle of providential

---

41. See *Dispensations*.
42. See pp. 140-43.

preventive suffering. Paul says only that God permitted Satan to dispatch a demon to constantly torment him. The work of this "thorn demon" illustrates God's total ability to care for His own. God's provisions are far superior to any possible challenge. He is able to make even our enemies benefit us (Ps. 76:10).

If God [is] for us, who [can be] against us?'' (Rom. 8:31b)

There is a fine irony in Paul's suffering. The thorn demon wanted to destroy Paul but could only force him to rely on God's superior provisions. God used Satan's attack to keep Paul from falling into the same pattern of arrogance that originally caused the fall of Satan. God has a wonderful sense of humor; with marvelous finesse, He lets the devil defeat himself. Only omnipotent God has the power to turn suffering into blessing, and this power has been made available to us through residence and function in the divine dynasphere. God can use adversity to our advantage, even pressures our foes have designed to harm us.

While Paul was suffering intensely and wondering why God did not relieve the pain, God was masterfully demonstrating His preeminence to Paul. The apostle was hurting and sought relief, but "underneath [were] the everlasting arms" (Deut. 33:27). Through this experience Paul's personal love for God increased. But before he reaped the benefits of providential preventive suffering, Paul applied a false solution and made a wrong application of doctrine.

A FALSE SOLUTION AND WRONG APPLICATION

As the first stage of spiritual adulthood, spiritual self-esteem is still an awkward phase in which the believer has not yet developed the true instincts of spiritual maturity. That is why Paul reacted emotionally to the pain of providential preventive suffering. In an understandable human reaction, he was momentarily affected by the discomfort before regaining his composure and passing the test.

Concerning this [thorn in the flesh] I appealed to the Lord three times that it might depart from me. (2 Cor. 12:8)

Paul's use of prayer was a false solution to suffering for blessing; his request that the suffering be removed was a wrong application of doctrine.

Providential preventive suffering is essential to the adult believer's spiritual advance. He should never ask God to remove the means of his growth. He should never pray for the removal of suffering for blessing by which the protocol plan of God is fulfilled.

We think we know when we have had enough suffering, but God knows us better than we know ourselves. He never sends more pressure than we can bear (1 Cor. 10:13), but on the other hand He sends enough pressure to accelerate our growth. Only when He sees that we have passed the test or that we have flunked so badly that we need time to regroup does He remove or reduce the suffering. What God does not remove He intends for us to bear.

God has a unique plan for each believer. His timing is perfect for every individual. He makes the sovereign decision to nurture the positive Christian's growth with the right kind, the right intensity, and the right duration of suffering or prosperity. Too much or too little adversity, too much or too little prosperity, the wrong combination, or the wrong timing would retard the believer's spiritual progress. A believer who tells God how and when to administer suffering for blessing claims to have greater wisdom and a better plan than God. This is blasphemy. We do not dictate to God. We are told to "come boldly before the throne of grace" (Heb. 4:16), but we have no right to question the sovereignty of God, much less to ask for the cancellation of divine wisdom.

Paul made a false application of doctrine by entreating God to remove providential preventive suffering. Worse yet, he made an even more basic error by employing prayer to accomplish what it was never designed to do.

Prayer is a powerful tool that has many effective applications, but the spiritually adult believer should not pray for strength or for relief under suffering for blessing. Why not? In this case prayer would violate divine protocol.

Billions of years ago God established the system for giving strength to the royal family. That system is the divine dynasphere. The believer does not need to ask for what has already been provided. Therefore, any Church Age believer who prays for strength when pressure assails him is insulting God. He implies that divine omnipotence, which God has made available in the divine dynasphere, is insufficient to enable spiritual royalty to live the Christian life under all circumstances.

The utilization of divine assets is a matter of learning and applying Bible doctrine, not a matter of prayer. Too often the believer does not understand his suffering because he has neglected or resisted doctrine. He remains ignorant of the powerful problem-solving devices that belong to the royal family.

Frequently, believers under pressure entreat God for a miracle, but miracles are no solution to suffering for blessing. By performing a miracle involving the sudden removal of pressure, God would be canceling His own system for accelerating the believer's spiritual advance. For sovereign, omnipotent God, nothing is easier than a miracle. Miracles express only His sovereign decision; they do not require man's positive volition or any function of human free will.

Blessing is far more difficult for God to bestow when the Christian's volition is involved, yet that is precisely what God has achieved by creating the protocol plan.

The believer must freely choose to reside in the palace of the divine dynasphere. There he must learn and metabolize (ingest and digest) Bible doctrine. He also must consistently apply this metabolized doctrine throughout suffering for blessing. God will terminate the test in His own perfect time (1 Cor. 10:13). That is a divine promise, so that the believer's natural desire for relief from pressure becomes a matter for confidence in God, not an occasion for pleading for miracles. The believer with positive volition gains strength by using doctrine, by exercising his own mind which is inculcated with the thinking of God, not by observing supernatural events.

False solutions to one's own suffering include miracles and the misuse of prayer; all true solutions are integral parts of the divine dynasphere. We have already discussed these problem-solving devices for spiritual childhood and spiritual adulthood in chapter 1. They include rebound, the faith-rest drill, hope, virtue-love, and sharing the happiness of God.

DIVINE COUNSELING FOR PAUL

Obviously God did not answer Paul's prayers. He did not remove the thorn in the flesh, nor did He respond in any way except to perpetuate Paul's suffering. Finally, after Paul had repeated his urgent request on three occasions, God reminded the great apostle of a doctrine he already knew.

> Then He assured me: My grace [has been and still] is suffi-
> cient for you, for the power is achieved with weakness.
> (2 Cor. 12:9a)

We have already noted the pattern of achievement in this verse.[43] What is the "power" in this context, and what is the "weakness"? The *power* is divine omnipotence as it becomes available to the believer with each stage of spiritual adulthood through residence, function, and momentum in the divine dynasphere. Omnipotence operates in the adult believer in the form of spiritual self-esteem, spiritual autonomy, or spiritual maturity.

The *weakness* is the suffering for blessing which God applies to the believer in each of these stages of spiritual achievement. God sends the weakness of providential preventive suffering, momentum testing, or evidence testing. God has

---

43. See pp. 57-58.

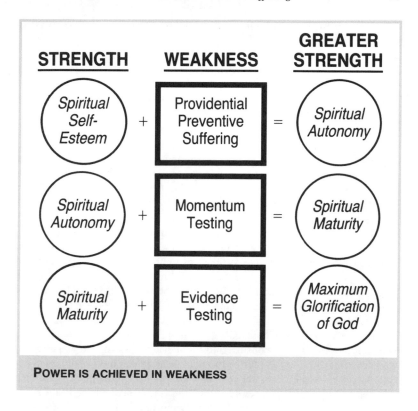

STRENGTH		WEAKNESS		GREATER STRENGTH
Spiritual Self-Esteem	+	Providential Preventive Suffering	=	Spiritual Autonomy
Spiritual Autonomy	+	Momentum Testing	=	Spiritual Maturity
Spiritual Maturity	+	Evidence Testing	=	Maximum Glorification of God

POWER IS ACHIEVED IN WEAKNESS

provided the power in the divine dynasphere; man experiences the weakness in suffering that is beyond human solution. God's power, which is employed by man in helplessness, produces accelerated spiritual growth.

> Therefore, I will boast all the more gladly about my weaknesses in order that the power of Christ may reside in me. (2 Cor. 12:9*b*)

This is boasting not in the sense of glorifying self but as a manifestation of *esprit de corps*. Paul's boasting expressed his delight in belonging to God's protocol plan. Such boasting indicates submission to God's system and is the antithesis of arrogance. Thus Paul demonstrates that providential preventive suffering has been effective in his life. Divine protection against arrogance had succeeded because of his positive volition in the application of metabolized doctrine in his soul. He had stopped feeling sorry for himself, as when he had begged God to remove the pain. Rather than being preoccupied with himself and his problems, Paul now has focused his attention on the person of Christ.

Paul's suffering had not changed. His human weakness had not changed. His old sin nature had not changed. The divine dynasphere had not changed. What had changed was Paul's attitude. He had begun to apply the doctrine he knew to the circumstances in which he found himself. He remembered doctrine, began to think objectively, utilized his problem-solving devices, and regained control of his life.

Suffering in itself has no virtue. The meaning and blessing in suffering lie in the demonstration of divine grace and power. Omnipotence operates through God's Word resident in the believer's soul. From doctrine comes personal love for God resulting in spiritual self-esteem, and that inner strength furnishes yet greater capacity to love God.

Suffering for blessing illuminates God's grace. Suffering converts self-glorification into a legitimate glorying which is worship, love, and appreciation of God. Paul's boasting was not the loud, overt bravado we normally associate with braggarts. Instead, he was confident and sure, not of himself, but of the efficacy of the divine dynasphere. He celebrated the essence of God, His protocol plan, and the fabulous assets available to every Church Age believer. Boasting, here, is an attitude of the soul that is the epitome of spiritual self-esteem.

Having been reminded of God's grace provisions, Paul expressed his total confidence in God's policy of suffering for blessing. Now that he was thinking Bible doctrine, he recalled a further point of doctrine that motivated him to endure his thorn in the flesh. He remembered that the prototype of the divine dynasphere sustained the humanity of the Lord Jesus Christ during His first advent. Paul refers to the prototype divine dynasphere as "the power of Christ."

In the prototype divine dynasphere Christ attained spiritual self-esteem, spiritual autonomy, and spiritual maturity. He perfectly fulfilled the Father's plan, which included suffering for blessing, for "although He was a Son, He learned obedience from the things which He suffered" (Heb. 5:8). The same policy of suffering for blessing that Paul was enduring in the operational divine dynasphere, and that we endure today, had been the means of accelerating the spiritual growth of the humanity of Christ.

> For this reason I find contentment in weaknesses, in
> slanders, in pressures, in persecutions, in stresses in behalf
> of Christ, for when I am weak, then I am powerful. (2 Cor.
> 12:10)

"Contentment" is capacity for happiness; it is the believer's satisfaction with the blessings that God has given him. The spiritually adult believer in the operational divine dynasphere can share the happiness of God in all circumstances, just as the humanity of Christ in the prototype divine dynasphere possessed inner happiness on the cross while being judged for the sins of mankind (Heb. 12:2). If God the Holy Spirit could sustain Jesus under the excruciating pain of being judged for our sins, certainly the ministry of the Spirit can utilize the assets of the operational divine dynasphere to sustain us in any hopeless situation in which we may find ourselves.

Some divine blessings involve prosperity; others come in the guise of adversity. The believer can be grateful for whatever he has in whatever state he finds himself (Phil. 4:11-12). This tranquillity of soul is derived from his personal love for God, for when a Christian loves the One who gives, he appreciates His gifts. "Contentment," or sharing the happiness of God, is the problem-solving device directed toward self. This inner happiness characterizes all three stages of spiritual adulthood, increasing in strength with the attainment of each successive stage.

WARM-UP EXERCISES FOR MOMENTUM TESTING

Several types of providential preventive suffering are listed in 2 Corinthians 12:10, setting up a distinct pattern. As Paul has already stated, each category of suffering for blessing creates a situation of helplessness. The believer cannot use his human intelligence, experience, ingenuity, talent, or influence to resolve the problem. He must rely on divine assets. The word "weaknesses," therefore, expresses this helplessness and represents the overall concept of providential preventive suffering. The believer with spiritual self-esteem has the capacity to "find contentment" whenever suffering enters his life.

The next four categories of testing in 2 Corinthians 12:10 are precursors of the four momentum tests which we will study in connection with spiritual autonomy.[44] The growing believer is familiarized with these momentum tests— in advance, and at reduced intensity. God carefully prepares the believer for the future, when more intense suffering will be needed to perpetuate his spiritual growth. Here we discover again the truth that God will not test the positive believer "beyond what [he is] able [to bear]" (1 Cor. 10:13).

Providential preventive suffering not only suppresses arrogance and moves the believer into spiritual autonomy, but it also serves as a warm-up for the testings that will accelerate him beyond spiritual autonomy into spiritual maturity. "In slanders" corresponds to *people testing*. "In pressures" anticipates

---

44. See pp. 95ff.

WEAKNESSES as warm-ups for	MOMENTUM TESTING
SLANDERS	*People Test*
PRESSURES	*Thought Test*
PERSECUTIONS	*System Test*
STRESSES	*Disaster Test*

PROVIDENTIAL PREVENTIVE SUFFERING IN 2 CORINTHIANS 12:10

thought testing. "In persecutions" corresponds to *system testing.* And "in stresses" prepares the believer for *disaster testing.*

This entire system of spiritual advancement is said to be "in behalf of Christ." The principle that suffering is a key element in the glorification of Christ is also stated in Paul's epistle to the Philippians.

> For to you it has been given in behalf of Christ not only to
> believe in Him but also to suffer for His sake." (Phil. 1:29)

How does our suffering benefit Christ? By fulfilling the protocol plan of God we glorify the Lord Jesus Christ. He is exalted in our lives as we attain spiritual adulthood and proceed toward maturity so that we are qualified to receive maximum blessing. Christ is glorified by delivering special, tailor-made blessings to the mature believer.[45] We "suffer for His sake" in the sense that periodic suffering is essential to our advance. The emphasis is on spiritual growth and on Christ's glorification, not on suffering itself.

Personal love for the Lord Jesus Christ motivates us to desire His glorification. Our application of doctrine during providential preventive suffering accelerates spiritual growth, which contributes to the demonstration of His glory. Therefore, as Paul states in 2 Corinthians 12:10, we suffer for His sake "all the more gladly."

Our purpose in life is to utilize the assets of the divine dynasphere so that we advance to spiritual maturity. Much of this advance is spurred by suffering for blessing. Concluding his discussion of providential preventive suffering, Paul

---

45.   See pp. 136-39.

reiterates that when we pursue our destiny, moving step by step toward the goal, "then [we are] powerful" (2 Cor. 12:10). The omnipotence of God, available for our utilization in the divine dynasphere, sustains and empowers us at each stage as we move forward in His protocol plan.

Because 2 Corinthians 12:7-10 describes providential preventive suffering, the final word "powerful" in this passage refers to the next stage of advance after spiritual self-esteem. Paul has passed the test of providential preventive suffering and has attained new power. "Powerful" in this context becomes a synonym for spiritual autonomy.

VII
Spiritual Autonomy

THE DYNAMIC STATE OF
SPIRITUAL SELF-ESTEEM

PHYSICAL EXERCISE DEVELOPS STRENGTH, coordination, and stamina and is essential for good health. In the same way, adversity gives the believer the vital spiritual exercise that builds spiritual autonomy. According to this athletic analogy, spiritual autonomy is spiritual self-esteem with muscle.

The experience of using divine assets under providential preventive suffering strengthens all the characteristics of spiritual self-esteem. Success in handling pressure dramatically increases the believer's confidence in God. As a result, legitimate self-confidence also grows. The believer becomes keenly aware of belonging to God's protocol plan and of possessing tremendous divine assets that work in time of crisis or tranquillity. Occupation with Christ and sharing the happiness of God cause the believer with spiritual autonomy to conduct himself with confidence, graciousness, and unshakable poise.

Derived from the classical Greek noun *autonomia,* the word "autonomy" originally meant to live under one's own laws, to live in a state of being independent. In modern usage autonomy expresses independence, self-determination, self-direction. In the Christian way of life, spiritual autonomy is the freedom of exercising royal prerogatives within one's own palace, the divine dynasphere. Spiritual autonomy is the dynamic state of spiritual self-esteem.

The spiritually autonomous Christian knows that God has equipped him to meet the demands of life. Through his pastor's faithful teaching and his own experience of doctrinal application, he has learned to utilize invisible divine assets in his daily life. Furthermore, suffering for blessing has given him a new attitude toward other people. Spiritual autonomy gives the believer strength to love others consistently with impersonal love.

IMPERSONAL LOVE MANDATED BY GOD

*Im*personal love is defined by contrast to personal love. Personal love comes in two categories:

1. ROMANCE is personal love for a member of the opposite sex,

2. FRIENDSHIP is personal admiration for a member of either sex.

Personal love is attraction or admiration for someone else based on one's own standards. By falling in love or making a friend, however, a person creates a problem. The object of his love is imperfect, and sooner or later, for one reason or another, that person will become a source of suffering and testing. Because no one is perfect, the object of personal love will cause disappointment, frustration, and hurt. The problem is that no one is perfect, neither the subject nor the object. Both contribute their flaws to the relationship.

When God commands us to love all believers (John 15:12, 17), our neighbors (Matt. 19:19; Rom. 13:9), and all mankind (Luke 6:27-28, 35), obviously He cannot mean personal love. God is commanding us to *resolve* problems, not to *create* problems. In fact, the only personal love with inherent virtue is personal love for God. God is the only perfect object of love.

What category of love fulfills the divine mandate? Impersonal love directed toward all mankind has inherent virtue and problem-solving characteristics. Impersonal love is unconditional with regard to its object. This means that no merit is assigned to the object of love; the motivation for impersonal love is not attractiveness, rapport, or worthiness. Motivated by the believer's own virtue, impersonal love is, therefore, tolerant, unprejudiced, courteous, and objective in the face of hostility and antagonism. Impersonal love is the attitude of the spiritually adult Christian resulting from the filling of the Holy Spirit and the perception, metabolization, and application of Bible doctrine inside the palace of the divine dynasphere.

DEFINITION AND DESCRIPTION OF IMPERSONAL LOVE

To understand the love that God commands every believer to have for all people, a distinction must be made between the subject and object of love. The subject is the one who loves; the object is the one who is loved. When love emphasizes the object, personal love is in view. When love emphasizes the subject, impersonal love is in view. Impersonal love is unconditional, emphasizing the virtue and spiritual status of the subject rather than rapport with the object. The greater the virtue of the subject, the greater the scope or range of its objects. The object of impersonal love can be known or unknown, friend or enemy, attractive or repulsive, honorable or dishonorable, good or evil, believer or unbeliever.

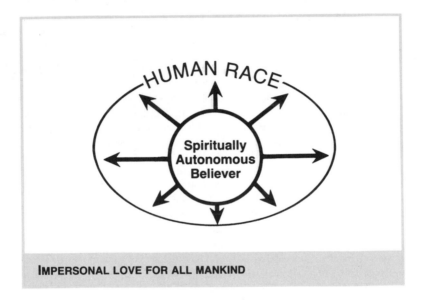

IMPERSONAL LOVE FOR ALL MANKIND

Impersonal love, therefore, is defined as the virtue of the subject resulting from residence, function, and momentum in the divine dynasphere. Impersonal love develops in stages, specifically the three stages of spiritual adulthood: spiritual self-esteem, spiritual autonomy, and spiritual maturity. Impersonal love is a sign of spiritual adulthood, since all three stages possess impersonal love in some degree. The Christian's impersonal love is not fully developed in Gate 5 of the divine dynasphere but becomes stabilized in Gate 6 and maximized in Gate 8.

Personal love for God, which is the source of spiritual self-esteem, is also the source of impersonal love for all mankind. In other words, Gate 5 of the divine dynasphere precedes Gate 6.

If someone should allege, ''I love God,'' and yet he hates his fellow believer, he is a liar. For he who does not love his fellow believer, whom he has seen, is not able to be loving God, whom he has not seen. Furthermore, we have this mandate from Him, that he who loves God [personal love for God, Gate 5 of the divine dynasphere] should also love his fellow believer [impersonal love, Gate 6]. (1 John 4:20-21)

Spiritual self-esteem is prerequisite to the function of impersonal love. The mandates to ''love your neighbor *as yourself*'' imply that spiritual self-esteem is the essential foundation for impersonal love (Matt. 22:39; Mark 12:31; Gal. 5:14). Then, as the believer advances to spiritual autonomy, he builds the spiritual muscle to comply with every divine mandate regarding impersonal love for all mankind. Capacity for impersonal love is *acquired* through providential preventive suffering, which carries the believer into spiritual autonomy. Impersonal love is then *tested* through the people test as part of momentum testing on the way to spiritual maturity.[46]

Impersonal love is not indifference or a lack of compassion. It is the virtue at the core of all successful personal relationships in friendship or romance.

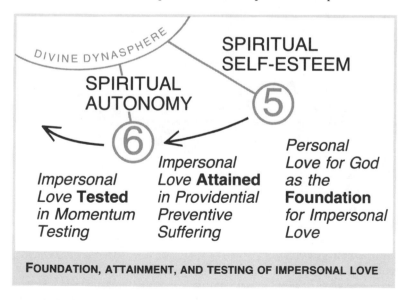

DIVINE DYNASPHERE

SPIRITUAL SELF-ESTEEM

SPIRITUAL AUTONOMY

(6) (5)

Impersonal Love Tested in Momentum Testing

Impersonal Love Attained in Providential Preventive Suffering

Personal Love for God as the Foundation for Impersonal Love

FOUNDATION, ATTAINMENT, AND TESTING OF IMPERSONAL LOVE

46. See pp. 98-100.

Impersonal love is a virtue from God attained in the fulfillment of the protocol plan, whereas personal love is an expression of man's ego that may not involve virtue. Impersonal love emphasizes the virtue, integrity, and spiritual adulthood of the subject; personal love emphasizes the attractiveness and desirability of the object. Impersonal love encompasses the entire human race; personal love is reserved for a few. Impersonal love is sustained by Bible doctrine; personal love is sustained by rapport and mutual admiration. Impersonal love is imperative, mandated by God of all believers toward all mankind; personal love is optional and exclusive. Impersonal love requires fulfillment of the protocol plan of God; personal love requires no qualifications: anyone can fall in love. Impersonal love is a problem-solving device; personal love is a problem manufacturer.

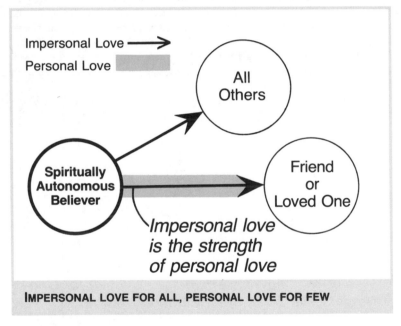

IMPERSONAL LOVE FOR ALL, PERSONAL LOVE FOR FEW

While personal love for members of the human race can be a distraction to the believer's relationship with God, impersonal love for all mankind is a manifestation of personal love for God as the highest motivation in life. Impersonal love brings virtue to all problems of love and hate, friendship and enmity, attraction and animosity. Impersonal love perpetuates its own honor, virtue, and integrity without retaliation, reaction, prejudice, discrimination, or revenge. Impersonal love cannot be destroyed by hatred, persecution, unjust treatment, vindictiveness, or any other category of antagonism.

Impersonal love is the effective basis for dealing with all mankind. It is the quality of not allowing one's personal feelings or emotions to motivate discourtesy and thoughtlessness. Impersonal love is the mental attitude that does not react in a personality conflict but treats others on the basis of one's own honor, integrity, and objectivity.

Spiritual autonomy *is* that honor, integrity, and objectivity in the believer. Although impersonal love begins to emerge in earlier stages of Christian growth, it is erratic prior to reaching spiritual autonomy. In fact, the distinguishing quality of spiritual autonomy is impersonal love for all mankind. An overview of the characteristics of spiritual autonomy will describe the inner strength which animates impersonal love.

CHARACTERISTICS OF SPIRITUAL AUTONOMY

As the Christian advances in the divine dynasphere, he utilizes available divine omnipotence on a consistent basis in more areas of his life. When compared with the qualities previously listed under spiritual self-esteem, the more powerful characteristics of spiritual autonomy reflect this greater utilization of divine omnipotence.

1. CONTINUATION OF CONTENTMENT. The believer possesses increased capacity for happiness and tranquillity of soul. He can appreciate the grace of God at work in every circumstance of his life. The believer's happiness increases in strength and becomes more constant in each stage of spiritual adulthood.

2. PERPETUATED MENTAL STABILITY. Mental attitude improves with each stage of spiritual advance.

> He who gets wisdom [Bible doctrine] loves his own soul [spiritual self-esteem from metabolized doctrine]; he who cherishes understanding prospers [advances beyond spiritual self-esteem to spiritual autonomy]. (Prov. 19:8)

> Keep on having this thinking in you which also resided in Christ Jesus. (Phil. 2:5)

The believer with spiritual autonomy is no longer as vulnerable to pressure as he was upon first entering spiritual adulthood. He now has greater ability to concentrate so that he can apply Bible doctrine more consistently in adversity as well as in prosperity.

3. IMPERSONAL LOVE FOR ALL MANKIND. The consolidation of impersonal love is the most dramatic difference between spiritual self-esteem and spiritual autonomy. Christian integrity enables the believer to treat all people on the basis of his own virtue rather than borrow their strength or depend on their merits or attractiveness.

4. COGNITIVE SELF-CONFIDENCE. In spiritual self-esteem the knowledge factor was called epistemological rehabilitation, the process of renewing the mind with the hundreds of doctrines the believer had metabolized over the years in spiritual childhood. In spiritual autonomy the knowledge factor is cognitive self-confidence, which involves a more complete understanding of doctrine from having utilized divine problem-solving devices under providential preventive suffering. The spiritually autonomous believer knows that doctrine works. He has greater confidence in God and in his own ability to recall and accurately apply doctrine without distorting either the doctrine or the application.

5. GRACE ORIENTATION TO LIFE. While spiritual self-esteem also includes grace orientation, spiritual autonomy involves a deeper appreciation for the grace policy which God administers to all believers. Grace totally excludes human effort, human strength, human merit, human ability. Human advantages do not contribute to the execution of the protocol plan of God. The Christian way of life is a supernatural way of life demanding a supernatural means of execution. The spiritually autonomous believer understands his total dependence on divine omnipotence. Orientation to God's grace frees him from the last vestiges of legalism. With spiritual autonomy he does not abuse the freedom that grace gives him. Instead, he uses that freedom to comply with God's will, purpose, and plan for the Church Age. He utilizes available divine omnipotence to perpetuate his spiritual growth.

6. DOCTRINAL ORIENTATION TO REALITY. The utilization of divine omnipotence keeps the believer on the path of reality and avoids any arrogant drive toward unreality. Because arrogance and subjectivity have been reduced to a minimum by providential preventive suffering, the spiritually autonomous believer is able to habitually utilize available divine power. In dramatic contrast to the neurotic or psychotic Christian, he enjoys the full effectiveness of all divine problem-solving devices. Spiritual autonomy is the epitome of sanity and mental stability.

7. GREATER DECISIONS FROM A POSITION OF STRENGTH. Right thinking (Bible doctrine) and right motivation (personal love for God) lead to right decisions. In each successive stage of spiritual adulthood, the believer makes a higher percentage of good decisions. More good decisions mean more right actions, fulfilling the principle that a right thing must be done in a right way in order to be right. In contrast, a right thing done in a wrong way is wrong, and a wrong thing done in a right way is also wrong. A wrong thing done in a wrong way obviously is wrong. Specifically, all spiritual momentum and advance is a right thing done in a right way. This is the essence of divine protocol. The basis for good decisions is the perception and metabolization of Bible doctrine; the good decision itself is the application of doctrine.

8. PERSONAL CONTROL OF ONE'S LIFE. The spiritually autonomous Christian understands and accepts his own limitations. He also recognizes that the grace provision of invisible assets has removed all limitations to his advance to spiritual maturity, which is the ultimate objective. The advancing believer understands that he cannot manipulate others and at the same time maintain control over his own life. No one can tamper with the decisions of others and be objective in his own decisions. The spiritually autonomous Christian, therefore, refrains from interfering in the lives of other people. Spiritual autonomy restrains jealousy, possessiveness, defensiveness, and the inordinate desire to dominate others. Spiritual autonomy remains righteous without becoming self-righteous, and moral without entering into moralistic orgies of crusader arrogance.

9. A PERSONAL SENSE OF DESTINY. In spiritual autonomy the Christian becomes increasingly aware of his own destiny within the protocol plan of God. God is his destiny. God has designed a powerful plan for blessing him to the maximum, a plan that enables his life to glorify Jesus Christ both now and forever. Once a believer is free from possessiveness and from seeking to control others, he can concentrate on exercising his God-given prerogatives within the framework of his own royal priesthood. He has learned to respect the privacy of others. He has become tolerant of the flaws and foibles of those whom he would ordinarily resent. His impersonal love means that he can interact with others from the high ground of Christian integrity while concentrating on the fulfillment of God's purpose for his own life.

10. COMMAND OF SELF. As the powerful extension of spiritual self-esteem, spiritual autonomy stabilizes the believer's self-control, self-restraint, poise, and self-regulation. His soul is so inculcated with Bible doctrine that, under the filling of the Holy Spirit, his reason is sovereign over his life. He is not

controlled by emotion or by the subjective aberrations of others. Consequently, in command of himself, the believer has a quality of communication with others that avoids inordinate ambition and competition.

11. QUALIFICATION FOR MOMENTUM TESTING. Because God never places more pressure on a believer than he can bear, spiritual autonomy is a prerequisite for momentum testing. By achieving spiritual autonomy, the believer is ready to proceed into the next phase of his advance to spiritual maturity.

12. ATTAINMENT OF A NEW PHASE OF THE UNIQUE LIFE. The *modus vivendi* of the believer with spiritual autonomy is described by the phrase "Christ [is] at home in your hearts," that is, in the thinking portion of the mentality of the soul (Eph. 3:16-17).

SPIRITUAL AUTONOMY AND THE COMPLETION OF VIRTUE-LOVE

Spiritual autonomy is not an isolated virtue. It is an integral part of a greater, compound virtue, called virtue-love, all parts of which have now been introduced so that the overall concept may be presented.

Spiritual autonomy marks the attainment of Gate 6 of the divine dynasphere and the consolidation of virtue-love. As the combination of Gates 5 and 6, virtue-love creates marvelous capacity for life. Furthermore, energized by divine omnipotence through the believer's residence in the divine dynasphere, virtue-love also becomes the most versatile problem-solving device in the protocol plan of God.

> Now remain faith [the faith-rest drill], hope [confidence in promised blessings], and love [virtue-love], these three, and the greatest of these [is] love. (1 Cor. 13:13)

Faith-rest and hope are useful methods of problem solving that become operational in spiritual childhood.[47] These two systems of applying Bible doctrine to experience continue to be effective in spiritual adulthood.

Virtue-love, however, is greater than faith-rest or hope because it expresses strength that belongs exclusively to spiritual adulthood. Virtue-love solves problems in the believer's relationships with God and with others. In Gate 5, personal

---

47. See pp. 10-11.

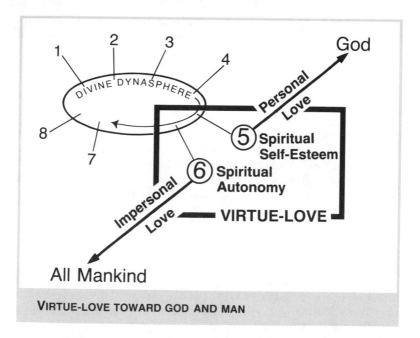

VIRTUE-LOVE TOWARD GOD AND MAN

love for God is *virtue-love directed toward God.* This is the highest motivation in life. Personal love for God automatically gives the believer spiritual self-esteem. Providential preventive suffering then strengthens spiritual self-esteem, developing spiritual autonomy in Gate 6. This becomes the inner strength that manifests itself in impersonal love for all mankind, or *virtue-love directed toward others.*

The significance of virtue-love can hardly be overemphasized. Although believers of previous dispensations were commanded to love God and man (Matt. 22:35-40), virtue-love is unique to the Church Age. Sustained by the power of the indwelling Holy Spirit, fueled by a depth of doctrinal resources never available before the canon of Scripture was completed, designed to follow the precedent of the glorified Christ, virtue-love is an integral part of the operational divine dynasphere. It is a problem-solving device far more effective than even the considerable divine assets available to the heroes of the Old Testament.

More than a problem-solving device toward God and man, virtue-love is also the believer's capacity for life, love, and happiness. Virtue-love equips him to enjoy life while facing all categories of momentum testing. Without this tremendous system of virtue, no member of the royal family could advance the final distance into spiritual maturity and the maximum glorification of Jesus Christ.

This multifaceted, composite virtue is discussed in detail in *Christian Integrity*.[48] Here we will summarize and note how impersonal love is the final item which completes the construction of virtue-love.

VIRTUE-LOVE DEFINED

Gates 5 and 6 of the divine dynasphere represent a single virtue, divided according to its objects and presented to indicate the sequence in which this overall virtue is acquired. Personal love for God comes first. As personal love for God increases, the believer's attitude toward self improves: spiritual self-esteem becomes spiritual autonomy. Finally, as this inner strength becomes established in his soul, he is able to deal more consistently with others from impersonal love.

As previously noted, *im*personal love is defined by contrast to personal love. Both of these categories of love can be illustrated in the sentence "I love you." In personal love, the emphasis is on the "you," on the attractiveness, character, intelligence, and personality of the object of love. Personal love depends on rapport with the object. Obviously, personal love is exclusive. Only a few people receive any particular believer's personal love, which requires a degree of intimacy, knowledge, trust, and reciprocation. For compatibility to exist, the "I" and the "you" must perceive one another as fulfilling each other's norms and standards.

Impersonal love, on the other hand, is entirely a function of the "I," the subject of the sentence, the one who loves. What is his character? Does he possess virtue? The term *impersonal* love acknowledges that no compatibility, familiarity, reciprocation, or intimacy of any kind is required between the subject and object. Impersonal love is the spiritually autonomous believer's unconditional attitude toward *everyone* he meets. It is the expression of his integrity, which is manifested by tolerance, patience, compassion, courtesy, and generosity. Impersonal love excludes prejudice, hypocrisy, insensitivity, and rudeness.

The believer's impersonal love is inherently virtuous because it can exist only when he has virtue. By contrast, personal love for another human being has no virtue in itself and does not necessarily involve virtue of any kind. Any irresponsible fool can fall in love. Falling in love requires no intelligence, talent, ability, or integrity. Personal love depends on the object rather than the subject of love; the one who loves may be deceived in his judgment of the object or may fantasize qualities in the object which do not exist. Personal love is often a problem manufacturer with no inherent problem-solving capability.

There are two sources for inserting virtue into personal love. For believers and unbelievers, adherence to the divine laws of establishment can support

---

48.   Pp. 112-38.

personal love. For believers, attainment of spiritual autonomy creates the impersonal love that sustains personal love. The only category of personal love that is inherently virtuous and does not need to be sustained by impersonal love is the believer's personal love for God. By the very perfection of His essence, God is eternally worthy of the Christian's love. The very idea of tolerance toward perfect God is ludicrous and blasphemous.

Therefore, The believer's personal love for God, which is inherently virtuous, and his impersonal love for all mankind, which is also virtuous in itself, constitute the composite strength of character which I call virtue-love.

GENERAL CATEGORIES OF LOVE

The value of virtue-love becomes dramatically clear when we understand that there are three general categories of human love:

1. PSEUDO-LOVE,

2. VIRTUE-DEPENDENT LOVE (personal love for man),

3. VIRTUE-LOVE (personal love for God; impersonal love for man).

Pseudo-love is arrogance hidden behind a facade of emotion or hypocrisy of words. Pseudo-love uses others for self-gratification, for personal advancement, or as props to hold up one's weaknesses. Much that is passed off as genuine love is not love at all. A notorious cause of human suffering, pseudo-love is removed by spiritual growth in the divine dynasphere, which results in virtue-love and capacity for virtue-dependent love.

Virtue-dependent love includes romance and friendship. In romance especially, but also in friendship, a person tends to idealize the object of love. But no one is perfect. An image of perfection imposed on anyone is certain to cause disappointment and frustration. Reality inevitably emerges. Even if the object of love is treated as a person and is not expected to meet unattainable standards, still his or her independence, vacillations, foibles, and flaws of the old sin nature will periodically strain the relationship. But this is only half the problem.

Actually, the difficulties in personal love arise from far greater complications than those caused by the volatility of one who is loved. The person who loves is also changeable and imperfect. His or her own quirks, instabilities, and sin nature collide with the imperfections and fluctuations in the object of love. The intimacy and honesty of personal love, by their very nature, multiply the odds against a successful relationship. In personal love, each party's problems are compounded by the other person's problems. If a person cannot handle his own problems, he will never be able to deal with the problems of someone with whom he is intimate. Apart from spiritual autonomy, personal love is an uncontrollable, unsustainable problem maker.

Personal love between imperfect human beings is perpetually in a state of flux. Alterations in emotions, moods, physical health, intellectual preoccupations, perceptions, misperceptions, reactions to external influences and demands—all these conspire to disrupt the relationship. Petty irritations continually intrude. In the eyes of the one who loves, the object of love may change from being attractive to unattractive to attractive again, from responsive to reactive, from charming to annoying. Beneath the emotional turbulence inherent in personal love, however, impersonal love remains as constant as the spiritually autonomous Christian's own character.

The complex difficulties inherent in romance and friendship can be overcome. Wonderful relationships can be sustained, but the prerequisite is virtue. Romance and friendship are virtue-dependent. Each individual must bring his or her own virtue into the relationship.

For the believer, God has provided the system by which to acquire and maintain this individual virtue. The system is the *divine dynasphere,* the believer's royal palace, the protocol plan of God. The virtue is found in Gates 5 and 6, called *virtue-love.*

By the time a believer reaches spiritual autonomy, he has the full exercise of virtue-love as the key problem-solving device of the entire divine dynasphere. Virtue-love—toward God and others—is the strength of character that enables him to continue his spiritual advance. With virtue-love he can pass through the valley of momentum testing, which is the next category of suffering for blessing, and advance to the high ground of spiritual maturity.

VIII
Momentum Testing

NO ASCETICISM IN SUFFERING
FOR BLESSING

ALTHOUGH THIS STUDY FOCUSES ON ADVERSITY in the life of the believer in Jesus Christ, suffering is *not* the basic characteristic of Christianity. Instead, spiritual autonomy gives the believer capacity to enjoy life in spite of any adversity that comes his way. His happiness does not depend on environment, possessions, or people. He can appreciate the pleasant details of life and cope with the disasters because he is not enslaved to circumstances. The problem-solving devices of the protocol plan of God enable the believer to equate prosperity and adversity, living and dying.

Metabolized doctrine in the believer's soul causes him to personally love God. That ever-increasing love produces contentment and happiness, which he brings with him into every situation. Indeed, sharing the happiness of God in spiritual adulthood is the most effective problem-solving device in the protocol plan of God. The believer advances by applying Bible doctrine under pressure, but it is the doctrine he applies, not the suffering he endures, that causes his growth.

Bible doctrine explains suffering, and metabolized doctrine alleviates suffering in the soul. But Christianity is not a religion of suffering. There is no asceticism in the protocol plan of God. Despite false teaching to the contrary, suffering for its own sake is not a legitimate Christian objective.

Tragically, many Christians never learn the doctrine of suffering. To their way of thinking, adversity creates an aura of spirituality. Presumptuously claiming to follow Christ in His sufferings, they attach importance to their own pain as if it brought them closer to God. They distort their lives to fit a crippling false doctrine: they assume God honors self-sacrifice and commands them to suffer. This malignant idea breeds arrogance, destroys capacity for life, and blasphemes the character of God.

Legalism, asceticism, and a martyr complex impose unnecessary suffering on believers, but such self-induced misery has no place in divine protocol. The saving work of Christ eliminates all human works for salvation (Eph. 2:8-9); rebound by grace excludes all penance (1 John 1:9); the marvelous doctrines of royal privilege and opportunity expose the arrogance of self-abnegation, self-flagellation, self-mutilation (Gal. 5:12).

God retains sovereign control over suffering in the protocol plan, which He will administer only to the right believer at the right time and to the right degree. God, not self, administers suffering for blessing. In other words, the believer must not look for trouble. On the contrary, he is to utilize divine provisions for problem *solving*. Even divine discipline exists for the purpose of blessing, but ascetic Christians ignore God's purpose and cling to suffering as an end in itself. Their misguided, false attempts to earn God's approbation incur only divine wrath. These legalistic believers reject God's grace, refuse to utilize the invisible assets of divine omnipotence, and instead function in Satan's cosmic system under religious evil. [49]

Under unusual circumstances a Christian may suffer for his beliefs. Truth arouses animosity in those with hardened negative volition (Matt. 10:34-36), but the believer should not provoke animosity just to prove his loyalty to the truth. Such suffering merely feeds a perverse form of arrogance. The antagonism a believer endures is neither an indication of spiritual growth nor a proof of his effectiveness as a witness for Christ. Every Church Age believer is an ambassador of Jesus Christ in the devil's world (2 Cor. 5:20). He is *in* the world but not *of* the world, and he is commanded "not [to] love the world, nor the things in the world" (1 John 2:15). However, neither is he to cause unnecessary suffering by making himself *persona non grata*.

The Christian's royal ambassadorial commission does not call upon him to be obnoxious and to cause resentment in order to claim that he "suffers for Jesus." The spiritually autonomous believer is motivated by love for God, not by a desire to prove himself to God or man. Furthermore, the Bible doctrine in

---

49. See *Christian Integrity*, p. 169.

his soul is far too great a treasure to be flaunted before the enemies of the truth (Matt. 7:6). He finds opportunities to present the Gospel in order to pass on the good news. His purpose is neither to gain God's approbation nor to expose himself to the world's hatred (John 15:18-21).

Second Corinthians 6 teaches that we are to give "no cause for offense in anything, in order that the ministry be not discredited" (2 Cor. 6:3). The function of the divine dynasphere (2 Cor. 6:6-7) and the attainment of spiritual autonomy give the believer excellence, quality, and class as a royal ambassador of the Lord Jesus Christ. With spiritual autonomy the royal ambassador can surmount "endurance, afflictions, hardships, distresses, beatings, imprisonments, tumults, labors, sleeplessness, and hunger" if and when such testings occur (2 Cor. 6:4-5). Whether in prosperous or adverse circumstances (2 Cor. 6:8), his love, loyalty, and happiness are related to the Lord whom he represents.

SUFFERING IN FOUR CATEGORIES OF MOMENTUM TESTING

Spiritual autonomy not only gives the believer capacity for life as Christ's representative on earth but also prepares him for the final approach to spiritual maturity. In order to accelerate the believer's momentum to the final objective of maturity, God periodically inserts momentum testing among the advancing believer's blessings. Four categories of momentum testing characterize Christian suffering in the advance from spiritual autonomy to spiritual maturity:

1. PEOPLE TESTING

2. THOUGHT TESTING

3. SYSTEM TESTING

4. DISASTER TESTING

The believer with spiritual autonomy does not fear this formidable catalog of suffering. He has previously passed a warm-up exam for each of these tests. Now that his spiritual self-esteem has become spiritual autonomy, providential preventive suffering has prepared him for the four categories of momentum testing he is about to encounter.

At this stage in his spiritual life, the believer should not be caught off guard by suffering. The pain will not be less than before. In fact, the suffering may be more intense, but he has the problem-solving devices necessary to take suffering in stride.

PEOPLE TESTING

APPROBATION AS A TEST OF MOMENTUM

People testing challenges the believer from two antithetical directions: approbation and antagonism. In either case, the danger lies in relinquishing spiritual autonomy and turning over control of one's life to someone else. A person the believer loves or admires may inordinately influence his life and happiness. Anyone he hates definitely usurps control.

Personal love in the human race is virtue-dependent. Lacking inherent virtue, it relies on the integrity of impersonal love as a problem-solving device. This very dependence on virtue-love makes every personal love relationship a test of the believer's faithfulness to divine priorities. Will he overemphasize the object of love to the point of compromising his personal sense of destiny in the protocol plan of God? Or will he integrate his human relationships into a consistent, balanced Christian life?

Personal love emphasizes the object of love, but if a believer elevates the human object of his love above God, he fails the people test. In his desire to please the woman he loves, a man may turn over control of his life to her. He makes himself a slave, living by her whim rather than by the strength of his own soul. Ironically, as a slave he renounces all possibility of pleasing her. He ceases to be the man to whom she originally was attracted. The same may be true of a woman. Although a wife lives under her husband's authority, she should not renounce her responsibility for her own life out of her desire to please him.

Personal love does not require either party to surrender his or her autonomy to the other. God has a unique plan for each believer. Each is a royal priest before God and remains an individual. In a personal love relationship both the subject and the object must maintain integrity and contribute virtue-love if the relationship is to have hope of success.

The key to passing the people test is that people emphasis must not take precedence over God emphasis. In other words, among the many legitimate activities and involvements in the believer's life, Bible doctrine must receive first priority. Human relationships are important in any normal life, but the Christian's relationship with God in the divine dynasphere enables human personal love to succeed. Therefore, the believer must learn to say no when even legitimate activities challenge the top priority of doctrine.

A believer may make his own choices in the selection of his friends and loved ones, but thereafter they will make many decisions for him unless he maintains his spiritual autonomy.

> Be not deceived; evil friends corrupt good morals. (1 Cor. 15:33)

He who walks with wise men will be wise,
But the friends of fools will suffer evil. (Prov. 13:20)

Personal love may not sound like a particularly unpleasant momentum test. Everyone wants to be in love. Personal love, however, is a problem manufacturer with no inherent problem-solving capability. When a person reveals his soul to someone he loves, the intimacy between one imperfect person and another creates vulnerability to suffering. Some of the greatest anguish in life comes from personal love. Personal love can avoid becoming misery and slavery only when accompanied by the virtue of impersonal love. Spiritual autonomy, therefore, is the inner strength that makes personal love a marvelous blessing.

ANTAGONISM AS A TEST OF MOMENTUM

Like personal love, antagonism can also cause the believer to surrender the control of his life to someone else. He may be driving down the freeway when another motorist cuts in front of him. The immediate reaction may be anger at that discourteous so-and-so, but anger is ridiculous in this situation. Suddenly the believer is upset and irritated; his whole attitude is distorted by this petty incident. He has turned over the custody of his happiness to a total stranger. If he refuses to recover from the mental attitude sin of hatred through rebound, he may escalate his initial reaction into a foolish and potentially violent feud with the other driver.

Any time a believer reacts to people with jealousy, bitterness, vindictiveness, or implacability, he immediately grants them control over his life. In an irrational attempt to regain control, he may vent his antagonism in gossip, maligning, false accusation, or even physical violence. But by attacking the person to whom he has surrendered his happiness, the believer attacks his own happiness. Each antagonistic reaction carries him deeper into self-induced misery.

When other people control a believer's life, whether or not they want control or even realize they have such influence, he blames them for his discontent. But blaming others for self-induced misery cuts off the possibility of solution and, under the law of volitional responsibility, intensifies the suffering. With spiritual growth, the believer becomes aware of this pattern of unhappiness. He uses rebound for forgiveness of the sins involved, but the specific solution to people testing is impersonal love, in which the believer's own inner strength is the basis for toleration of others. Impersonal love is crystallized as an active component of virtue-love only after the believer has attained spiritual autonomy.

Ultimately, the solution to all momentum testing is the believer's happiness. Happiness as a problem-solving device is the monopoly of God and His plan.

The believer cannot depend on people for happiness; he must depend on God. The believer must follow divine protocol to avoid undue influence from those he loves and to keep from falling into hatred toward those who irritate him. Spiritual momentum in the protocol plan of God will bring the believer to spiritual autonomy where his contentment is stabilized and where he can utilize impersonal love as a solution to his problems with people.

THOUGHT TESTING

THE IMPORTANCE OF DOCTRINAL THINKING

Thought determines the believer's life. Thought has such a powerful effect on the believer's success or failure in the Christian life that thinking must be considered a major momentum test. In all stages of Christian growth the believer will face the pressure of thought conflicts in his soul.

Human viewpoint will conflict with divine viewpoint. False concepts will challenge Bible doctrine. Arrogance will intrude upon humility. Expedients of all kinds will compete with the protocol plan of God. Fear will paralyze reason. These are essentially private conflicts which the believer must resolve in his own soul. Quandaries, confusions, and unanswered questions motivate the positive believer to apply the resources of Bible doctrine he has learned. Concentration on doctrine accelerates his spiritual growth.

Thought testing may exist when circumstances are overtly prosperous and tranquil. A person is not always what he appears to be on the surface; the real person is the thought content of his soul.

> For as he [a person] thinks within himself, so is he. He says
> to you, "Eat and drink," but his heart [the place of thought]
> is not with you. (Prov. 23:7)

Because a believer is what he thinks, a thought can make or break him, depending on the nature of the thought. If his thought is consistent with Bible doctrine, he advances in the protocol plan of God. If his thought is contrary to doctrine, he is distracted from his true destiny in life. His mental attitude toward life is the function of his thinking, the composite of all he knows and believes.

Prayer illustrates the importance of thought in fulfilling the believer's private responsibilities before the Lord.[50] Each member of the royal family is a priest with the tremendous privilege of representing himself before God. With privilege comes responsibility. God has established the protocol which the

---

50. See *Prayer*.

believer must follow in using prayer. The believer's prayers must be consistent with God's essence, objectives, and *modus operandi*. Hence, accurate and careful doctrinal *thinking* is the basis for effective prayer. When his prayers reflect God's own thoughts and desires, the believer can be confident of receiving affirmative answers (John 15:7).

Jesus explained that wrong and sloppy thinking guarantees failure in prayer.

> And when you are praying, do not use meaningless repetition as the Gentiles do, for they think that they will be heard for their many words. (Matt. 6:7)

THINKING EVIL AND THINKING GOOD

Rational thinking is the essential human activity that distinguishes man from animals. Like the angels, man was created with a soul capable of rational thought. Therefore, the mentality of the soul is the battlefield of the angelic conflict.[51] When the believer thinks evil, he is evil. He resides in Satan's cosmic system. From evil thinking comes evil motivation; from evil motivation, evil actions.

> And Jesus, knowing their thoughts, said, "Why are you thinking evil in your hearts?" (Matt. 9:4)

In contrast, thinking that is consistent with the truth has enormous repercussions for good. Salvation itself is appropriated by a right thought, by nonmeritorious positive volition toward the Gospel of Jesus Christ.

> What do you think about the Christ? (Matt. 22:42*a*)

Mankind's great enemy is a thought called arrogance. Arrogance can inflate or deflate man's opinion of himself. He thinks he is better or worse than he actually is. Both self-aggrandizement and self-denigration distort and deny reality, which is the realm in which God's plan is effective. God's grace deals with us as we are, but an egocentric believer who does not live in objective reality will never use God's grace provisions to advance in the protocol plan.

> For if anyone thinks he is something [arrogance] when he is nothing, he deceives himself. (Gal. 6:3)

---

51. See pp. 140-43.

There is a grim irony in arrogance. A person who thinks more of himself than he has a right to think is actually depriving himself of his greatest advantages, the benefits that come with the fulfillment of God's plan for his life.

> For I say through the grace of God which has been given to me, to everyone who is among you, stop thinking of self in terms of arrogance beyond what you ought to think, but think in terms of sanity for the purpose of being rational without illusion, as God has assigned to each one a standard [of thinking] from doctrine. (Rom. 12:3)

Arrogance is illusion, unreality, and when perpetuated, arrogance becomes insanity. The preventive is the truth of Bible doctrine.

> Therefore, let him who thinks he stands take heed [of Bible doctrine] lest he fall. (1 Cor. 10:12)

The divine mandates that the believer must obey in order to consistently pass thought testing are summed up in Romans 12:2.

> Stop being conformed to this age, but be transformed by the renovation of your thought, that you may prove what the will of God is, [namely] the good, the well-pleasing, and the complete. (Rom. 12:2)

"The renovation of [one's] thought" is accomplished over a period of time by giving Bible doctrine number one priority, by organizing one's life around the daily perception of the Word of God. "The good, the well-pleasing, and the complete" is the protocol plan of God, executed in the palace of the divine dynasphere. Only in the divine dynasphere can the believer receive all the blessings God has prepared for him—in prosperity or adversity.

HUMILITY IN CONTRAST TO FALSE SOLUTIONS

The paragon of right thinking is the humanity of Jesus Christ, who constantly lived and functioned inside the prototype of the divine dynasphere.

> Keep on having this mental attitude in you, which was also in Christ Jesus. (Phil. 2:5)

Our Lord's mental attitude of humility was manifested by His total conformity to the plan of the Father. Humility, which is obedience to divine authority and orientation to God's grace, should be the attitude of every member of the royal family of God.[52]

Humility excludes false solutions to thought testing. What are some of the pseudo-solutions which genuine humility avoids?

RATIONALIZATION is self-justification while blaming others for one's own failures and sufferings.

ANGER attacks a problem with temper and tantrums, which manifest total irresponsibility. Unjustified anger ignores the problem, diverting attention instead to self, and attempting to cower people and control them with threats or violence. Power lust and approbation lust are often expressed through anger, which arises from feelings of inferiority that are temporarily assuaged by revenge or by injuring those who challenge one's inflated opinion of self.

DEFENSE MECHANISMS attempt to insulate the believer's mind from overpowering pressures. But such sociopathic functions as drug abuse, lasciviousness, and drunkenness merely compound the original problem by divorcing the believer from reality.

DENIAL ignores the problem in the blind hope that it will go away. Believers who plead with God for miracles often fall into this false system of problem solving.

SUBLIMATION reacts to frustration by finding a new outlet for pent-up emotions. A bored believer may seek happiness in social life, sex, or a pursuit of money when he actually needs to develop love for God through Bible doctrine. Most sublimation is directed into activities that are moral and normal but which have been given a false priority above Bible doctrine and the plan of God.

WORSHIP AND MENTAL COMBAT

Paul depicts thought testing as a battle in the soul. But this is a battle for which God has devised brilliant strategy and tactics. He has powerfully armed and amply supplied the believer to win this inner warfare against erroneous thinking.

> For the equipment and weapons of our warfare [are] not human attributes but attributes of power by means of God [the utilization of divine omnipotence in the divine dynasphere] against the destruction of fortifications [Satan's multifaceted systems of false thinking], assaulting and

---

52. See *Christian Integrity,* pp. 60-82.

> demolishing speculations and every obstacle of arrogance against the knowledge of God, even making a prisoner of every thought to the obedience of Christ, holding in readiness [doctrine in the soul] to punish all deviation when your obedience has been fulfilled [obedience to the mandates of God's protocol plan resulting in spiritual adulthood]. (2 Cor. 10:4-6)

Although divine viewpoint thinking searches out and destroys false human viewpoint, the destruction of incorrect ideas and attitudes is not the ultimate victory in thought testing. Victory lies in possessing the true perspective, thinking with true ideas, understanding and applying true doctrines.

> Jesus therefore was saying to those Jews who had believed Him, "If you abide in My word [Bible doctrine], then you are truly disciples of Mine; and you shall know the truth, and the truth shall make you free." (John 8:31-32, NASB)

In other words, worship of God is a mental attitude.

> God is a Spirit, and those who worship Him must worship in Spirit [the filling of the Holy Spirit, Gate 1 of the divine dynasphere] and in truth [knowing and thinking Bible doctrine, Gate 4]. (John 4:24)

All aspects of worship are based upon accurate, doctrinal thinking. In the Eucharist the believer concentrates on Christ, remembering the doctrines that reveal His person and saving work.[53] Music praises God in doctrinal lyrics. Giving is a mental attitude, and the privilege of contributing to the Lord's service is extended to believers who understand God's grace (2 Cor. 9:7-8).[54] But by far the most important form of worship is concentrating on the teaching of God's Word.

As a result of victories on the battlefield of thought testing, the believer deepens his personal love for God, shares the happiness of God, and acquires inner beauty. This inner beauty, which Paul describes as "sanity of mind" or "stability of mind," characterizes the believer in spiritual adulthood (1 Tim. 2:9-10, 15*b;* 2 Tim. 1:7).

---

53. See *Blood of Christ,* pp. 31-34.
54. See Thieme, *Giving: Gimmick or Grace* (1973).

SYSTEM TESTING

SYSTEMS DEFINED, THE PROBLEM STATED

A system, as the term is used here, is an organization composed of people under the *authority* of other people, which functions according to a *policy* designed to fulfill a specific *objective*. Human society is a web of systems. Every individual belongs to many of these organizations, formal and informal. There are business corporations, military services, ecclesiastical organizations, athletic teams, professional associations, universities, governmental departments, marriages, families, and many other systems. All of these are characterized by:

1. PERSONNEL UNDER AUTHORITY

2. THE OBJECTIVES OF THE ORGANIZATION

3. POLICY OF THE MANAGEMENT

There are good and bad systems, which may be successful or unsuccessful. The personnel—in authority and under authority—may be accomplished or incompetent. Objectives may be legitimate or dubious, lucid or ill-defined. Policy may encourage employees to produce or may oppress them. Problems inevitably exist in the complex of interlocking and overlapping systems that constitute human society. All these organizations involve people, no two of whom are alike and not one of whom is perfect. With so many old sin natures jostling against one another and expressing themselves day after day, no wonder system testing is an inescapable form of suffering that poses a major challenge to the Christian's spiritual advance.

What is a believer to do when he is treated unfairly by someone in authority over him? How should he respond to bias and favoritism that promote people who do inferior work? What if he has a personality conflict with his boss? Or how does he maintain his motivation and integrity when policies serve someone's personal interests rather than strengthening the organization, when they conflict with normal living, or when they seem arbitrary and stupid? How does he cope with conflicting, vague, or impossible objectives?

The dynamics and problems of organizations have been studied and written about by many distinguished authorities. Most problems boil down to arrogance, expressed in incapacity, laziness, distraction by wrong priorities, and ignorance. The purpose of this study of Christian suffering is not to diagnose the weaknesses of particular systems and to prescribe organizational remedies. Instead, the objective is to describe the believer's mental attitude and *modus operandi* as a result of utilizing divine problem-solving devices. Spiritual autonomy enables him to survive and benefit from system testing.

QUIT OR COPE

Two courses of action usually are open to the believer when confronted with system testing. He can quit or he can cope with the pressure, using the dynamics of available divine omnipotence. Certainly there are times to separate oneself from an organization. If a system's objectives or policies are clearly evil, the believer should disassociate himself from it. This would apply to groups like the Communist Party, the Nazi Party, certain apostate churches and cults, criminal organizations, and paramilitary groups that undermine the authority of government through civil disobedience or terrorism.

Separation is required in extreme cases, but quitting because of pressure is often a poor decision from a position of weakness. If the believer succumbs to the pressure, if he quits on relatively mild provocation, he has flunked the system test.

> If you falter in times of trouble,
> How small is your strength. (Prov. 24:10)

If the believer perseveres in a situation even when circumstances are less than perfect, and continues to do a good job, he will be vindicated and promoted spiritually by the Lord. The vindication comes from residence in the power of the divine dynasphere. The believer's royal palace is strong enough to weather any storm, if he will remain inside and use his divine assets.

Spiritual autonomy gives the Christian the power to put the problem in the Lord's hands and continue to function without an arrogant reaction. Bitterness, implacability, self-pity, hatred, jealousy, and revenge do not need to control the believer's life simply because problems exist in a system to which he belongs.

SPIRITUAL AUTONOMY IN SYSTEM TESTING

By remembering the component parts of spiritual autonomy, the believer discovers the assets he needs in facing system testing. Spiritual autonomy is:

1. IMPERSONAL LOVE FOR ALL MANKIND and

2. Strengthened SPIRITUAL SELF-ESTEEM derived from

3. PERSONAL LOVE FOR GOD, which is the result of

4. BIBLE DOCTRINE in the soul.

The believer will need all these qualities when confronted with system testing.

In spiritual autonomy the believer is motivated by his love for God. In any system to which he belongs, he does his job "not as pleasing men but unto God" (1 Thess. 2:4). He does not rely on the organization to furnish his motivation because he is self-motivated. The organization cannot destroy motivation that it did not create in the first place. Only the believer himself can destroy his own motivation through negative volition to the protocol plan of God. With personal love for God as his motivational virtue, the spiritually autonomous Christian can contribute to the organization even when it may treat him unfairly. Needless to say, he does the best possible job regardless of injustice, unfair criticism, or job discrimination. He does not complain or join in organizational conspiracies.

Man is frequently unfair, but God is always fair. Man's systems are flawed, but God's protocol plan is perfect. Human beings in authority may be despicable, but God is always worthy of respect. The spiritually autonomous believer's personal love for God motivates impersonal love for mankind, which enables him to be tolerant of the weaknesses and failures of others. When he is a victim of unfair leadership, unjust management, or an inefficient system, he deals with personality conflicts on the basis of impersonal love. In other words, he takes the attitude that the people who inflict system testing on him are simply contributing to his spiritual advance. Since he loves God, God is working "all things together for good" in his behalf (Rom. 8:28).[55]

The inventory of Bible doctrine in the believer's soul enables him to submit to authority and be an asset to any organization. That same doctrine strengthens him to endure system testing and through his professionalism to be a stabilizing influence for others who also may suffer from the organization's pettiness, shortsightedness, or ineptitude.

In the epistle to the Colossians, Paul states the principle, then illustrates from a variety of systems, and finally presents the correct application of doctrine to system testing.

> And whatever you do in word or deed, do it all in the name of the Lord Jesus, giving thanks to Him through God the Father. Wives, submit to the authority of your husbands as is fitting in the Lord. Husbands, love your wives and stop being bitter against them. Children, obey your parents in

---

55. See *Integrity of God*, pp. 172-89.

everything, for this pleases the Lord. Parents, do not embitter your children, or they will become discouraged. [Children, lacking inner resources, are adversely affected by too much system testing from unfair, inconsistent parents.] Labor, obey management in everything, not with eye-service as men-pleasers but with virtue of heart [doctrine in the thinking of the soul], respecting the Lord.

Whatever you do, keep functioning from [your own] soul as to the Lord [spiritual autonomy] and not to man, since you know that you will receive the reward of your inheritance [your focus extends beyond the objectives of any human organization]. You serve the Lord Christ. Anyone who does wrong will receive the consequences of his wrong, and there is no partiality [under the law of volitional responsibility]. (Col. 3:17-25)

The doctrine of God's impartiality applies to system testing.[56] After the believer has used the appropriate problem-solving devices, he places his case before the supreme court of heaven. God is the perfect judge. There is no reason to complain and whine about unfairness.

The believer is highly immature if he entertains the illusion that fallen, totally depraved human beings will always be enlightened and fair. This is the devil's world. Injustice and discrimination are the norm under Satan's arrogant administration. Rather than focus his attention on the stupidity, cowardice, and evil of mankind, the spiritually autonomous Christian will regard human weaknesses in the context of God's plan.

God is always fair to the believer. God has furnished powerful and effective divine assets, and He intends for the believer to bear the testing that He does not remove. When separation from a flawed system is not justified, spiritual autonomy gives the believer the strength to put the case before God, leave it there for divine solution, and cope with the situation as unto the Lord.

DISASTER TESTING

THE MOST OBVIOUS TEST

People testing, thought testing, and system testing may exert an insidious pressure on the believer. He must be alert to recognize these challenges to his

---

56. See *Integrity of God*, pp. 42-46.

spiritual advance. When he has identified the nature of the test, he then can apply the appropriate problem-solving devices and pass the test.

Disaster testing, however, is anything but subtle. The problem is not to identify the threat but to endure the shock and to maintain poise for decision-making under extreme duress.

There are two categories of disaster testing:

1. PERSONAL DISASTER

2. HISTORICAL, OR NATIONAL, DISASTER

A personal disaster may be physical pain caused by injury, disease, handicap, or genetic weakness. It may be mental anguish, caused by loss of loved ones, reputation, success, employment, money, or property. The privations of hunger, thirst, or exposure to heat or cold may be classified as personal disasters. Arrogance spawns personal disasters: disdain for authority breeds criminals who trample the rights, privacy, and property of their victims. Those who break the law must suffer from the administration of justice (Matt. 26:52; Rom. 13:4).

A historical disaster is a situation that brings grief to many people. A large number of people may suffer from the weather in heat and drought or in extreme and prolonged cold. Blizzards, hurricanes, tornadoes, and floods cause widespread damage as do powerful earthquakes, tidal waves, or volcanic eruptions. Insects or plant diseases may kill crops. Epidemics can decimate a population.

The cycles of a free economy or adjustments in governmental policy may cause immediate hardships for large portions of society. Injustice victimizes many people where self-aggrandizement corrupts the integrity of leadership. When a nation declines, the evils of crime, terrorism, and drug abuse inflict terrible suffering upon the entire society. Arrogance, revenge, greed, inordinate ambition, and power lust pit group against group, nation against nation, ultimately unleashing the violence of war with all its attendant suffering.

THE DISASTER OF ECONOMIC DEPRESSION

How does the spiritually autonomous believer deal with a disaster that affects his entire nation? For example, how can he pass the test of economic depression?

Throughout the centuries during which the Bible was written, the Jewish economy was agricultural. Famine was tantamount to depression. Hence, I will use the term "economic depression" in translating "famine" in certain passages of Scripture.

The economic health of a client nation to God is a rough index of the nation's spiritual condition. Economic prosperity is promised for nations that follow the divine laws of establishment concerning economic freedom.

> This will be the sign for you, O Hezekiah [king of Judah]: "This year you will eat what grows by itself, and the second year what springs from that. But in the third year sow and reap, plant vineyards and eat their fruit. Once more a remnant of the house of Judah will take root below and bear fruit above. (Isa. 37:30-31, NIV)

Economic recovery accompanies spiritual recovery in the client nation. But when the economy is chronically depressed, the nation is usually in spiritual decline. A client nation declines spiritually when the "remnant," the pivot of growing and mature believers in that nation, shrinks while the number of believers who reject the plan of God increases. Furthermore, when the remnant becomes too small to counterbalance the spiritual influence of negative believers, God punishes the client nation with collective divine discipline.

Five cycles of discipline are administered to the client nation whose believers refuse to recover their spiritual momentum. The second cycle of discipline is economic recession (Lev. 26:18-20); the fourth cycle is economic depression (Lev. 26:23-26; Deut. 28:15, cf. 28:23-24). The malaise of economic depression often is the weakness that brings on the fifth cycle, military conquest by a foreign power (Lev. 26:27-35; Deut. 28:25-26).[57]

THE ADVANCING BELIEVER IN DISASTER

Even while the nation suffers under divine discipline, God never disregards the faithfulness of individual believers. Under the disaster test of economic depression, the spiritually autonomous believer uses all the problem-solving devices of spiritual adulthood. He directs his *hope* toward doctrine, his *personal love* toward God, his *impersonal love* toward mankind, and his acquired divine *happiness* toward himself. With these powerful divine assets he can not only survive the storm but even enjoy it—with total confidence in God's plan for his life.

Abram failed to use any problem-solving devices in economic depression, but the Lord still supplied his every need (Gen. 12:10—13:1). By neglecting to

---

57. The five cycles of national discipline are delineated in Leviticus 26:14-39. See *Dispensations*, p. 4n.

use the doctrine he knew, Abram manufactured unnecessary pressure for himself and was unable to enjoy God's provision as he could have.

The proper attitude in economic disaster is described by Peter.

> These [momentum tests of all kinds] have come so that your faith [the application of Bible doctrine in utilizing God's problem-solving devices]—of greater worth than gold, which perishes even though refined by fire—may be proved genuine and may result in praise, glory, and honor when Jesus Christ is revealed [the Rapture, or resurrection, of the Church as a preliminary to the Judgment Seat of Christ, where eternal rewards will be based on spiritual growth]. Though you have not seen him, you love him; and even though you do not see him now, you believe in him [use the assets of the divine dynasphere] and are filled with an inexpressible and glorious joy. (1 Pet. 1:7-8, NIV)

In disaster testing, the spiritually adult believer uses the greatest of all problem-solving devices, the happiness of God, which is described here as "inexpressible and glorious joy." God shares His happiness with the believer first in spiritual self-esteem, then more powerfully in spiritual autonomy, and most effectively in spiritual maturity. The believer inculcated with the thinking of God is happy or content in whatever circumstances he finds himself and can therefore cope with any pressure in life.

Knowledge of Bible doctrine gives the believer a sense for historical trends so that he is alert to pending economic disasters. Common sense in preparation for economic depression is illustrated by Joseph, the prime minister of Egypt. Joseph understood the importance of liquidity, or its ancient equivalent in grain, and stored up reserves for use in lean years (Gen. 41:46-57). Inflation as a cause of depression is described as a factor in the fourth cycle of discipline (Lev. 26:26). When depression is divine discipline, only the spiritual recovery of the believer can deliver the client nation. As go believers, so goes the nation.

> If disaster comes, whether the sword of judgment [war] or disease or economic depression, we will stand in Your presence before the temple that bears Your name [where doctrine was taught to the Jews by means of ritual] and will cry out [pray] to You in our distress. Then You will both hear us and deliver us. (2 Chron. 20:9)

God protects the growing believer in disaster testing. The spiritually autonomous believer has the privilege of understanding these doctrines and of appreciating the One who protects and delivers him.

> In economic depression He [God] will ransom you from death, and in battle from the power of the sword. (Job 5:20)

> Who shall separate us from the love of Christ? Shall disaster or anguish or persecution or economic depression or privation or danger or sword?...But in all these things we win the supreme victory through Him who loves us. (Rom. 8:35-37)

PAUL'S MENTAL ATTITUDE: CURSING TURNED TO BLESSING

When a believer suffers momentum testing, he is closing in on the objective of the Christian way of life. Spiritual maturity is the next step. In people testing, thought testing, system testing, or disaster testing, the Christian's mental attitude can be characterized by eager anticipation and stimulation despite the pain he suffers. Metabolized Bible doctrine enables him to see how close he is to achieving maturity.

Paul himself is an example of the believer's attitude when beset by momentum testing after a major personal failure. He had reached spiritual self-esteem, which is vulnerable to arrogance, and had successfully faced providential preventive suffering so that he gained spiritual autonomy. Then, in a resurgence of arrogance, he assumed that his own plan for his life was better than God's plan. In defiance of the doctrine he knew (Rom. 11:2-5, 13; Gal. 2:7), the warnings of other people (Acts 21:10-14), and his own common sense (Gal. 2:11-13; Phil. 3:2), Paul abandoned his thriving ministry to the Gentiles in the Aegean Quadrangle and returned to Jerusalem.

Paul blended arrogance with sentimentality, producing a disastrous result. He remembered his celebrity as a brilliant young Pharisee and wished to go back and have an impact for Christ among his old associates. He failed miserably. His unbelieving countrymen were adamantly negative to the Gospel, as they had previously opposed Christ, and the legalistic Jewish Christians were negative to doctrine. To gain an audience with the Jews, Paul went so far as to compromise his integrity, taking a blasphemous religious vow in the Temple (Acts 21:23-26).

Beginning with a riot in the Temple and an assassination plot against him, a two-year imprisonment ensued, which carried Paul to Rome. Paul quickly recognized his failure and rebounded so that the purpose of this long period of suffering changed from cursing to blessing. In the midst of suffering, he regained his spiritual momentum. In fact, providential preventive suffering rapidly strengthened his spiritual self-esteem into spiritual autonomy. In Philippians 3, Paul was describing himself retrospectively: he expressed the viewpoint of spiritual self-esteem in verse 10 and the perspective of spiritual autonomy in verse 11. The adversity he had been undergoing was momentum testing. From a position of spiritual maturity, he recalled when he had not yet arrived at maturity but was well on his way. As a mature believer Paul was remembering the grace of God that had delivered him from his own self-induced misery and had accelerated his advance to maturity.

Paul had initiated a sequence of suffering with his own arrogant decisions, but God converted cursing into blessing as soon as Paul used rebound and reentered his palace of the divine dynasphere. The apostle did not dwell on his failure. He evaluated his situation long enough to learn his lesson, then gratefully pressed forward in the plan of God.

MOMENTUM TESTING IN PHILIPPIANS 3

LEAVING FALSE CONFIDENCE BEHIND

Paul opens Philippians 3 by repeating a warning that he himself had disregarded in his Jerusalem fiasco. Believers must beware of religion with all its emotional appeal, self-righteousness, coercion, and potential violence. In particular, Paul cites his own aristocratic background, zeal, and fame in Judaism. Religion had channeled his intellect and energy, had flattered and promoted him, had given him tremendous "confidence in the flesh" (Phil. 3:4). Through his personal faith in Christ and inculcation with Bible doctrine, Paul had renounced his old, misplaced confidence in man. His power lust and his self-righteous zeal to impose his own legalism on others had been replaced by spiritual autonomy. Instead of self, Christ was now the focus of his attention. Personal love for God had superseded arrogance as the foundation of his attitude toward himself.

> But whatever things were gain [profit] to me, those things [his status symbols in Israel] I now consider loss for the sake of Christ. More than that, I conclude all things to be loss compared to the surpassing greatness of knowing Christ Jesus my Lord, for the sake of whom I have suffered the loss of all things [his Jewish celebrity] and conclude them [to be] excrement that I may gain Christ. (Phil. 3:7-8)

"Gain[ing] Christ" is a synonym for fulfilling the protocol plan of God. Paul expresses his desire to advance in the operational divine dynasphere all the way to Gate 8, spiritual maturity, just as the humanity of Christ set the precedent for the royal family by attaining maturity in the prototype divine dynasphere.

PARENTHESIS: HOW TO ATTAIN SPIRITUAL MATURITY

In verses 9-11, Paul inserts a parenthesis, explaining how to "gain Christ."

> That I may be found in Him [as a member of the royal family, in union with Christ] not having a righteousness of my own from the Law [no salvation by keeping the Mosaic Law] but that [divine righteousness] acquired through faith in Christ, that righteousness from God on the basis of faith. (Phil. 3:9)

To "gain Christ" a person must first believe in Christ (Phil. 3:9). At the moment of faith, God permanently imputes His own absolute righteousness to every believer, eliminating any need to earn God's approbation with the human righteousness of religion or of good deeds. Man appropriates salvation only according to divine protocol: "by grace are you saved through faith [in Christ], not of works lest anyone should boast" (Eph. 2:8).

After salvation the believer must continue to follow divine protocol. Human works cannot earn salvation, nor can human good works earn God's love or blessings after salvation. God's grace policy is consistent. The believer lives the Christian way of life by following God's mandates, not by striving to fulfill his own legalistic idea of what ought to please God. As a teaching aid, the divine dynasphere consolidates God's mandates, making His grace policy understandable, systematically presenting the means by which we "grow in grace and in knowledge of our Lord and Savior Jesus Christ" (2 Pet. 3:18).

> That I may know Him and the power of His resurrection and the fellowship of His sufferings, having become like [Him] with reference to His death. (Phil. 3:10)

In Philippians 3:10 Paul emphasizes suffering, but he begins by stating the importance of post-salvation epistemological rehabilitation related to spiritual self-esteem. Although Paul is in spiritual maturity as he writes, he is giving us the benefit of his experience in spiritual self-esteem. Therefore, he begins verse 10 with the infinitive of purpose of the verb *ginosko,* "to know." The infinitive of purpose indicates the objective or purpose of the action of the main verb, which is found in verse 8, "I conclude all things to be loss...that I may know Him."

Paul reached this conclusion through post-salvation epistemological rehabilitation and cognition of the doctrine of spiritual adulthood. Knowing Christ, or occupation with Christ, is one of the characteristics of spiritual self-esteem. From the viewpoint of spiritual self-esteem, Paul now turns his attention to the power of God in resurrection.

THE GREAT POWER EXPERIMENT

Jesus Christ experienced two unique deaths on the cross. The *substitutionary spiritual death* of Christ provides eternal salvation for the human race. The *physical death* of Christ involved a unique trichotomous separation of body, soul, and spirit which set the stage for a demonstration of divine power in resurrection.

Our Lord's body went into the grave (Luke 23:50-53). His human spirit went into the presence of the Father in heaven (Luke 23:46; John 19:30). And His soul was taken by the Holy Spirit into Paradise, which is a compartment of Hades in the heart of the earth (Luke 23:43; Acts 2:27, 31; Eph. 3:9).[58]

In the resurrection of Christ from His unique physical death, two categories of divine power were displayed. The omnipotence of God the Father restored our Lord's human spirit from heaven to His body in the grave. The Father thereby became an agent of the resurrection of Christ (Acts 2:24; Rom. 6:4; Eph. 1:20; Col. 2:12; 1 Thess. 1:10; 1 Pet. 1:21). The omnipotence of God the Holy Spirit restored Christ's soul from Hades to His body in the grave. Hence, the Holy Spirit also became an agent of Christ's resurrection (Rom. 1:4; 8:11; 1 Pet. 3:18).

So vital is the issue of power in the life of Christ, and so magnificent is the doctrine of divine omnipotence, that our Lord's first advent can be characterized as a *great power experiment*. In this use of the word, an experiment is a demonstration of a known truth. Here the known truth is Bible doctrine related to the total availability of divine power to the humanity of Christ in hypostatic union.[59] The great power experiment of the hypostatic union demonstrates the infinite power of God the Father and God the Holy Spirit in sustaining the humanity of Christ throughout His first advent.

---

58. See Thieme, *Victorious Proclamation* (1977).

59. In theological terminology, the *hypostatic union* is the God-Man, the Lord Jesus Christ. See *Christian Integrity*, pp. 193-96.

The great power experiment of the hypostatic union is extended as the great power experiment of the Church Age. The power that raised Jesus Christ from the dead is now available to every member of the royal family for the execution of the protocol plan of God. For the Church Age believer, an experiment is not only a demonstration of known truth, but also an operation undertaken to discover some unknown principle or effect. While the delegation and distribution of divine power is well-known to God, this magnificent grace provision is unknown to the believer until discovered in the New Testament and communicated by the pastor under the ministry of God the Holy Spirit. When the believer's soul is inculcated with Bible doctrine, yet another definition of "experiment" applies. The great power experiment of the Church Age is the tangible result of a policy, the unique divine policy of making divine omnipotence totally and equally available to every member of the royal family.

One of the results of the baptism of the Holy Spirit at salvation is the creation of a new spiritual species, the royal family of God (2 Cor. 5:17). The purpose of creating this new spiritual species is to enable the Church Age believer to utilize divine power, which is made available in three categories:

1. The OMNIPOTENCE OF GOD THE FATHER related to our portfolio of invisible assets,

2. The OMNIPOTENCE OF GOD THE SON related to sustaining the universe and perpetuating human history,

3. The OMNIPOTENCE OF GOD THE HOLY SPIRIT related to life in the divine dynasphere.

Never before in human history has so much divine power been made available to so many believers as in the great power experiment of the Church Age. The utilization of this divine omnipotence by the believer is the basis for invisible impact during the Church Age. There are three categories of impact:

1. PERSONAL IMPACT as blessing by association with the mature believer,

2. HISTORICAL IMPACT as blessing by association with the pivot of mature believers in a client nation to God,

3. INTERNATIONAL IMPACT as blessing by association for non-client nations through spiritually mature missionaries sent out from a client nation.

This briefly explains what Paul means when he declares that his purpose is to "know Him and the power of His resurrection." Paul now addresses the subject of suffering as he continues to describe his purpose in life: "and [that I may know] the fellowship of His sufferings," referring to our Lord's suffering for blessing during His first advent.

THE FELLOWSHIP OF CHRIST'S SUFFERINGS

As an extension of the great power experiment of the hypostatic union into the Church Age, three categories of suffering for blessing are available to every believer who reaches spiritual adulthood.

1. PROVIDENTIAL PREVENTIVE SUFFERING challenges the believer's spiritual self-esteem, forestalls arrogance, and serves as a warm-up for momentum testing.

2. MOMENTUM TESTING exercises the believer's spiritual autonomy through people testing, thought testing, system testing, and disaster testing.

3. EVIDENCE TESTING demonstrates the divine dynamics of spiritual maturity and glorifies God to the maximum.

These unique systems of suffering for blessing were first experienced by the humanity of Christ in the prototype divine dynasphere. These same systems of suffering for blessing are now available to accelerate the momentum of every spiritually adult believer as he advances inside the operational divine dynasphere. "The fellowship of His sufferings" describes the Church Age believer's utilization of spiritually adult problem-solving devices. The consistent application of these problem-solving devices equates adversity and prosperity, living and dying.

Paul cites the supreme example of our Lord's suffering when he speaks of "having become like [Christ] with reference to His death." The Greek compound verb *summorphizo,* in the passive voice, means "to take on the same form as, to be conformed with, to become like." The spiritually adult believer takes on the same form as Christ during His substitutionary spiritual death on the cross. The spiritually adult believer produces the action of the verb through the omnipotence of the Holy Spirit in the divine dynasphere and through sharing the happiness of God as a problem-solving device.

While Jesus Christ was being judged for the sins of the world, He utilized these same two factors to remain on the cross in a state of impeccability.

> Christ...through the eternal Spirit [the omnipotence of the Holy Spirit in the prototype divine dynasphere] offered Himself without blemish to God. (Heb. 9:14)

> Who [the humanity of Christ] because of the present exhibited happiness [utilization of divine happiness as a problem-solving device], endured the cross [substitutionary spiritual death], despising the shame [of coming into contact with sin and judgment in a state of impeccability]. (Heb. 12:2)

The final three hours in which Jesus hung on the cross were the most agonizing for any man in the history of the human race. Even the anticipation of such pain caused our Lord horrible anguish in Gethsemane (Matt. 26:38-39). Arrested, unjustly tried, tortured to the point of extreme debilitation, nailed to a cross, He suffered all without complaint (Mark 15:2-5; Acts 8:32-35). Then, when imputed with the awful burden of human sin and judged by the justice and omnipotence of God, Jesus broke the dignity of His silence and screamed with pain (Matt. 27:46). How did the humanity of Christ endure the Father's judgment? At any moment Jesus could have shouted "Enough!" and stepped down from the cross. What kept Him there until the last sin of the last member of the human race was judged and salvation was provided for all?

In the midst of His unspeakable anguish, the humanity of Christ persevered on the cross in the power of the Holy Spirit inside the prototype divine dynasphere and in the exercise of divine happiness as a problem-solving device.

The same power that sustained Jesus on the cross is now available to every member of the royal family. As a result of Christ's strategic victory on the cross, four dynamic problem-solving devices were made available to every Church Age believer who achieves spiritual adulthood through residence, function, and momentum inside the divine dynasphere.

1. TOWARD GOD: personal love for God as the motivational virtue of spiritual self-esteem.

2. TOWARD PEOPLE: impersonal love for all mankind as the functional virtue of spiritual autonomy.

3. TOWARD DOCTRINE: hope as the goal-orientation of spiritual adulthood.

4. TOWARD SELF: sharing the happiness of God.

While all four of these problem-solving devices were used by the humanity of Christ on the cross, sharing the happiness of God is emphasized in Hebrews 12:2. When we utilize these divine problem-solving devices, we are using the resources that sustained our Lord's humanity in purchasing our so great salvation.

God was glorified by Christ's strategic victory in the angelic conflict. God is also glorified when members of the royal family win tactical victories as they utilize divine assets under pressure en route to spiritual maturity. [60] At maturity the believer acquires capacity to receive special blessings and to pass evidence testing, both of which glorify God to the maximum.

CONFIDENCE FROM THE DOCTRINE OF RESURRECTION

The pattern of maximum glorification of God continues in every generation of the Church Age until the royal family is completely formed. When complete, the entire royal family is resurrected at the Rapture of the Church. This terminates the great power experiment of the Church Age. Having discussed the resurrection of Christ in Philippians 3:10, Paul turns his attention in verse 11 to the resurrection of the Church, the concluding event of the Church Age. The power that raised Jesus Christ from the dead is the same power that will resurrect the royal family of God (1 Cor. 6:14).

> If by any means I will arrive with reference to the out-resurrection [the Rapture of the Church], that one from the dead. (Phil. 3:11)

Two enclitic particles in the Greek, translated "if by any means," indicate that Paul did not doubt the *fact* of the Rapture but was wondering about the *manner* in which he will participate. Two possibilities existed: Paul would be either physically dead or physically alive at the moment of resurrection. He would be either among "the dead in Christ" who "shall rise first" or among those "who are living, who remain" on earth at the time of the Rapture, who "shall be caught up together with them in the clouds to meet the Lord in the air, and so we shall always be with the Lord" (1 Thess. 4:16-17).

God the Father will be the agent of resurrection for "the dead in Christ," those Church Age believers who die before the Rapture occurs. God the Holy

---

60. Strategic and tactical victories are described in *Christian Integrity,* pp. 175-77.

Spirit will be the agent of resurrection for "those who are alive" at the time of the Rapture.

Paul's speculation is rhetorical, for the benefit of the readers, because he seemed to understand that he would receive resurrection out from the dead. By the time he wrote "I have finished the course" in 2 Timothy 4:6-8, he was certain that the resurrection would occur after his death. In writing to the Philippians, therefore, Paul was acknowledging the two possibilities regarding the Rapture as a means of teaching the doctrine of the imminency of the Rapture.

"Rapture" is an act or fact of being transported, a state of emotional ecstasy, a state of being rapt or carried out of oneself. "Rapture" is not a biblical word, but the Rapture of the Church is a technical theological term for the resurrection of the royal family of God. During the Church Age, God is forming a royal family to complement the new royal title awarded to Jesus Christ as a result of the cross. When the royal family is complete, the Rapture will occur. At the Rapture every Church Age believer, whether dead or still living, whether winner or loser, will receive his resurrection body (1 Cor. 15:50-53; Phil. 3:20-21). At that moment, the Church as a spiritual building is transformed into a spiritual temple (Eph. 2:20-22). The Rapture achieves ultimate sanctification for every member of the royal family (Eph. 5:26-27).[61]

"Imminency" means to be impending, and is also used as a technical theological term. The imminency of the Rapture recognizes that no prophecy must be fulfilled before the resurrection of the Church occurs. The next eschatological event will be the Rapture itself. In the biblical statements that Christ is coming soon, the word "soon" connotes imminency (Rev. 22:7, 12, 20).

The Church Age is unique in many respects, among them the fact that this is the only dispensation devoid of prophecy. The Church Age began with the Day of Pentecost, A.D. 30, which was prophesied (John 14:17; Acts 1:5, 8), and will conclude with the Rapture, which is also prophesied. There is no intervening prophecy between these termini of the Church Age.

Although members of the royal family can look beyond the Rapture to events of the Tribulation and Millennium, no event of prophecy occurs during the Church Age. Consequently, we must evaluate history in terms of historical trends, such as those illustrated in the local churches of Revelation 2-3. The emphasis in the great power experiment of the Church Age is not the visible impact of prophetic events but the invisible impact of individual believers who utilize divine omnipotence.

The doctrine of the imminency of the Rapture is illustrated by the principle that "no one knows the day or the hour" (Matt. 24:36). There will be no

---

61. See *Christian Integrity,* p. 49.

advance warning of the Rapture, which might have occurred in Paul's day, may take place today, or may not happen for another thousand years. Therefore, the believer should not search for eschatological significance in historical events. Instead, he should concentrate on the execution of the protocol plan of God (1 Cor. 1:4-8; 1 John 3:2-3). Distortion of the imminency of the Rapture causes instability from foolish speculation concerning the time of the Rapture (James 5:7-8).

The verb *katantao* in Philippians 3:11 means to arrive at something, as one would reach the destination of a journey. This entire journey will occur in a moment of time, the moment of resurrection for the completed royal family of God. *Katantao* appears in the subjunctive mood, which implies a future reference qualified by an element of contingency. The future event is the Rapture; the element of contingency will exist in every generation as believers do not know whether they will be resurrected with the dead or with the living. Paul speaks for the entire royal family as he dramatizes the imminency of the Rapture.

One of the primary results of applying the doctrine of the Rapture is increased confidence. The believer can face his own death in the certainty that one day he will receive his resurrection body in "conformity with the body of [Christ's] glory according to the exertion of His power that enables Him to bring everything under His control" (Phil. 3:21). Furthermore, the believer gains confidence regarding Christian loved ones and friends who have died, "that [he] may not grieve as do the rest [of the world] who have no hope" (1 Thess. 4:13). The doctrine of the Rapture removes fear and, therefore, constitutes one application of hope as a problem-solving device.

> Therefore, comfort each other with these doctrines [of the Rapture]. (1 Thess. 4:18)

Paul was a mature believer when he wrote Philippians, but for our benefit he wrote parts of chapter 3 from the viewpoint of his experience in the early stages of spiritual adulthood. Philippians 3:9-11 views the Christian way of life from the perspective of spiritual self-esteem. Verses 12-14 represent the attitude of spiritual autonomy. Paul's retrospection ends with verse 15, where he describes the thinking of a mature believer.

In spiritual adulthood, suffering for blessing accelerates growth. This does not exclude prosperity from the believer's life. Overt prosperity poses difficulties of its own and is actually a form of momentum testing. The spiritual adult will face distractions in prosperity and in adversity, just as he will share the happiness of God through the utilization of divine assets—in prosperity or in adversity. The principle is that periodic suffering for blessing is a means of spiritual momentum whereas inner prosperity, regardless of circumstances, is a result of momentum.

END PARENTHESIS: PAUL'S SPIRITUAL AUTONOMY

With Philippians 3:11 Paul closes the parenthesis begun in verse 9. He has finished describing how to "gain Christ" (Phil. 3:8). We gain Christ, or advance to spiritual maturity, through the three stages of sanctification: positional, experiential, and ultimate sanctification.

Sanctification is the work of God in making each member of the royal family like Jesus Christ. *Positional sanctification* is union with Christ through the baptism of the Holy Spirit at the moment of salvation. Paul expressed this initial stage of sanctification in verse 9, "that I may be found in Him." *Experiential sanctification* is the execution of the protocol plan of God on earth, as we follow our Lord's precedent in the prototype divine dynasphere through our residence in the operational divine dynasphere. This second stage of sanctification is described in verse 10, "that I may know Him and the power of His resurrection and the fellowship of His sufferings." *Ultimate sanctification* is the possession of a resurrection body like the resurrection body of Jesus Christ. This final stage of sanctification is anticipated in verse 11, "I will arrive with reference to the out-resurrection [the Rapture]."

Having closed the parenthesis, Paul resumes in verse 12 from where he left off: "I have suffered the loss of all things and conclude them dung that I may gain Christ..." (Phil. 3:8).

> Not that I have already received [spiritual maturity, or have "gain[ed] Christ"] or have already accomplished [maturity], but I keep on pursuing [the objective of spiritual maturity] that I may overtake it, for which I also was [pursued and] overtaken by Christ Jesus. (Phil. 3:12)

According to Paul's autobiographical retrospection, when he attained spiritual autonomy his mental attitude was genuine humility. The great apostle did not rest on his laurels or become arrogant about his spiritual stature. Instead, he recognized that he had not reached the final objective. He had not yet fulfilled the protocol plan of God by advancing to spiritual maturity. No believer attains spiritual maturity until in the status of spiritual autonomy he passes the four parts of momentum testing: people testing, system testing, thought testing, and disaster testing.

LOSING AND REGAINING SPIRITUAL MOMENTUM

Many years earlier, Paul had passed the first category of suffering for blessing: providential preventive suffering, which is a warm-up for momentum
testing. With arrogance effectively checked, spiritual autonomy gave him the
ability to accurately evaluate his own spiritual status. Objective self-evaluation
is necessary to avoid the hazard of living in the past and bogging down before
achieving the goal.

The danger of losing spiritual momentum was familiar to Paul. In fact, he
is describing his *second* attainment of spiritual autonomy. The first time he
reached spiritual autonomy, he lost his spiritual impetus and retrogressed in the
plan of God. By learning the hard way, Paul came to understand the wisdom of
the Roman maxim: *Qui non proficit deficit.* "He who does not go forward goes
backward."

Paul's failure began when he ignored the will of God and assuaged his own
sentimentality by returning to Jerusalem. He compromised his integrity, incited
the fanatical hatred of the religious Jews, and endured two years of incarceration
in Caesarea before being transported as a prisoner to Rome. Paul suffered intensely. Initially, divine discipline motivated rebound, followed by momentum
testing which accelerated Paul's renewed spiritual advance. As a result of suffering for blessing, Paul arrived in Rome as a mature believer.

During the two years in Caesarea and in the shipwreck on the coast of Malta,
Paul passed all four parts of momentum testing. We can trace his momentum
testing. *People testing* included the vicious attitude of Ananias, the high priest
(Acts 23-24) and the rejection of the Gospel by King Herod Agrippa II, his sister
Bernice, and the court that attended them (Acts 25-26). *System testing* frustrated
Paul through the malfunction of Roman justice under Felix and Festus, the two
successive procurators of the Roman province of Judea (Acts 24:22—25:12;
26:32). *Thought testing* challenged Paul's mental attitude when he had to face
the unthinking panic of passengers and crew during the storm at sea (Acts
27:31-44), when he was bitten by the poisonous snake after saving everyone's
life in the shipwreck (Acts 28:3-6), and when he was rejected by the Jews upon
finally reaching Rome (Acts 28:23-31). *Disaster testing* threatened Paul's life in
the assassination plot against him in Jerusalem (Acts 23:12-14) and in the storm
and shipwreck (Acts 27).

While still a prisoner in Rome, Paul wrote Philippians in the status of
spiritual maturity. This fact is implied in the increments of momentum testing
that he passed prior to reaching Rome. His spiritual status is confirmed by comparing the Greek verb *teleiöo,* translated "or have already *accomplished*
[maturity]" in verse 11, with its cognate noun *teleios,* translated "as many as are
mature" in verse 15. Paul had completely recovered from his failure. As a

mature believer living entirely within the will of God, he embarked on his fourth missionary journey after his acquittal by Caesar. Paul's evidence testing began during his first Roman imprisonment and probably continued during part of the fourth missionary journey through the Roman provinces of Asia, Gaul, and Spain (Phil. 2:23-24; Philemon 22; Rom. 15:24, 28).

In looking back over his recent recovery, Paul remembered that when he was still in spiritual autonomy he knew he had not "already achieved" maturity. He also recalled being keenly aware that he was closing in on the goal. Consequently, he took the offensive in his advance to the high ground of spiritual maturity.[62] "I keep on pursuing [the objective]," he wrote. Refusing to be discouraged, Paul would not be hindered by past failure. He had learned to rebound and keep moving. His aggressive action in spiritual autonomy took the form of persistence in positive volition, the accumulation of metabolized doctrine, the utilization of divine omnipotence, and the use of problem-solving devices in momentum testing. He thus followed the example that the humanity of Christ had established during the Incarnation for every Church Age believer.

STEADINESS OF PURPOSE

Paul interjects a classical Greek grammatical construction as an expression of purpose and expectation. His purpose is "to overtake, to seize, to attain" the objective of spiritual maturity, and he confidently expects to fulfill that purpose. He anticipates his advance to spiritual maturity through the valley of momentum testing. In other words, Paul in spiritual autonomy knows that suffering is coming. He knows the pattern. Just as spiritual self-esteem plus providential preventive suffering equals spiritual autonomy, so also spiritual autonomy plus momentum testing equals spiritual maturity. Rather than be caught off guard and victimized by suffering, he takes an aggressive approach to adversity.

When Paul writes "I keep pursuing [the objective] in order that I may overtake [it]," he uses military terminology. He steadily advances by his continual reception, retention, and recall of Bible doctrine. He moves forward by using the problem-solving devices of hope in doctrine, personal love for God, impersonal love for all mankind, and sharing the happiness of God within himself. He presses on, knowing that God will accelerate his advance through the suffering of momentum testing.

No arrogant illusions remain in Paul's thinking. He may be pursuing the goal, but he always remembers whose goal it is and in whose power he is able to attain this goal. He returns to square one, the first step into the Christian way

---

62. See pp. 13-14.

of life, the perspective of salvation by grace. The objective that he concentrates on overtaking is the same goal "for which [Paul] also was [pursued and] overtaken by Christ Jesus." Jesus Christ's objective has become Paul's objective. That goal is the maximum glorification of God.

For Paul's advantage Jesus Christ pursued and overtook Saul of Tarsus, as Paul was then known, on the road to Damascus. Our Lord's purpose in inflicting the pain of blindness on that young, overzealous Pharisee was that Saul might believe in Christ. Likewise, God's purpose in imposing momentum testing on the great apostle was that Paul might fulfill the protocol plan of God by attaining maturity. The intended (and accomplished) result of administering suffering to Paul was glorification of God to the maximum.

Philippians 3:12 documents the fact that spiritual maturity is the objective of the Christian life. Paul is not practicing false humility by declaring that he has not reached the goal. In this retrospective verse, he recalls that when he was in spiritual autonomy he knew that he had not yet arrived at spiritual maturity. He possessed the strong self-esteem that belongs to the believer in spiritual autonomy, but he entertained no illusions about himself. He accurately evaluated his spiritual life and recognized his need to keep pursuing the objective. A believer who overestimates himself hinders his own advance; a believer who evaluates himself objectively perpetuates his momentum and eventually reaches maturity.

THE BASIS FOR OBJECTIVE SELF-EVALUATION

> Brethren [fellow members of the royal family], I do not evaluate myself as having overtaken [obtained the objective], but one thing [I do]: forgetting what [is] behind and straining forward toward what [is] ahead, I press on toward the goal for the prize [blessings in time and eternity for the mature believer] of that upward call [the saving ministry of the Holy Spirit, designated "efficacious grace," which converts the believer's faith into salvation] from God [the Father as author of the protocol plan] in Christ Jesus [union with Christ as the basis for spiritual royalty]. (Phil. 3:13-14)

The Greek verb Paul uses to describe his self-evaluation is *logizomai* which has a prominent place in Greek philosophical discourse. This verb connotes nonemotional thinking according to strict logical rules, apprehension of something actually present, representation of facts as they are.

There are two objective standards for self-analysis available to every member of the royal family of God:

1. Perception, metabolization, and application of BIBLE DOCTRINE,

2. The doctrine of SUFFERING.

The believer's attitude toward Bible doctrine changes as a result of post-salvation epistemological rehabilitation. Doctrine in the soul creates a desire for more doctrine. Initially the immature Christian listens to Bible teaching for a variety of motives that carry over from his life as an unbeliever, but gradually human viewpoint is replaced by divine viewpoint. The believer's academic discipline and concentration on the Word of God become stronger as he develops personal love for God, the highest motivation in life.

The spiritually adult believer approaches the perception of doctrine with a new mental attitude. He concentrates on the Mind of Christ (1 Cor. 2:16) because he is occupied with the person of Christ (Phil. 1:21) and has begun to share the happiness of God (John 15:11). The believer knows that he has attained spiritual adulthood because his perception, metabolization, and application of doctrine cease to be a means to an end and instead become ends in themselves. He takes genuine pleasure in the Word of God. The perception of Bible doctrine is the highest form of worship.

The Christian's second standard for objective self-evaluation is the doctrine of suffering. This spiritual yardstick must be used with caution because many variables are involved. The overt circumstances of life have a wide variety of causes. Comparing the experience of one believer to that of another is never precise. Two believers may experience similar disasters, but in one case the pressure is suffering for blessing while in the other it is divine discipline. The difference lies in the spiritual advance or retrogression of the believer, not in the overt circumstances of life. Therefore, no suffering in itself conclusively indicates a Christian's spiritual status. Furthermore, the blend of adversity and prosperity is unique in every life by divine design. Yet even prosperity can have at least three legitimate sources: blessing by association, logistical grace, or escrow blessing. Of these three sources, only escrow blessings are connected with a specific spiritual status. Blessing by association can prosper anyone in the periphery of a mature believer, and logistical grace is guaranteed to every believer, whether winner or loser.

Neither adversity itself nor prosperity itself is necessarily a sign of spiritual progress. In fact, Paul's self-evaluation emphasizes the stage of growth he has *not* attained rather than the stage he *has* attained.

A believer can use suffering as a barometer of spiritual growth only in the sense that pressure forces him to apply the Bible doctrine in his soul. His ability to utilize the doctrinal inventory in his soul under stress indicates his level of advance. If he falls apart in every crisis, he has a long way to go before reaching spiritual maturity. If his occupation with Christ, reliance on doctrine, and utilization of divine omnipotence enable him to take suffering in stride, he is making progress in spiritual adulthood.

From Paul's experience of the reality of doctrine under momentum testing, he knew that he had reached spiritual autonomy and was closing in on spiritual maturity. The purpose of this self-knowledge is not to compare oneself with other Christians but to motivate continued momentum in the protocol plan of God. There is no substitute for Bible doctrine as the only measure and standard for self-analysis in the plan of God. The successful application of doctrine under pressure demonstrates the efficacy of divine provisions, and as a result, increases the advancing believer's personal love for God and spiritual self-esteem.

AN ATHLETE'S DETERMINATION

Following Paul's self-evaluation, he uses ellipsis in an idiom of concentration—an abbreviated interjectional clause—to eliminate the negative and emphasize the positive. "But [I concentrate on] one thing" indicates that he has blotted out, forgotten, or disregarded past failures and is pressing on to maturity as the final objective. Paul used rebound and rapidly recovered from his Jerusalem fiasco. By "forgetting the things [which are] behind," Paul demonstrates a principle that applies to every believer.

Recalling past failures causes bitterness, self-pity, and a guilt complex, and hence further involvement in Satan's cosmic system. When remembered and pored over, failures compound current problems and hinder advance in the protocol plan of God. God has a purpose for every believer, and that purpose is to rebound and keep moving. Paul's retrospective exposition is designed to encourage believers to confess their sins to God, to keep short accounts with Him, to forget past failures, to concentrate on present momentum in the divine dynasphere. The Christian must not handicap himself. Past punitive suffering, whether self-induced misery or divine discipline, must not hinder his execution of divine protocol in present suffering for blessing. All believers periodically fail; only losers allow past failures to hinder their current progress in the protocol plan of God.

On the one hand, Paul forgets past failures, and on the other hand, he "stretches out or strains forward toward the goal or finish line." In Philippians 3:13-14 Paul uses an athletic analogy. Just as an olympic class runner maintains his form in spite of physical agony, so also the believer continues to follow divine protocol in the midst of suffering. Paul has rounded the final turn of spiritual autonomy and is sprinting down the home stretch toward spiritual maturity. Just as the athlete drives for the finish line, so also the believer concentrates on the objective, unhindered by distractions, as he undergoes momentum testing. "Straining forward" and "pressing on" portray the aggressive mental attitude of the believer who has nearly reached spiritual maturity. His goal is the maximum glorification of God which will become a reality in his life in spiritual maturity.

God glorifies Himself by distributing the special blessings He created for each believer in eternity past, but only the mature believer has the capacity to receive these fabulous blessings.[63] Blessings for time and eternity are the "prize," the goal, the purpose for which the believer was saved.

The "upward call from God" refers to the ministry of God the Holy Spirit at the instant an individual first believes in Christ. Every member of the human race is born spiritually dead, unable to comprehend spiritual things and totally incapable of a relationship with God. We have a spiritually dead understanding and a spiritually dead faith. The ministry of the Holy Spirit is necessary, first, to make the Gospel clear and, second, to make our faith in Christ effective for salvation. In itself our faith has no power to save us; the Holy Spirit must take our faith and make it effectual or effective in establishing an eternal relationship with God (John 16:8-11; Rom. 10:14).

We receive no credit even for believing in Christ; all glory belongs to God. We are saved exclusively by the power of God. The "upward call" is the work of the Holy Spirit in the lucid presentation of the Gospel. This call is designated *common grace* because it is extended to every individual. The Holy Spirit's ministry in converting the believer's faith into eternal salvation is called *efficacious grace*. In every case where common grace is not followed by faith in Christ, efficacious grace does not occur. The work of God the Holy Spirit in common and efficacious grace is emphasized as a gift from God (Eph. 2:8). The divine purpose in saving us is that we might reach the goal and attain the prize of spiritual maturity. Spiritual maturity, divine blessings, and the glorification of God form the complete package awarded to the spiritual winner.[64]

> Therefore, as many as [are] mature, let us keep on thinking
> this [aggressive mental attitude under pressure], and if you
> think differently on some point, even this God will reveal to
> you. (Phil. 3:15)

Paul has completed his retrospective exposition and now writes from his current status of spiritual maturity. He infers from the preceding verses, which

---

63. See pp. 136-39.
64. See *Integrity of God,* pp. 126-64.

describe spiritual self-esteem and spiritual autonomy, that in every generation a certain number of positive believers will continue their momentum until they attain spiritual maturity. These magnificent Christians represent a special group. Once they understand the objective of the Christian way of life, they do not waver. Instead, they organize their lives and priorities for the purpose of glorifying God to the maximum. As a result of passing that portion of momentum testing classified as thought testing, the mature believer has fulfilled the biblical mandates related to divine viewpoint mental attitude (Rom. 12:2-3; Phil. 2:2).

"Let us keep on thinking" refers to an action that began in the past and continues into the present. The same process of utilizing metabolized Bible doctrine in the power of the divine dynasphere, which enables the believer to attain maturity, is the means of facing maximum suffering for blessing after reaching maturity. Paul is urging readers, at every stage of spiritual growth, to join him in the system of thinking that leads to spiritual maturity. A dynamic and powerful mental attitude is required for the mature believer who is facing evidence testing.

FAILING A TEST

Philippians 3:15 warns the believer that even after he fulfills the protocol plan of God by reaching spiritual maturity, he must not let up. He must continue to utilize available divine omnipotence and cognition of doctrine. By acknowledging that the mature believer might "think differently on some point," Paul assumes that spiritual maturity has its vulnerabilities which could result in failure to pass evidence testing. The believer cannot approach evidence testing with a cocky attitude or with a propensity toward self-pity and bitterness. Indulgence in some form of arrogance causes even the mature believer to fail under pressure.

The ability to think under pressure perpetuates the believer's momentum through each stage of spiritual adulthood. The spiritual winner thinks; the spiritual loser emotes without thought. Courage is thinking under pressure; cowardice is failing to think under pressure—and falling apart emotionally. Under suffering for blessing, the believer's content of thought is the Bible doctrine he has metabolized over many years. Right thinking from metabolized doctrine and the right motivation from personal love for God create the positive determination and *esprit de corps* needed to fulfill the protocol plan of God.

No matter how far a believer advances in God's plan, he is still human. No believer on earth is perfect; we are all prone to failure, especially under the pressure of suffering for blessing. Failure can come from a lack of doctrine or from a particularly difficult thought test. The believer may have resisted or rejected the specific principle of doctrine that he now needs under pressure. More likely, however, he has learned the doctrine but has become disoriented by fear or emotionalism under momentum testing.

When a believer "thinks differently," that is, when his endurance flags and he is unable to think clearly, he may flunk any test connected with suffering for blessing. The solution after failure is to rebound and keep moving, as Philippians 3:13 commands. Immediate rebound keeps the believer from losing ground. Although he fails to advance, he retains his current level of spiritual growth, ready for another administration of testing at the proper time.

The spiritually adult believer learns quickly from failure. When his attitude has wavered or when he has made a wrong application of doctrine, he uses rebound if necessary to reenter the divine dynasphere. Inside his invisible palace he either draws upon the doctrine he already knows to make a correct application or he is receptive to learning the doctrine he previously may have resisted. "God will reveal" the truth through the perception and application of Bible doctrine accurately and faithfully taught by the orthodox pastor. God reveals the truth through intermediary means. There is no direct communication from God during the post-canon period of the Church Age.[65] After the canon of Scripture was completed, direct divine revelation ceased, placing emphasis instead on the power of Bible doctrine resident in the royal believer's soul.

A SOLDIER'S STEADY ADVANCE

Although provision is made for failure, the purpose of momentum testing is not failure but success.

> However, as a result of what we have attained, keep advancing in ranks by means of the same [system of spiritual momentum inside the divine dynasphere].[66] (Phil. 3:16)

Paul has shifted from an athletic to a military analogy. The verb *stoicheo* connotes marching in ranks. Members of the royal family are executing a powerful plan when they obey the mandates of the divine dynasphere. The objective of this plan is no less than to demonstrate the eternal glory of God. This verse establishes that there are stages of spiritual adulthood, stages in the fulfillment of God's protocol plan.

---

65. See Thieme, *Canonicity* (1973).

66. The King James Version adds "let us mind the same thing," but this phrase is not found in the best manuscripts.

"What we have attained" is *spiritual self-esteem* when the believer is undergoing providential preventive suffering. "What we have attained" is *spiritual autonomy* when undergoing momentum testing, as is Paul in this context. "What we have attained" is *spiritual maturity* when the believer receives evidence testing.

The same system that the believer uses to pass providential preventive suffering and momentum testing must also be used to pass evidence testing. "Advancing in ranks" is a most significant translation. Far too many Christians fall out of ranks and become casualties in the angelic conflict. They are losers who fail to execute the protocol plan of God and fail to glorify Him in the great power experiment of the Church Age. We must remain in ranks, which is tantamount to the following:

1. Residence, function, and momentum inside the DIVINE DYNASPHERE,

2. Consistent and prompt use of REBOUND to avoid prolonged residence in Satan's cosmic system,

3. AVOIDANCE OF DISCOURAGEMENT by any failure or setback in any category of suffering for blessing,

4. Consistent use of the PROBLEM-SOLVING DEVICES of spiritual adulthood, and

5. Unrelenting perception, metabolization, and application of BIBLE DOCTRINE.

The believer advances in ranks from one stage of spiritual adulthood to the next. As he progresses, he scores tactical victories in the angelic conflict. This spiritual warfare will come into dramatic focus in the final category of suffering for blessing. Spiritual maturity puts the believer in position for the most significant and beneficial of all suffering for blessing: evidence testing that glorifies God to the maximum.

IX
Spiritual Maturity

THE CHARACTERISTICS OF SPIRITUAL MATURITY

A CATEGORICAL DESCRIPTION OF SPIRITUAL MATURITY indicates the happiness and inner strength related to this final stage of spiritual growth. These characteristics mark the highest attainment of the Christian way of life. The purpose of this summary is not to establish a model of behavior for the immature believer to legalistically imitate. Instead, these characteristics, when compared to the previously described characteristics of spiritual self-esteem and spiritual autonomy,[67] enable the advancing believer to accurately anticipate the marvelous benefits of faithful persistence in the protocol plan of God.

1. MAXIMUM CONTENTMENT. Sharing the happiness of God is the highest of all problem-solving devices in the protocol plan of God (Phil. 4:11-13). The advancing believer began to share the happiness of God upon entering spiritual adulthood in Gate 5 of the divine dynasphere. Now in spiritual maturity at Gate 8, his "happiness [is] fulfilled" or complete (John 15:11). Suffering, which would normally be difficult, becomes relatively easy through residual happiness in the soul.

---

67. See pp. 67-69, 87-90.

Happiness is a mental attitude which equates adversity and prosperity, living and dying. Maximum capacity for happiness enables the mature Christian to face every challenge in his experience. God strengthens the believer through metabolized Bible doctrine *and* suffering for blessing so that His own shared happiness may be tested, developed, and completed in the believer's soul in adversity as well as in prosperity. God shares His happiness with the believer for the believer's own benefit; therefore, happiness is the problem-solving device directed toward self.

2. MENTAL STABILITY. Bible doctrine saturates the mature believer's thinking. He has maximum application of doctrine to every experience. Cognizance of doctrine enables him to give divine viewpoint precedence over empirical experience. Consequently, his mental attitude is stabilized by the doctrine he knows rather than destabilized by the circumstances of his life. The mature believer views his life in the light of God's plan, which gives him tremendous confidence regarding time and eternity. This confidence in God's ability to provide for him and to bless him in any future contingency is the biblical definition of "hope" (Rom. 8:24-25). Hope is the mature believer's problem-solving device directed toward Bible doctrine and related to his mental stability.

3. MAXIMUM USE OF VIRTUE-LOVE AS A PROBLEM-SOLVING DEVICE. Virtue-love includes personal love for God as motivational virtue (Gate 5 of the divine dynasphere) and impersonal love for all mankind as functional virtue (Gate 6). The mature believer has maximum use of both categories of virtue-love. Therefore, he is occupied with the person of Christ (Phil. 1:21). Furthermore, because virtue-love for God motivates virtue-love toward others, personal love for God in spiritual maturity becomes the dynamic basis for resolving all kinds of problems. Virtue-love is the problem-solving device directed toward God, toward self, and toward other people.

4. COGNITIVE INDEPENDENCE. The mature believer can think and apply doctrine for himself from the truth stored within his own soul. As a result of post-salvation epistemological rehabilitation and persistence in the perception of doctrine, the mature believer has a superior understanding of the mechanics of the protocol plan by which he attained maturity. The mature believer understands God's plan for his life and can face his problems with clarity of thought.

5. MAXIMUM GRACE-ORIENTATION TO LIFE. Orientation to the grace of God characterizes the mature believer's thinking, motivation, decisions, and actions. He understands that the principle of grace in salvation is

parlayed into the policy of grace after salvation. We were saved under the principle of grace; we live under the policy of grace. Rather than superimpose his own opinions on God's wisdom and generosity, the believer is delighted to do things God's way. He is free from the fanaticism, legalism, emotionalism, self-effacement, and asceticism which result from ignorance, arrogance, and habitual cosmic involvement.

6. MAXIMUM DOCTRINAL ORIENTATION TO REALITY. Capacity for prosperity and the ability to apply doctrine to experience give the mature believer spiritual common sense. Spiritual common sense is an astute outlook on life that can penetrate confusing, complicated situations and discern the key issues. The mature believer is realistic. He is not easily deceived. He has the wisdom to synthesize the situation and identify the best course of action, and the courage to do a right thing in a right way.

7. THE GREATEST DECISIONS IN LIFE FROM A POSITION OF MAXIMUM STRENGTH. Every decision by a mature believer can be a great decision. He has a full, practical understanding of the mechanics of God's protocol plan so that he can relate his decisions to the invisible but real assets that God has provided. Because he has established the right scale of values, the mature believer consistently makes right decisions. For him, doctrine takes number one priority.

8. MAXIMUM CONTROL OF ONE'S LIFE. No one who tampers with the lives of others can at the same time control his own. Therefore, the mature believer does not seek to coerce or manipulate others. He is not possessive with those whom he loves and thus avoids the pitfall of jealousy. He does not give expression to power lust. Instead, he fully utilizes the privacy of his priesthood; God is the focus of his life. Personal love for God motivates impersonal love for others.

He eliminates false applications from his life: no competitiveness from arrogance, no comparativeness from subjectivity, no conspiracy from inordinate ambition. In other words, he neither demands superiority over everyone else, nor derives his self-esteem from comparisons with others, nor demeans others in order to elevate himself. He controls his own life by faithfulness in the execution of God's protocol plan. God has control over his life. Because his thoughts, motives, decisions, and actions are consistent with God's plan, the believer lives in a state of sharing the happiness of God. He makes decisions with the full understanding that he bears the responsibility for their consequences.

9. MAXIMUM DYNAMICS IN LIVING. The mature believer has an unwavering personal sense of destiny. He knows that God has a purpose for his life; he understands God's purpose; he applies his understanding of God's plan to the particular circumstances of his life, whether good or bad. Self-command, poise, self-restraint, and self-control are established traits of his character. He recognizes that he continues to fulfill his destiny by executing the protocol plan of God. This results in a life of maximum spiritual production. The mature believer will have far greater production in a short period of time than will a legalistic believer over a long Christian life.

10. ESCROW BLESSINGS. The first stage of the maximum glorification of God in spiritual maturity is the distribution of escrow blessings. In eternity past God created an inheritance of special blessings for each believer (Eph. 1:3; 1 Pet. 1:4). These blessings are the "prize of that upward call from God" described in Philippians 3:14. The distribution of these unique blessings demonstrates the matchless grace of God and glorifies Him in the angelic conflict. He placed this unique treasury on deposit, as if in escrow, to be distributed to the believer when he acquires the capacity to enjoy God's "greater grace" (James 4:6). The believer gains capacity to receive, utilize, and enjoy his escrow blessings through the execution of the protocol plan of God resulting in spiritual momentum and the attainment of spiritual maturity. Capacity for blessing is a characteristic of spiritual maturity; therefore, the distribution of escrow blessings is also a characteristic of maturity.

11. QUALIFICATION FOR EVIDENCE TESTING. The second stage of the maximum glorification of God in spiritual maturity is evidence testing. Never before in history has God made so much of His omnipotence available to the believer as in the Church Age, and never before in the believer's lifetime does he have greater exercise of God's power as in spiritual maturity. These tremendous divine dynamics are necessary for the final increment of suffering for blessing. As a result of reaching maturity and achieving maximum utilization of his problem-solving devices, the dynamics of the believer's life are manifest in both living and dying, in both prosperity and evidence testing—under the consistent utilization of divine omnipotence.

12. ATTAINMENT OF THE FINAL PHASE OF THE UNIQUE LIFE. Spiritual maturity is characterized by that phase of the unique life described as "Christ [being] glorified in [the] body" (Phil. 1:20-21). This glorification of Christ occurs through escrow blessings and evidence testing.

THE GLORIFICATION OF GOD IN SPIRITUAL MATURITY

CONVEYANCE OF ESCROW BLESSINGS

There are two stages in the maximum glorification of God by the believer on earth. Both are exclusive privileges of spiritual maturity.

1. God is glorified when the believer attains SPIRITUAL MATURITY, Gate 8 of the divine dynasphere. At this point the believer begins to receive distribution of the ESCROW BLESSINGS that God created in eternity past.

2. God is glorified when the mature believer passes EVIDENCE TESTING.

Every Church Age believer belongs to a unique plan designed by God in eternity past. The objective of this plan includes blessing for the believer "beyond all that [he can] ask or imagine" (Eph. 3:20). In the distribution of these blessings, God is glorified by blessing the believer.

The first thing God ever did for us is the means of glorifying Him: He created the believer's blessings before He created the believer. "Before the foundation of the world" (Eph. 1:4), God the Father tailored fabulous blessings specifically for each individual Christian and, as it were, deposited those blessings in escrow.

> Worthy of praise and glorification is God, even the Father of
> our Lord Jesus Christ, who [the Father] has blessed us with
> every spiritual blessing in the heavenlies in Christ. (Eph. 1:3)

God's plan for blessing the believer may be compared to an escrow contract. An escrow is a deed, bond, or other agreement by which one person conveys some form of property to another person. Rather than being conveyed directly, however, the property is deposited with a third party, to be delivered when the intended recipient fulfills certain conditions set forth in the terms of the escrow agreement.

Just as an escrow agreement has three parties, so also Ephesians 1:3 mentions three parties: God the Father, Jesus Christ, and the believer. God the Father is the *grantor*. In eternity past He created each believer's blessings for time and for eternity and deposited them with Jesus Christ, who acts as a *depositary or escrow officer*. Each believer is the *grantee* of an escrow contract from God.

If you have believed in Christ, you are the grantee of blessings that stagger the imagination. However, part of divine wisdom is the principle that capacity

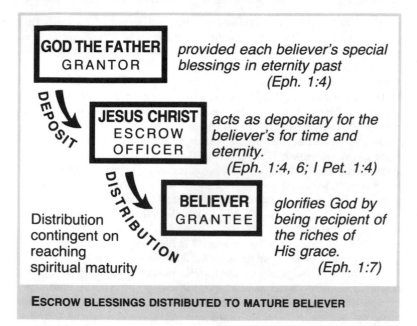

GOD THE FATHER
GRANTOR

provided each believer's special blessings in eternity past (Eph. 1:4)

DEPOSIT

JESUS CHRIST
ESCROW
OFFICER

acts as depositary for the believer's for time and eternity. (Eph. 1:4, 6; I Pet. 1:4)

DISTRIBUTION

BELIEVER
GRANTEE

glorifies God by being recipient of the riches of His grace. (Eph. 1:7)

Distribution contingent on reaching spiritual maturity

ESCROW BLESSINGS DISTRIBUTED TO MATURE BELIEVER

for blessings must precede the conveyance of blessings. God, therefore, designed the protocol plan to produce that capacity which makes the distribution of blessings meaningful, enjoyable, and glorifying to God.

Blessing does not begin at spiritual maturity. As part of His logistical grace policy, God has designed a system of lesser blessings which He distributes during the entire earthly experience of the believer.[68] This means that logistical grace is not simply a vehicle for sustaining the believer's life on earth but is a system of providing undeserved blessing whose enjoyment can be surpassed only by the ultimate distribution of escrow blessings for time. Furthermore, whatever capacity we have for blessings in time is far exceeded by our escrow blessings for eternity. Between the logistical blessings of spiritual childhood and early spiritual adulthood and the escrow blessings of the eternal state is this fantastic grace provision of God for the believer who executes His plan, purpose, and will, by the attainment of spiritual maturity. Obviously, God is glorified when any believer executes this plan, and as a sign of His pleasure He conveys escrow blessings for time.

The path to these magnificent blessings involves undeserved suffering. These blessings come through suffering as well as through prosperity.

---

68. See *Christian Integrity*, pp. 55-57.

The believer who attains spiritual maturity is classified as a winner. The question arises as to what happens to the escrow blessings of the Christian who is classified as a loser, the believer who fails to attain spiritual maturity. To illustrate the biblical answer to this question, we again return to the analogy of the escrow agreement. In the state of Texas, escrow contracts are irrevocable. From the date the contract is signed, the property in escrow cannot be retrieved by the grantor, and the contract cannot be canceled. Likewise, the believer's escrow contract with God is irrevocable (1 Pet. 1:4). The only reason a believer's escrow blessings are not delivered to him is that he fails to fulfill the conditions of the escrow agreement. The only condition is that the believer advance to spiritual maturity. The loser's escrow blessings belong to him irrevocably, but they will remain undistributed, on deposit forever as a memorial to lost opportunity and as a monument to the eternal bounty of God's grace. While the believer cannot lose his salvation, he can lose the conveyance of escrow blessings for time and eternity.

Escrow blessings are called "spiritual" in Ephesians 1:3, not because they are ethereal and intangible, but because God is emphasized as their source (John 4:24a). Escrow blessings may include material prosperity and temporal success as well as invisible impact and the spiritual strength of maturity itself. The characteristics of spiritual self-esteem, which are strengthened in spiritual autonomy, become yet stronger in spiritual maturity and constitute fabulous blessings in the inner life. In addition to this marvelous stability and capacity of soul, Jesus Christ as the depositary commences with the conveyance of escrow blessings for the mature believer's life on earth.

A treasury of blessings for time and eternity has your name on it. Your personal blessings are irrevocable, "imperishable, and undefiled and will not fade away"; neither you nor anyone else can cancel them (1 Pet. 1:4). The location of the deposit is "in the heavenlies"; no repository could be more secure (1 Pet. 1:4). The date of the deposit is "before the foundation [creation] of the world"; no other fortune has an older heritage. The depositary is Christ; no one could be more personally interested in delivering your blessings to you. The creator and grantor of your blessings is God the Father; there is no greater giver.

> He [God the Father] who did not spare His own Son, but delivered Him up for us all, how will He not [the Father] with Him [Christ, the escrow officer] freely give us all things [our escrow blessings]? (Rom. 8:32, NASB)

Because God is glorified by blessing the believer, the purpose of the believer's life is to receive escrow blessings. What must he do to receive them? Grace excludes all human works. Therefore, the Christian's responsibility under the conditions of the escrow contract is to utilize the assets of the divine dynasphere and advance to spiritual maturity. Only in maturity is he able to receive the marvelous blessings that God has placed on deposit for him.

EVIDENCE TESTING AND THE MAXIMUM GLORIFICATION OF GOD

Suffering plays an essential role in advancing the believer to maturity. After he reaches maturity, and after he has received many escrow blessings, suffering then makes a unique and specialized contribution to the maximum glorification of God. Undeserved suffering in the life of the mature believer furnishes evidence in a courtroom drama that has been unfolding since long before human history began. In the appeal trial of Satan, a summary of which follows, God calls mature believers to the witness stand to testify concerning His matchless grace. Evidence testing is Satan's attempt to discredit their testimony.

Like escrow blessings, evidence testing is the privilege of the mature believer and the final category of suffering for blessing. Evidence testing follows the pattern of all suffering for blessing in that "God is faithful, who will not allow you to be tested beyond what you are able" to bear (1 Cor. 10:13). Only spiritual maturity has the strength to endure, benefit from, and even enjoy evidence testing. In short, God can glorify Himself to the maximum through escrow blessings and through evidence testing only in the lives of mature believers. This is another reason spiritual maturity is the objective of the Christian way of life.

X
Evidence Testing

THE APPEAL TRIAL OF SATAN

All human suffering, regardless of category, is linked to the chain of events that began in prehistoric times. When God created the universe, He formed a race of supercreatures, classified in the Bible as angels. Angels are rational beings with the ability to travel throughout the vast universe God created for them. God made them perfect, without sin, totally acceptable to His absolute righteousness. Because volition is a necessary component of a rational mentality and of capacity for love, God gave the angels free will so that they might understand His character and worship Him.

Furthermore, God established a system of angelic authority and organization within which the angels lived and functioned. He perfectly blended freedom, authority, and responsibility, creating a structured environment within which each angel could express his own volition.[69]

In the beginning the most exalted of all the angels was the anointed cherub, called Lucifer, the Son of the Morning (Isa. 14:12). He was entrusted with responsibilities and was granted privileges beyond those of any other angel, but he abused his freedom through arrogance and rebellion against God (Ezek. 28:12-19). Arrogance is the worst of all sins; it is the distorter and obscurer of

---

69. The angelic College of Heralds and Order of Battle are presented in tape-recorded Bible classes, available as indicated on page iv.

reality, an enemy of every rational creature. Arrogance was the self-deception that caused magnificent Lucifer to compete with God rather than love and worship Him. Arrogance is the reason for Lucifer's horrible future suffering (Matt. 25:41), just as arrogance already has caused his frustration and discontent through the thousands of years since he revolted against God.

We do not know how long ago Satan fell, but in spite of his protracted arrogance and suffering, he remains the most talented, attractive, and personable creature to come from the hand of God (Ezek. 28:12; 2 Cor. 11:14). His force of persuasion is as compelling today as when he convinced one third of all the angels to join his prehistoric revolution against God (Rev. 12:4*a*). Satan's fall and his leadership of myriad angels in revolt inaugurated the prehistoric warfare that I call the angelic conflict, a conflict that continues to this day and that will be concluded only with the final judgment at the end of human history.

A comparison of Scripture with Scripture leads to the conclusion that God held a trial in eternity past. In the prehistoric trial God was the judge and the prosecution; Satan was the defense. God considered all the evidence and pronounced a guilty verdict. He sentenced Lucifer and all the fallen angels to "eternal fire" (Matt. 25:41).

Further biblical evidence for the prehistoric trial of fallen angels is found in Satan's titles. The words "devil" and "Satan" are not names but titles, both of which mean "accuser" or "adversary" as an attorney accuses someone in court. His proper name, Lucifer, means "translucent, light of the dawn," identifying a creature of exceeding beauty. He is called the devil and Satan because he was the defense attorney who represented himself and the fallen angels at the prehistoric trial and because he continues to act as an attorney now that the trial has entered its appeal phase during human history (Job 1:6-12; 2:1-5; Zech. 3:1-2).

"Eternal fire...has been prepared for the devil and his angels" (Matt. 25:41), but because the sentence was not immediately executed—and, in fact, will not be carried out until the end of human history (Rev. 20:10)—we can accurately infer that Satan appealed the sentence. The elapse of time between the sentence and its execution indicates that human history is part of this momentous trial, the appeal trial of Satan.

What is Satan's appeal argument? What case could he possibly construct to reverse the verdict of perfect, omniscient, and just God? Perhaps we can speculate from a common objection that is frequently repeated in the devil's world. Satan's appeal probably followed this line of argument: How can a loving God cast His creatures into hell?

Human history provides the answer. When Satan appealed his sentence, God convened an appeal trial which is coterminous with human history. Consequently, man was created to resolve the angelic conflict.

Before He created man, God anticipated his fall and in His matchless grace designed a plan of salvation for all mankind through faith in Jesus Christ. Furthermore, God created fabulous assets, privileges, and opportunities for every believer so that he might enjoy fellowship with God. God's grace is freely available to every human being. For anyone who refuses to believe in Jesus Christ, the only alternative is divine judgment. Human history displays God's magnificent character and gracious policy to Satan, to all the angels, and to mankind. History also demonstrates that no one goes to hell but by his own negative volition (John 3:18, 36).

Restricted to one small corner of the universe called planet Earth, man was created a lower creature than the angels, limited in strength, intelligence, and mobility. But like the angels man is rational and possesses the same free will that angels possess. The resolution of the angelic conflict lies in man's exercise of volition for or against the Lord Jesus Christ, for or against the plan of God. Angels observing human beings will witness proof after proof of Satan's own culpability and proof after proof of God's perfect justice and grace (Job 1:6; 2:1-3; Luke 15:7, 10; 1 Cor. 4:9; 11:10; Eph. 3:10; 1 Tim. 3:16; 5:21).

The appeal trial of Satan is coterminous with human history. In human history God is duplicating every situation that Satan used as a basis for argument and objection in his prehistoric trial. Apparently a major issue in that trial was the concept of suffering. The two categories of evidence testing, as the final stage of Christian suffering for blessing, correspond to Satan's major lines of argument, and the mature believer's utilization of divine assets to pass evidence testing totally demolishes the devil's case.

First, Satan argues that men, like angels, will not be able to handle suffering, especially if they consider the suffering unjust. The only reason anyone remains faithful to God, Satan charges, is because God blesses him. This was the argument in the book of Job. Job, however, discredited Satan's theory and was entered as evidence in God's case against Satan. Despite a period of failure, Job remained faithful to God not because God was blessing him but because of the doctrine he had learned and eventually applied. As a mature believer, Job possessed the resources to take extreme suffering in stride and to identify his circumstances as suffering for blessing rather than punitive suffering.

Satan likewise was given tremendous assets prior to his fall. He did not fall through any fault or negligence on God's part; he failed through rejection of all God had provided. Satan has no legitimate case, no excuse. Numerous figures in Old Testament history—Abraham, Moses, David—suffered intensely, but their suffering did not reduce them to being miserable, whining creatures. Their strength in suffering demonstrated the power of metabolized doctrine to sustain great happiness under every circumstance of life, to equate living and dying, prosperity and adversity. Only Satan is to blame for the state to which he has fallen.

Satan's second principal argument is that no one will remain faithful to God if offered sufficient wealth or power. In other words, everyone has his price. This argument is a direct defense of Satan's own fall from his office of anointed cherub, the highest ranking status among angelic creatures. The issue: Will creature lust for power, fame, wealth, or any other attainment be more powerful than the plan of the Creator? Will man choose self-aggrandizement independent of God, or will he execute God's plan and allow God to promote him? This is the evidence test Satan leveled against the humanity of Christ during the Incarnation (Matt. 4:1-11).

THE PHASES OF THE APPEAL TRIAL

GOD PRESENTS HIS CASE

The terminology of United States jurisprudence provides analogies for the appeal trial of Satan. The structure of a trial can be superimposed upon the structure of human history.[70]

A trial has three phases. First, there is the *formal presentation of the case:* the prosecution presents its case, followed by the defense. Next is the *rebuttal* phase: the rebuttal arguments of the prosecution followed by the rebuttal arguments of the defense. Finally comes the *closing argument and summary:* by the prosecution and then by the defense.

The formal trial in Satan's appeal trial corresponds to Old Testament history. God created man as a rational creature lower than angels, duplicating at a reduced scale the conditions of the prehistoric angelic conflict. The courtroom is planet Earth. The human race provides evidence, arguments, and precedents in the appeal trial. God entered His evidence by creating man just as the angels were created: innocent (or perfect) with the potential to love and worship God through right decisions and the potential to become imperfect by wrong decisions.

Human history provides the same circumstances and options which belonged to angelic history before man's creation. Satan had been created in perfect innocence; Adam was created in perfect innocence. The angels have free will; man has free will. Adam freely and deliberately chose to follow the pattern of arrogance which characterized Satan's original revolution. The fall of Adam duplicates the fall of Satan. The rebellion of Satan in the Garden of God resulted

---

70. Dispensations, depicted in the figure on page 144, are periods of human history differentiated according to divine revelation. They are the divine outline and interpretation of history. A study of dispensations is available on tape. See also *Dispensations*.

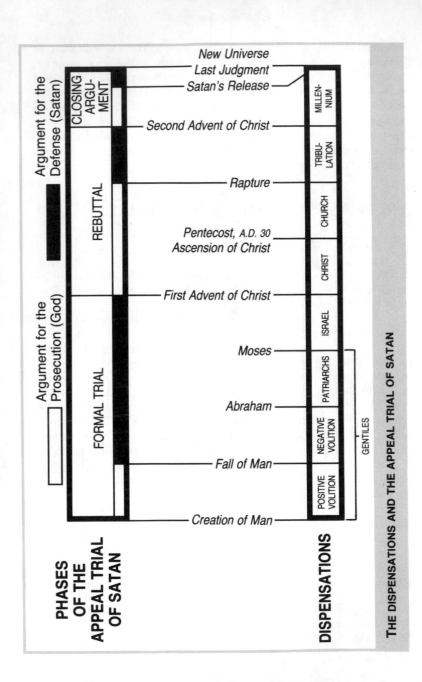

THE DISPENSATIONS AND THE APPEAL TRIAL OF SATAN

in the fall of angelic creatures (Rev. 12:4*a*); the disobedience of Adam in the Garden of Eden resulted in the fall of mankind (Rom. 5:12*a*).

In angelic history God had provided a decision-making process by which angels could express nonmeritorious positive volition. Likewise, God provided salvation for all mankind so that man can express nonmeritorious positive volition through faith in Christ (John 3:16). Through the exercise of free will, angelic creatures are divided into two categories: elect and fallen (Heb. 2:2; Rev. 12:7). Through free will mankind is divided into believers and unbelievers (John 3:36).

SATAN'S CASE

With the fall of Adam, Satan became ruler of the world. After usurping Adam's rule over the earth, Satan presented his case in his many attempts to establish control over his kingdom so that he might create perfect environment on earth. Just as in the prehistorical angelic conflict, his purpose in the historical extension of the angelic conflict is to prove himself equal with God, to be "like the Most High" (Isa. 14:14). Satan wishes to demonstrate that arrogance is not arrogance but a viable alternative to God's plan. However, Satan lacks the ability, brilliant though he is, to produce the utopia he wishes to establish.

The formal phase of the appeal trial includes angelic observation, participation, and interference in the affairs of mankind (Gen. 6:1-4; Job 1:1-3). These angelic activities continue throughout all phases of the trial.

GOD'S REBUTTAL

The formal phase of Satan's appeal trial has been followed by the rebuttal phase, in which we live. This most dramatic phase of the appeal trial coincides with the great power experiment. Therefore, God's rebuttal is twofold.

1. THE GREAT POWER EXPERIMENT OF THE HYPOSTATIC UNION resulted in strategic victory of the humanity of Christ over Satan at the cross.

2. THE GREAT POWER EXPERIMENT OF THE CHURCH AGE is resulting in tactical victories of those believers who fulfill the protocol plan of God.

As the prosecution, God has presented an astonishing rebuttal to Satan's unsuccessful attempts to prove his own superiority. In the strategic action that had been prophesied since the fall of man (Gen. 3:15), God the Son "became flesh" (John 1:14). "When the fullness of time came, God sent forth His Son, born of a woman" as the God-Man in hypostatic union forever (Gal. 4:4).[71] Satan had tried desperately but failed to prevent the first advent and Incarnation of the Lord Jesus Christ.

Our Lord attained strategic victory through residence, function, and momentum inside the prototype divine dynasphere. The spiritual winner in the Church Age attains tactical victory through residence, function, and momentum inside the operational divine dynasphere.

As Paul indicated in Philippians 3:10-11, both increments of the great power experiment conclude with resurrection. The great power experiment of the hypostatic union terminated with the resurrection of Christ. The great power experiment of the Church Age will terminate with the resurrection or Rapture of the Church. Both the first advent of Christ and the Church Age are documented in terms of power which is demonstrated by resurrection.

> Who [Jesus Christ] was demonstrated the Son of God by means of power belonging to the Holy Spirit, by means of the resurrection from the dead—Jesus Christ our Lord. (Rom. 1:4)

> And [I pray that you members of the royal family may know] what is the surpassing greatness of His [the Father's] power to us, who have believed, for the working of His superior power which He put into operation by means of Christ when He raised Him from the dead and seated Him at His right hand in heavenly places. (Eph. 1:19-20)

Between the resurrection of Christ and the resurrection of the Church, greater power is available to every believer than in any previous era of human history. The power that raised Jesus Christ from the dead is now available to every Church Age believer for the execution of the protocol plan of God. Divine omnipotence is available in three categories in the laboratory of human experience:

1. THE OMNIPOTENCE OF GOD THE FATHER who designed the portfolio of invisible assets,

2. THE OMNIPOTENCE OF GOD THE SON who sustains the universe and perpetuates human history, and

---

71. See *Christian Integrity,* pp. 193-96.

3. THE OMNIPOTENCE OF GOD THE HOLY SPIRIT who provides the energy within the divine dynasphere.

The glorification of God through the utilization of divine power is part of the uniqueness of the Church Age.

> Now to Him [God the Father] who is able to do infinitely more than all we could ever ask or think on the basis of the power which is working for us [the omnipotence of each Member of the Trinity], to Him [be] the glory by the Church [tactical victory in the great power experiment of the Church Age] and by Jesus Christ [strategic victory in the great power experiment of the hypostatic union] with reference to all generations of this [unique] age of the ages [some believers in every generation of the Church Age will utilize divine power to execute the divine plan and glorify God]. Amen. (Eph. 1:20-21)

As the God-Man, Jesus Christ did not use His own omnipotence independent of the plan of God the Father for the first advent. He lived among men with their human limitations. In fulfillment of the Father's plan of salvation, Christ did not exercise His divine attributes to benefit Himself, to provide for Himself, or to glorify Himself. He veiled His preincarnate glory, without surrendering any divine attribute, and voluntarily restricted the independent use of His omnipotence in compliance with the Father's plan for the great power experiment of the hypostatic union. Instead, the humanity of Christ relied on the omnipotence of God the Father and of God the Holy Spirit, made available in the prototype divine dynasphere (Matt. 12:18, 28; Luke 4:14, 18; John 3:34). In this tremendous power system the perfect humanity of Christ maintained His impeccability throughout His life on earth. On the cross, while still impeccable Himself, He bore the sins of all mankind and was judged in our place. The omnipotence of the Holy Spirit sustained our Lord while the omnipotence and justice of the Father judged Him.

The prototype divine dynasphere not only sustained Jesus Christ in the most intense suffering man will ever know but enabled Him to endure the pain of the cross with uninterrupted inner happiness.

> Be concentrating on Jesus, the author and perfecter of our doctrine [the humanity of Christ tested and proved the prototype of the same divine dynasphere revealed to us in Church Age doctrine], who because of the present exhibited

happiness [the greatest problem-solving device in the divine dynasphere] endured the cross, having disregarded the shame [Jesus Christ remained impeccable while being judged for the sins of mankind], and sat down at the right hand of the throne of God. (Heb. 12:2)

The virgin birth of Jesus Christ initiated the great power experiment of the hypostatic union and totally separated the formal trial from the rebuttal phase of the trial. Although Christ was "made a little lower than the angels" in His unglorified humanity, in His resurrected humanity He is "crowned with glory and honor" far higher than the angels (Heb. 2:9-10). When the victorious Christ was awarded His new royal title, King of Kings and Lord of Lords, and was seated in the place of highest honor in heaven, God the Father then presented the most dramatic evidence in the entire appeal trial.

Totally unannounced in Old Testament prophecy, God inaugurated the Church Age with its mystery doctrine (Rom. 6:25-26; Eph. 3:1-7; Col. 1:25-27). During the Church Age He is creating, through the ministry of the Holy Spirit, a new spiritual species in union with Christ, a royal family to complement our Lord's new royal title. In so doing, God the Father extended the great power experiment from Christ's first advent into the Church Age. The prototype divine dynasphere designed for Jesus Christ has been bequeathed to us as the operational divine dynasphere. Through the baptism of the Holy Spirit, we have been created a new spiritual species, capable of utilizing available divine omnipotence. The great power experiment of the Church Age will reveal whether or not believers will use the omnipotence of God, power that has been made totally available to every believer.

Satan was caught entirely off guard when the mystery doctrines of the Church Age were unveiled. Like the bylaws of the ancient Greek mystery fraternities, the doctrines of the Church are known only to members of the organization. Church Age truths were revealed only to the royal family of God. The first hints of something marvelous at hand were given in Christ's prophecies just before the Church Age began (Matt. 16:18; John 14-17). Prior to our Lord's prophetic statements, no one knew about the baptism of the Holy Spirit and union with Christ, about the filling of the Holy Spirit, about all the powerful assets of the royal believer's palace. As never before, each member of the royal family is his own priest. Each is the heir of God, a joint heir with Jesus Christ.

The benefits and advantages of spiritual royalty defy description. The first advent and saving work of Christ constitute God's first rebuttal argument, and the formation of the royal family, along with God's brilliant protocol plan for the Church Age believer's advance to maturity, is the prosecution's second rebuttal argument. God's matchless grace in creating a palace and a royal protocol for every believer goes far beyond merely duplicating prehistorical divine sustenance for angelic creatures. But our fabulous assets glorify the essence and person of God, as did divine provisions for the angels in eternity past.

The royal family has the greatest opportunities that God has ever extended to the human race. Every Church Age believer has privileges and opportunities unimagined by Abraham, Moses, David, Elijah, or any other mature Old Testament believer. Although the royal family has assets that far exceed those held by any other believers since creation, believers today complain, fail to use their advantages, and default on their Christian lives. Rather than consistently learning Bible doctrine and developing spiritual self-esteem, spiritual autonomy, and spiritual maturity, they seek counseling and rely on others for strength. Ignorant of the Word of God, they have no spiritual resources in the content of their souls with which to face suffering. They are casualties in the angelic conflict even though all suffering in their lives is designed for correction, blessing, and happiness.

Jesus Christ's work of salvation was entered into evidence for the prosecution. He created the potential of salvation for the entire human race, demonstrating the absolute grace and justice of God. The provision of eternal salvation for man apparently duplicates a similar but unrevealed issue of volition in the prehistoric angelic conflict (Col. 1:20). Through faith in Christ, mankind gains a permanent relationship with God, similar to the eternal status of elect angels. Every time a human being believes in Christ, his decision is entered as evidence for the prosecution (Luke 15:7, 10). Moreover, every time a believer reaches maturity, he is called to the witness stand to provide conclusive evidence of God's grace and justice. This call to the witness stand is tantamount to evidence testing.

SATAN'S REBUTTAL

Satan's rebuttal argument is contained in the violence of the Tribulation, including demon invasions of the world and the worst anti-Semitism of human history. Truly, the Tribulation is the time of Satan's desperation, for he has no rational arguments to meet the witness of evidence testing given in every generation of the Church Age.

Characteristically, Satan's rebuttal in the Tribulation will include attempts to control his own kingdom through political and religious machinations. He will concentrate all his power in this frantic, seven-year attempt to overthrow God's verdict against him. These unsuccessful plots will end in shocking violence on an unprecedented worldwide scale (Rev. 6-19). Even though Satan is a supergenius, he lacks the rationale to meet the arguments of evidence testing. Violence indicates his failure to answer the rebuttal argument of the prosecution.

GOD'S CLOSING ARGUMENT

The closing argument for the prosecution will begin with Jesus Christ's second advent. Our Lord will return triumphant to earth as the King of Kings and Lord of Lords, superseding Satan as the ruler of this world (Ps. 110:1; Rev. 20:1-6). After incarcerating Satan (Rev. 20:2-3), Christ will restore Israel and establish His Jewish kingdom as the client nation of the Millennium (Isa. 5:26-30; Zech. 8:20-23). As a result of assembling the scattered Jews, He will fulfill God's unconditional covenants to the believers of Israel (Dan. 9:24). Israel, therefore, will be part of the prosecution's case both in the formal trial during Old Testament times and in the closing argument at Christ's second advent.

God's closing summary will be the millennial reign of Christ. The perfect environment of the Millennium will duplicate the prehistoric perfect environment of the universe before the fall of Satan. The Millennium will demonstrate that even under conditions of perfect environment man is still not satisfied; he cannot enjoy God's bounty apart from regeneration. Environment is never the solution to man's problems. If a believer makes environment a panacea, he cannot handle suffering. Arrogance rejects the grace of God and ruins perfect environment, which explains why Satan is incapable of creating perfect environment on earth.

This further proof of Satan's culpability will be found in man's negative volition while Satan himself is imprisoned and unable to influence human history. When truth is lucidly and universally taught, negative volition will still exist. Although Christ will be present on earth in resurrected glory, providing perfect environment during His millennial reign, some human beings will reject Him as Savior and will manufacture their own misery (Zech. 13:2-6). The Millennium will demonstrate that environment is neither the solution to man's problems nor the source of his happiness. If perfect environment will not provide happiness, neither will the improved environment that man seeks today for solutions to the problems of suffering.

The Millennium will reveal that the solution to man's problems resides in his thoughts, his mental attitude, his decisions rather than in external circumstances. Even if Satan could succeed in creating an overtly perfect environment, he still would not be equal with God who alone can create spiritual self-esteem, spiritual autonomy, and spiritual maturity within the soul. The inner dynamics of spiritual adulthood enable the believer to cope with the most intensified categories of suffering and to convert them into the greatest of blessings.

As part of the prosecution's case, perfect environment began and will end human history. Both Eden and the Millennium demonstrate that without a permanent relationship with God through faith in Jesus Christ, mankind will revolt against perfect environment as did angelic creatures. Consequently, even in perfect environment, rational creatures cannot survive independent of God.

SATAN'S CLOSING ARGUMENT

The closing argument for the defense, when Satan is released from prison after a thousand years, will show that Satan has learned nothing from his imprisonment. Ingrained arrogance does not respond to or profit from punishment. Upon his release Satan will discover many unbelievers living on earth in perfect environment under Christ's perfect rule. These people will have rejected the Gospel and denied all the evidence of Christ's magnificent saving work on their behalf. They will have ignored or opposed evangelism in many forms and will be primed for Satan's deceitful leadership.

Satan will rally these unbelievers (and negative believers as well) into a conspiracy that will quickly ignite as the Gog Revolution (Rev. 20:7-8). As in the Tribulation, Satan's final summary argument will be violence. The sheer violence of the Gog Revolution will parallel Satan's revolt against prehistoric perfect environment and will demonstrate once again the self-destructiveness of arrogance.

Satan has no argument but violence; the Gog Revolution will be his admission of defeat. Every possible shred of an excuse will have been stripped away; his guilt will be confirmed, as will the guilt of every creature who exercises his free will in revolt against God. Satan's final outburst of violence will utterly destroy his case, which is also the case of all fallen angels and of all human unbelievers as well. God will put down this last satanic revolt and thus will terminate human history (Rev. 20:9; 21:1).

THE FINAL VERDICT

In the long and thoroughly just appeal trial of Satan, the verdict will be: appeal denied. The sentence of the original prehistoric trial will be carried out (Matt. 25:41). Satan and all fallen angels will be cast into the Lake of Fire (Rev. 20:10-15), and Jesus Christ will convene the great white throne judgment (Rev. 20:11-14) where all human unbelievers will be resurrected, tried, and judged (Rev. 20:12a).

At this last judgment unbelievers will not be condemned for their sins because all human sins have previously been judged in Christ on the cross. Instead, Jesus Christ the judge will condemn them for their negative volition expressed in rejection of His saving work on their behalf. In their trial, unbelievers will rely on their good works as evidence to earn divine approbation, but only Christ's work on the cross is acceptable to God for salvation. The human good works of unbelievers, "written in the books, according to their deeds," will be judged as unacceptable. Relative human righteousness has no fellowship with absolute divine righteousness. Lacking equivalent righteousness, fallen man is unqualified to live with God forever. Whom the righteousness of God rejects, the justice of God can only condemn. Each human unbeliever, therefore, will be cast into the Lake of Fire, eternally separated from God (Rev. 20:12b-15). The universe of human history will then be destroyed by fire (2 Pet. 3:10; Rev. 21:1). New heavens and a new planet Earth, with New Jerusalem as its capital city, will be created for the eternal state (Rev. 21:1-2).

This summary of human history in the angelic conflict provides the background for evidence testing of mature believers.

EVIDENCE TESTING AS CROSS-EXAMINATION BY SATAN

Satan rules the world, but he does not control man's volition. Man is a free agent in the devil's world, as proven by the existence of evangelism in the Bible. Satan therefore conspires to prevent human beings from believing in Christ (2 Cor. 4:3-4). Failing that, he tries to prevent believers from attaining spiritual maturity, and failing that, he does everything he can to discredit the mature believer whom God has presented as evidence for the prosecution in the appeal trial of Satan.

Each mature believer is a witness for the prosecution. He is another proof of God's grace and of the efficacy of divine assets against all obstacles and distractions along the route of spiritual advance. Once God has presented a mature believer as evidence, Satan has the right of cross-examination. He uses suffering in the attempt to break down the believer, to force him to abandon God's resources. After reaching maturity, the believer receives some of the most intense pressure he will face in his lifetime. Because no believer could pass this test without the strength of maturity, evidence testing is the monopoly of mature believers.

There are two categories of evidence testing. Some mature believers are tested in relation to the plan of God; others are tested in relation to the circumstances of life. The believer has no choice in this matter. God sovereignly decides which type of evidence testing an individual will receive.

Each category of evidence testing will be illustrated in this study. Both categories have three parts, which may come in rapid sequence or which may be spread out over a period of time. The believer may pass all three parts of evidence testing the first time he encounters them, or he may pass one or two and fail the rest. If he fails yet rebounds promptly, he will not lose his spiritual momentum; he will retain his mature status, ready for another opportunity to pass the test, which often presents itself immediately.

The humanity of Jesus Christ underwent evidence testing at the beginning of His three-year earthly ministry. He was tested in relation to the plan of God. The three parts of His evidence testing challenged His relationship to:

1. THE HOLY SPIRIT (Matt. 4:1-4)

2. THE WORD OF GOD (Matt. 4:5-7)

3. THE PLAN OF GOD (Matt. 4:8-10)

Job is the example of a mature believer who received evidence testing in relation to the circumstances of life. His testing was also in three parts:

1. LOSS OF PROSPERITY (Job 1)

2. LOSS OF HEALTH (Job 2:1-10)

3. LOSS OF FRIENDS (Job 2:11ff)

Evidence testing is generally, though not always, administered by Satan. God restricts Satan from taking unfair advantage of any mature believer. For example, God prohibits the defense attorney from taking the witness's life (Job 1:12; 2:6). Short of committing murder, the devil is permitted wide latitude in his cross-examination because spiritual maturity equips the believer to handle the pressure (1 Cor. 10:13). Satan can instigate intense suffering, but we find confidence and comfort in the knowledge that, regardless of what evidence testing comes our way, God has established the rules and remains ultimately in control.

EVIDENCE TESTING OF THE HUMANITY OF CHRIST

CHRIST'S SPIRITUAL MATURITY

Inside the prototype divine dynasphere, the humanity of Christ advanced through all stages of spiritual growth, reaching maturity at an early age (Luke 2:40). His attainment of spiritual self-esteem, characterized by love for God, and His attainment of spiritual autonomy, characterized by impersonal love for all mankind, are described in Luke 2:52.

> And Jesus kept increasing in wisdom [momentum in Gate 4
> of the prototype divine dynasphere] and age and in favor
> with God [personal love for God in Gate 5] and men [imper-
> sonal love for all mankind, Gate 6]. (Luke 2:52)

The background for the evidence testing of Christ's humanity is the declaration of His spiritual maturity.

> And the Word [eternal God] became flesh [the hypostatic
> union] and tabernacled among us, and we beheld His glory,
> the glory as of the unique One from the Father, full of grace
> and doctrine. (John 1:14)

Matthew 4 records the evidence testing of our Lord, which was the first
event in His public ministry. He had spent thirty years in preparation for a three-
year ministry, and now He was at the threshold of executing the plan of the
Father that would culminate in His death, burial, resurrection, ascension, and
session. The context in Matthew describes the shift of Christ's ministry from
private to public.

The humanity of Christ signified His positive volition to the Father's plan by
submitting to baptism by John, the herald of the King (Matt. 3:13-15). Although
John baptized many people, the baptism of Christ was unique. Immersion in the
water symbolized our Lord's obedience to the plan of the Father for His first advent, a plan that no one but the impeccable Lord Jesus Christ could execute.
Christ's declaration of His submission to God's will elicited the strongest possible attestation of our Lord's spiritual maturity.

> And behold, a voice out of heaven saying, "This is My
> beloved Son in whom I am well pleased." (Matt. 3:17)

As true humanity, Christ had utilized the prototype divine dynasphere and
fulfilled the pattern of spiritual growth. Now at the outset of His public ministry,
He was immediately taken into the desert, alone, to face evidence testing.

> Then Jesus [the title of His humanity] was led by the Holy
> Spirit into the desert to be tested by the devil. (Matt. 4:1)

A lesson for the believer can be found in the first word of Matthew 4:1.
"Then" indicates that evidence testing was the first item on the agenda for
Christ's public ministry. No believer is qualified for maximum Christian service
until he has advanced to spiritual maturity and passed evidence testing.

Service for God increases in quality as the believer grows spiritually. Zeal to serve the Lord does not automatically qualify the Christian for service. Enthusiasm can exist in the immature as well as in the mature, and in fact religious zeal can characterize even morally degenerate unbelievers. This is not to discourage Christian service by any believer at any level of spiritual growth but to anticipate maximum service as a result of maximum preparation.

Evidence testing is the final category of suffering for *blessing*. The benefit inherent in Christ's victory was that our Lord started His public ministry with a success. The believer derives a similar impetus when he passes each phase of suffering for blessing along the way to maturity and passes evidence testing after attaining maturity. The Christian life begins with growth, not with service. The quality of Christian service improves as the believer accelerates his spiritual growth through each increment of suffering for blessing.

Three persons were involved in the testing of Christ: the humanity of Christ, the Holy Spirit, and Satan. The humanity of Christ was residing inside the prototype divine dynasphere. He was therefore filled with the Holy Spirit, as He had been since His virgin birth. Jesus was led by the same enabling power of the Spirit that leads the mature believer in the operational divine dynasphere. The third party present was the defense attorney of the appeal trial. Although the humanity of Christ was led into the desert by the Holy Spirit, the devil would administer the testing.

Intense physical duress was part of the circumstances for Christ's evidence testing. In the desert He went without food for forty days.

> And when He had fasted for forty days and forty nights, He
> was hungry. (Matt. 4:2)

The humanity of Christ was hungry every day for all forty days He spent alone in the desert. He was famished and already was suffering sharp, constant physical pain when evidence testing began.

THE FIRST EVIDENCE TEST OF CHRIST

The first part of our Lord's evidence testing attacked His relationship with God the Holy Spirit.

> And then when the tempter had come, he said to Him,
> "Since You are the Son of God, speak so that these stones
> may become bread." (Matt. 4:3)

Satan knows theology. Although he lives to exalt himself and oppose God, Satan knows from observation a great deal of true doctrine. Disarmingly, he approached Jesus with a true point of doctrine only to suggest a false conclusion. Christ *is* the Son of God. That is accurate information. "Son of God" is our Lord's first royal title as divine royalty; His first royal family is the Trinity.

At the time Satan was speaking, Christ held two royal titles. His first royal title is eternal in nature; He has always been God. His second title, "Son of David," was acquired at the moment of His virgin birth, His entrance into the human dynasty of King David. Now at thirty years of age, He was embarking on the earthly ministry that would culminate with the strategic victory over Satan at the cross. Three years from the time of His evidence testing, Christ would win His third royal title, which would be awarded to Him upon His ascension and session at the right hand of the Father in heaven. Our Lord's title of battlefield royalty won through strategic victory in the angelic conflict is "King of Kings, Lord of Lords, The Bright Morning Star." As the eternal complement to this third royal title, all Church Age believers are His third royal family.

Satan took an audacious approach. He is such a brazen liar that he used the true doctrine of Christ's royalty as a weapon against our Lord. This was the very doctrine that most threatened Satan's arrogant plans. Indeed, Satan would be strategically and tactically defeated as part of the doctrine of Christ's royalty. In a subtle attempt to trip our Lord into defeat, Satan virtually granted Christ the victory in advance.

The basis for Satan's first attack was his knowledge that in hypostatic union the deity of Christ has the power to accomplish any miracle. The deity of Christ was faithfully sustaining the universe at that very moment (Col. 1:17; Heb. 1:3). The act of turning stones into bread would have been a small matter for divine omnipotence. This first part of our Lord's evidence testing was an attempt by Satan to persuade Jesus Christ as the God-Man to exercise His deity contrary to the Father's plan for the Incarnation. Satan tempted the Lord to operate independently of the Holy Spirit, who was the Father's provision in the prototype divine dynasphere for sustaining Christ's humanity during His first advent. To fulfill the mission that He voluntarily accepted from God the Father in eternity past, Christ had to rely on the system of provision that the Father designed for Him. He did not use His own divine attributes independently to benefit, sustain, or glorify Himself. This is the true doctrine of kenosis.[72]

All Satan wanted Jesus Christ to do was to use His deity independently of the Father's plan to show that in His humanity our Lord could not depend on the Father's provision. Furthermore, our Lord was preparing the way for the protocol plan of God and the Church Age believer's dependence on the omnipotence of God.

Turn stones into bread? Omnipotence could have turned the whole mountain

---

72. See *Christian Integrity*, pp. 196-202.

into gingerbread! However, this would have compromised the function of His humanity under the sustaining ministry of the Holy Spirit.

The first phase of Christ's evidence testing teaches that miracles are not a legitimate solution to evidence testing, just as miracles are never the solution to any category of suffering for blessing. One of the easiest things for God to do is to perform a miracle because it requires no cooperation from human volition. Dramatic displays of supernatural power do not fulfill the purpose of evidence testing. Miracles require only divine sovereignty, whereas evidence testing spotlights human positive volition in the utilization of divine problem-solving devices.

The real issues in evidence testing are:

1. Will the mature believer continue to rely on divine assets?

2. Will those assets sustain him under extreme suffering?

The temptation to turn stones into bread was unique to our Lord Jesus Christ. This would be no temptation to human beings, for we lack the power equivalent to the task. In fact, the *humanity* of Christ was powerless to command stones to become bread. Such power belongs to deity alone. Furthermore, the miracles that Christ did perform throughout His earthly ministry were accomplished not in His own omnipotence but in the energy of the Holy Spirit according to the Father's plan (Matt. 12:28; Luke 14:14-15, 17-18, 21).

Although His humanity was fainting with hunger, Christ did not panic and scramble for an independent solution. He was being sustained and always had been supported by all-sufficient logistical grace. The prototype divine dynasphere, which includes the filling of the Spirit and the truth of Bible doctrine, is a tremendous power system. Because the Father had provided a perfect set of invisible assets for the Incarnation, God the Son could voluntarily restrict the independent use of His deity in keeping with the Father's plan. These are the same assets available to Christ's royal family in the operational divine dynasphere.

CHRIST'S VICTORY IN THE FIRST EVIDENCE TEST

Jesus answered Satan with one verse of Scripture because the power of doctrine is greater than any miracle. Bible doctrine has more power than man can imagine. We deal with an invisible enemy, with satanic systems, with an evil genius far superior to our human minds. Yet we have been given a power superior to all the concentrated forces of evil in the universe. Jesus Christ contradicted quickly with a short answer that was directly to the point.

> But He answered and said, "It stands written, 'Man must
> not live for bread only, but for every word that comes from
> the mouth of God.'" (Matt. 4:4)

As true humanity, Jesus dealt with His first evidence test from His own metabolized doctrine, doctrine He had learned as a member of the human race operating within the prototype divine dynasphere. From His humanity He recognized the power of God's Word. Rather than speak to the stones, He spoke to Satan, quoting a passage from Deuteronomy that describes the *modus operandi* of Israel as client nation to God. Jesus Christ is the God of Israel and the coming human King of the Jews. Satan had acknowledged Christ's divine royalty; now Christ built on Satan's true premise with an answer appropriate to His Jewish royalty. He quoted part of Deuteronomy 8:3 from the Septuagint, the brilliant, first century B.C. Greek translation of the Old Testament by seventy scholars in Alexandria, Egypt.

> He humbled you [God's dealing with Israel as client nation]
> and caused you to be hungry, and then He fed you manna
> [the perfect food] that neither you nor your ancestors had
> known, to teach you [the food was a teaching aid as well as
> physical sustenance] that man does not live by bread [or
> food] alone but by every word that comes from the mouth of
> God. (Deut. 8:3, translated from the Septuagint)

If God permits suffering for blessing, He always provides the solution. Hunger had been a test for two million Jews of the Exodus. They were helpless in the desert. They could do nothing to satisfy their hunger, just as the believer is helpless in suffering for blessing (2 Cor. 12:9-10). God faithfully supplied the Jews with the perfect manna that sustained them each day for forty years (Ex. 16). The food, however, was not the most important divine provision. The Jews gathered manna every day (except the Sabbath) as an illustration of the greater value of knowing and metabolizing the doctrine of God's logistical grace (Ex. 16:14-36). The point is that doctrine must be assimilated and metabolized as part of the believer's daily routine.

God *will* provide. Logistical grace is a fact of reality based on divine promises that guarantee food for as long as God desires to keep the believer alive in this world. In other words, the metabolization of the *doctrine* of logistical grace is more important than the metabolization of the physical food provided by logistical grace.

Food is essential for life, but the ultimate purpose of food is to allow the believer to perpetuate his spiritual advance. What actually sustains the believer is the divine guarantee of the details of life, not the details themselves. God's grace always emphasizes the giver more than the gift, the source more than survival. No wonder Christ could respond with such confidence. There was no question in His mind. No immediate personal gain and no relief from discomfort compares with the matchless love and grace of God.

All spiritual victory in any category of suffering for blessing is related to the Word of God. Christ found all the strength He needed in Bible doctrine and in the prototype divine dynasphere. In His victory over Satan, our Lord emphasized doctrine over experience, doctrine over emotion, doctrine over circumstances. He did not lash out with a diatribe against Satan. He did not gloat over exposing Satan's lie. He displayed no anger, no indignation, no outburst of emotion. He had nothing to prove. He simply relied on doctrine by stating what was pertinent.

THE SECOND EVIDENCE TEST OF CHRIST

Satan was permitted to select the location of the second part of Jesus Christ's evidence testing.

> And then the devil took Him to the Holy City [Jerusalem] and caused Him to stand on the highest point of the Temple complex. (Matt. 4:5)

The highest point of the Temple complex was called Herod's Porch. From this area a vertical precipice fell away to the rocky floor of the Kidron Valley 450 feet below. The second evidence test required the humanity of Christ to stand at this precarious brink.

> And he [the devil] said to Him, "If you are the Son of God, jump [throw yourself down]. For it stands written, 'He will command His angels concerning you, and they will lift you up in their hands so that you will not strike your foot against a stone.'" (Matt. 4:6)

A fall from such a height would mean certain death, but how was the humanity of Christ to answer now that Satan was employing the exact procedure that Christ used to win the first test? In fact, Satan repeated the true doctrine he had previously stated concerning the deity of Christ, then he quoted Jesus' phrase verbatim "for it stands written," and cited a passage of Scripture. We saw the power of the Word of God in Christ's victory in the first test. Now Satan attacks Scripture by quoting Scripture.

The problem is that Satan stated a true doctrine but from it derived a false application. He distorted the Word of God by excluding a line from the passage he quoted and by removing the passage from its context. This allowed him to arrive at a conclusion that seems true but is not.

Satan quoted part of Psalm 91, which is a song of deliverance probably written by Moses. The devil skillfully chose an Old Testament reference to Christ Himself, and even quoted Moses, the same writer that Christ had quoted from Deuteronomy 8:3. The immediate context is as follows.

> For You, O Lord, are my refuge.
> You have made the Most High your dwelling place.
> No evil will approach you.
> No disaster will come near your tent.
> For He will command His angels concerning you
> To guard you in all your journey.
> They will lift you up in their hands
> So that you will not strike your foot against a stone.
> You will tread on the lion and the cobra;
> You will trample the great lion and the constrictor snake.
>   (Ps. 91:9-13)

This deliverance psalm was written for the Jews as they marched through the rugged, mountainous regions of the Sinai. Dangers threatened from behind every stone. Each misstep posed a hazard. Psalm 91 states that throughout forty years of trekking through the desert, the Jews had guardian angels assigned by God to protect them in that hostile and initially unfamiliar environment.

Satan quoted Psalm 91:11-12, but he carefully omitted the line "To guard you in all your journey" in order to obscure the interpretation of the passage. The humanity of Christ was not part of the wilderness wanderings of the Jews nor was He on a dangerous journey Himself when Satan administered this evidence test. Even if the promise of deliverance were pertinent by application, the passage makes no guarantee against foolhardiness. To "strike [one's] foot against a stone" describes an accident. The mastery of the Jews over the wild animals of the desert deals with accidental encounters or with challenges that they had to face rationally and courageously in the normal course of events. If one of the Jews in the wilderness had deliberately jumped off a cliff, the guardian angels would not have interfered.

Satan's distortion and misapplication of doctrine attempted to lure Christ into an impulsive state of mind. The devil wanted Jesus to believe for a moment that He was authorized to do what normally He would have considered inane and sinful. Because Jesus was standing so close to the edge of the precipice, a rash thought might have translated itself into one short step to destruction.

Satan was attempting to trip up our Lord's spiritual common sense. The human mentality of Jesus Christ was inculcated with divine viewpoint thinking; from doctrine in His soul, He had the instincts of truth which Satan was trying to subvert. This was a brilliant ploy. He taunted Christ to prove the superiority of divine power, but Jesus had absolute confidence in divine omnipotence. He did not feel threatened by Satan's challenge. With perfect self-esteem, our Lord had nothing to prove.

Satan used Scripture to tempt the humanity of Jesus Christ to act independently of Scripture. A 450-foot leap onto rocks would be tantamount to suicide, but no passage in the Bible authorizes suicide or guarantees divine protection against suicide. An individual's departure from this earth is a matter of the sovereignty of God. The time and manner of death is not the legitimate option of human volition. A believer who commits suicide does not lose his salvation, but neither does he have divine authorization to take his own life.

God does not advocate or condone senseless, unreasonable actions, regardless of which Scripture some clever individual may quote as authority. The Father's plan for Jesus Christ's Incarnation never required Him to do anything absurd. The protocol plan for the royal family is likewise a no-nonsense plan with a no-nonsense objective. This principle has been overlooked by many believers who, rather than learn Bible doctrine, will blithely follow the latest traveling preacher into one corny, ludicrous idiocy after another, all in the name of serving God.

A deeper problem exists in Satan's taunt. The devil implied that, as God, Jesus Christ does not control the forces of nature. Actually, the deity of Christ sustains the universe. He was perpetuating the law of gravity throughout the time His humanity was enduring evidence testing. The scientific laws of nature are treatises on the faithfulness of the Lord Jesus Christ ''in [whom] all things hold together'' (Col. 1:17). Satan's cross-examination had violated the rules God had established for evidence testing. The devil as defense attorney had a right to put the humanity of Christ to the test (Heb. 4:15), but no right to test His deity (James 1:13).

The question of common sense was merely the surface issue in this insolence of Satan. When the Lord replied, He addressed the real problem.

> Jesus replied to him once more, ''Do not put the Lord your
> God to the test.'' (Matt. 4:7)

Satan had quoted Scripture that did not apply and had therefore distorted Scripture. Jesus quoted Scripture that did apply, and He made correct and accurate application. The humanity of Christ ignored Satan's temptation concerning suicide but homed in on the devil's admission that Christ is the Son of God. Jesus quoted Deuteronomy 6:16 to remind Satan of who had created him and of who was sustaining him even as they spoke. The Person whom Satan had begun to test was the God of the universe and of all creatures in the universe, including those who reject Him.

Satan's administration of evidence testing under the permissive will of God is always slanderous and blasphemous, but when Satan exceeded his bounds, the humanity of Christ recognized the violation and used doctrine to cut off the debate. Christ was thus victorious in the second phase of evidence testing.

THE THIRD EVIDENCE TEST OF CHRIST

Satan was so confounded by Christ's answer that he completely changed his tactics in the third round of evidence testing. No longer would Satan mention the deity of Christ, and no longer would he attempt to use Scripture.

> Once more the devil transported Him to a very high vantage
> point and showed Him all the kingdoms of the world and
> their glamour. (Matt. 4:8)

The Greek word *oros* is usually translated "mountain," but no mountain on earth presents a view of all the kingdoms of the world. Perhaps they went into space, but wherever the vantage point was located, Satan as the ruler of the world made a bona fide offer to the humanity of Christ.

> Then he [the devil] said to Him, "All of these I will give to
> you, if you fall down and worship me." (Matt. 4:9)

Both Satan and Christ knew that the Father's purpose is to deliver all the kingdoms of the earth to Christ. The unconditional covenants to Israel demand that the Son of David return to earth as its king. Operation Footstool, announced in Psalm 110:1, depicts the victorious Messiah as the king of all the earth with His foot on the necks of His defeated enemies. Christ's coronation as ruler of the earth will occur at His second advent. His task in His first advent was to purchase the salvation of mankind so that He might fulfill God's eternal, unconditional covenants to the Jews, which require them to have eternal life. Eternal life must be provided before eternal blessings can be enjoyed. Therefore, eternal salvation through our Lord's first advent must precede fulfillment of the unconditional covenants to Israel at His second advent. Without salvation, no population would exist in Christ's eternal kingdom.

The cross must come before the crown, but Satan proposed a plan to bypass the cross. Although Christ had just indicated his obedience to the Father's plan through the ritual of baptism, Satan in his desperation offered an alternative plan. His brilliant arguments had run out. His game plan had been defeated, and his poise had been shaken. The subtle sophistication that characterized the first two tests disappeared in this third, blatant temptation.

The humanity of Christ retained His perfect poise. His personal love for the Father is implicit in His reply to Satan. Personal love for God motivated the humanity of Christ, not greed and not even a desire to put down Satan. Our Lord realized that in the power of the prototype divine dynasphere He had passed evidence testing. By quoting pertinent doctrine, He continued to base His attitude on the Word of God in victory as He had under testing.

> Then Jesus said to him, "Go, Satan, for it stands written, 'Worship the Lord your God; serve Him only.'" (Matt. 4:10)

This was the final word in the debate. Satan was defeated completely by a command that applied at the time of Jesus' evidence testing just as it had always applied throughout the prehistoric phase of the angelic conflict. Rather than worship God, Satan originally fell because he tried to elevate self to receive the worship that belonged to God. The devil stands condemned, guilty of the charges brought against him in the prehistoric trial.

Christ totally refused to gain the kingdoms of the world by any means other than by the plan of God the Father. Satan had long before failed in this matter of loyalty; he had made himself a loser. Christ was and would always continue to be loyal, a winner who utilized the prototype divine dynasphere to the maximum.

> Then the devil left Him, and behold angels came to Him and began to serve Him. (Matt. 4:11)

Satan, the most powerful of angels, could do nothing but obey the command of Christ and depart. The accurate interpretation and application of Bible doctrine not only sustains the one who uses it but is an insurmountable defense against his enemies. Christ quoted from Deuteronomy 6:13, adding His unique evidence testing victory to the victories of all the mature Old Testament believers who had correctly applied the Word of God.

Christ relied upon the Word of God rather than on the independent use of His own deity, thereby making Satan's temptations a legitimate evidence test addressed to His humanity. Furthermore, our Lord provided the exact means by which the mature Church Age believer passes evidence testing. Supplied with the prototype divine dynasphere by the omnipotence of the Father and sustained in the prototype divine dynasphere by the omnipotence of the Holy Spirit, the humanity of Christ withstood Satan's cross-examination by thinking and applying the Bible doctrine in His human soul. In doing so, He set the precedent for the royal family, whose royal privileges far exceed the assets of even the greatest Old Testament believer.

EVIDENCE TESTING OF JOB

JOB'S SPIRITUAL MATURITY

Job has an undeserved reputation for patience. The patience of Job is mythical; the *perseverance* of Job was real. Unlike the impeccable humanity of Christ who, many centuries later, would pass all three parts of evidence testing in rapid succession, Job passed the first two phases but failed the third. In that third test he received an onslaught of self-righteousness and bad advice from three friends—with whom he was *impatient*—before he marshaled the divine resources in his soul and passed the final test.

Job was tested, not in relation to the plan of God as Jesus would be, but in relation to the details and circumstances of life. The temporary losses of prosperity, health, and friends suffered by Job during the course of evidence testing establish a precedent: believers who pass evidence testing related to the details of life can anticipate a multiplication of escrow blessings after the testing is complete (Job 42:10-17).

The Book of Job is the most ancient in the Bible. Its archaic Hebrew is interspersed with Arabic expressions. Hebrew and Arabic had not yet developed as separate languages from their common Semitic root, suggesting that this book was written during the time of the Patriarchs or soon after, perhaps while the Jews were living in Egypt. God inspired Moses to record earlier historical events, but the Book of Job is pre-Mosaic. It lacks any reference to Moses, Israel, or the Mosaic Law.

The human author of the Book of Job lived outside the commonwealth of Israel, indicating that evidence testing was designed by God for both Jews and Gentiles, as well as for Christ and the Church. Any believer who uses divine assets and advances to spiritual maturity has the privilege of glorifying God by testifying for the prosecution in Satan's appeal trial.

Job had to be a mature believer to qualify for evidence testing. The first verse in the book declares his maturity: he was "blameless and upright; he feared God and shunned evil." Not only was Job mature, but he is one of three Old Testament believers, listed by Ezekiel, who dramatize the impact of mature believers on history.

> Then the word of the Lord came to me saying, "Son of man [a title for the prophet Ezekiel], if a nation sins against Me by being unfaithful [to the Word of God] and I stretch out My hand against it to cut off its food supply, send famine to it, and kill both man and beast, even if these three men— Noah, Daniel, and Job—were in it, they could only deliver themselves by their own integrity [by their status of spiritual maturity]." (Ezek. 14:12-14)

In Ezekiel's day Israel had declined. How strong would the pivot need to be to hold the nation together? If Noah, Daniel, and Job belonged to the same pivot at the same time, then despite their combined historical impact the nation would still require divine discipline. This is meant to be a dramatic statement, a stern warning to the rebellious Jews. Israel had grown so degenerate that not even the tremendous influence of these three believers could avert discipline and bring blessing to the nation. God would deliver Noah, Daniel, and Job as individuals, but He would not deliver their nation. The thrust of this passage places Job among the greatest believers of all time.

Because Job was a mature believer, his prosperity represents escrow blessing. God had blessed him with family prosperity, material prosperity, and personal prosperity (Job 1:2-5, 10). God had promoted Job to be "the greatest man in the East," that is, throughout all of Arabia.

The supreme attestation of Job's spiritual maturity, however, came directly from God. God had just heard Satan, as the defendant and defense attorney in the appeal trial, boasting that he was the ruler of the earth (Job 1:7). In answer to Satan's taunting arrogance, God presented Job as evidence for the prosecution.

> Then the Lord said to Satan, "Have you considered my servant Job? There is no one on earth like him; he is blameless and upright, a man who fears God and shuns evil." (Job 1:9, NIV)

There was no believer "like My servant Job" not only in all Arabia but throughout Satan's entire kingdom of the world. Job was a mature believer before evidence testing began. He was "blameless" in that he did not invite temptation or testing. Although he was not sinless, the doctrine in his soul gave him the wisdom to avoid temptation, or to "shun evil." His suffering was undeserved. The timing of his evidence testing was entirely a matter of the sovereignty of God.

Job had the clearly defined scale of values typical of a believer who has advanced through spiritual self-esteem and spiritual autonomy into spiritual maturity. His number one priority was his relationship with God. His personal love for God took the form of awe and respect.

Having presented His witness, God granted Satan the right of cross-examination. Satan immediately attacked Job's character. The devil slurred Job's motivation, contending that he was a hypocrite who served God only so that God would bless him. The more God blessed Job, Satan implied, the more self-righteous Job became. Job was accused of being a coward who led an exemplary life for fear of personal loss. Satan charged that if God removed the escrow blessings, Job would "curse [God] to [His] face" and be no different from Satan himself (Job 1:11). Satan's accusations against Job were an attempt to bolster the devil's own case for the defense.

Before allowing the cross-examination to proceed, God reminded Satan of the rules. Evidence testing could not involve the death of Job.

> The Lord said to Satan, "Very well, then, everything he has is in your hands, but on the man himself do not lay a finger." Then Satan went out from the presence of the Lord. (Job 1:12, NIV)

THE FIRST EVIDENCE TEST OF JOB

Personal commendation from God and divine inspiration in the Book of Ezekiel attest to the spiritual maturity of Job. His maturity is affirmed by the presence of escrow blessing in his life. The dynamics of spiritual maturity are now demonstrated by his response in the first two evidence tests.

While enjoying his prosperity, with no premonition of impending disaster, Job was ready for whatever life would bring. A believer does not need to be in a disaster in order to possess the strength to meet a disaster. In the appeal trial of Satan, a mature believer has testimony to give, if called to the witness stand, but he has nothing to prove. He does not look for trouble. Indeed, prosperity manifested Job's strength in the form of capacity to enjoy his blessings. When prosperity suddenly turned to adversity, that same strength enabled him to meet the shock of disaster with poise, gratitude, and unflagging personal love toward God.

Evidence testing comes to the believer without notice, without warning, without explanation. The initial shock is part of the test. When he is enjoying his relationship with God and appreciating escrow blessings, the mature believer is suddenly hit with intense suffering. Evidence testing is obviously undeserved suffering. Job knew that the sudden change in his fortunes was through no fault of his own, and he confidently maintained this true opinion throughout his testing.

The challenge of evidence testing is to consider the giver rather than covet His gifts, to remember the person of God even when escrow and logistical blessings seem to wither away. The challenge is to trust God no matter how unexplainable the situation may be. The challenge is to stand fast in the doctrine you know, for through the Scriptures God is more real than any suffering in life.

Evidence testing itself, although intended by Satan to discredit the believer, is converted by metabolized doctrine into a gift from God, a clear manifestation of His personal love for the mature believer. The mature believer has complete assurance "that [God] is working all things together for good" (Rom. 8:28) when no other explanation can make sense of his circumstances. All overt supports are kicked away; evidence testing focuses the mature believer's attention on God's person and grace.

Job's first test hit suddenly. In the middle of a wonderful party, messengers rushed in from different quarters of his vast estates announcing disaster after disaster. Sabean bandits from the south had attacked a large work crew, massacring Job's men and stealing his valuable work animals (Job 1:14-15). This was a horrible shock to Job who loved the men who faithfully served him.

This first messenger's report was not completed before a second desperate messenger brought word of a sudden electrical storm that had killed more members of Job's staff along with a large number of his sheep (Job 1:16). Not only was Job losing old friends and trusted associates, but his wealth was evaporating.

Yet another messenger arrived with news of a Chaldean raid from the east that attacked and destroyed another contingent of Job's men and animals (Job 1:17). Then word came of a violent desert storm that had collapsed the house in which Job's sons and daughters were enjoying a feast, killing all but the one who escaped to carry the news (Job 1:18-19).

Job had lost everything. The depths of his grief were unfathomable, but in the midst of his shock and sorrow, he did not forget God, the source of his prosperity. Job understood that God removes people from the earth only at the right time and in the right manner. He knew that God has a purpose in the death of every believer. Although Job did not know God's reason for the simultaneous deaths of so many people he loved, including his own children, he believed the truth that this was the best time for them to die, despite the vigor of their youth.

In deep anguish Job declared bankruptcy after the custom of the ancient Middle East (Job 1:20), and worshiped God. Job had passed the first evidence test with admirable poise.

> And [he] said,
> "Naked I came from my mother's womb,
> and naked I will depart.

> The Lord gave and the Lord has taken away;
> may the name of the Lord be praised.''
> In all this Job did not sin by charging God with wrongdoing.
> (Job 1:21-22, NIV)

THE SECOND EVIDENCE TEST OF JOB

Satan's first cross-examination had failed. His cynical opinion of Job had proven false. God then reiterated His case, repeating His formal commendation of Job. "There is [still] no one like him on the earth" (Job 2:3). In the context of praising Job, God states the definition and purpose of evidence testing.

> And he still maintains his integrity, though you [Satan] in-
> cited me against him to ruin him without any reason. (Job
> 2:3*b*, NIV)

Evidence testing is God permitting Satan to cross-examine the mature believer with suffering that is undeserved and inflicted for no apparent reason. This suffering "without any reason" becomes a demonstration of the glory of God. Evidence testing forces the mature believer to depend totally on the grace provisions of God. The believer's integrity is created and sustained by the integrity of God, through divine assets provided for his spiritual growth.

The devil paid no attention to the integrity of Job. Arrogance is interested only in self. Satan was not impressed by the magnificent spiritual dynamics of Job or by the glorification of God in the life of this mature believer. Satan refused to admit that he had been wrong about Job. Instead, the devil strode back into the courtroom continuing to boast.

As the defense attorney, Satan now claimed that Job had not been thoroughly tested. Satan suggested that as long as Job were physically sound and relatively comfortable, he could find the human strength to keep up his hypocritical facade. As long as there is health there is hope, was Satan's subtle inference. God permitted the devil to continue this line of reasoning, which became the second part of Job's evidence testing.

At Satan's instigation Job broke out in ulcers. He contracted a particularly loathsome type of skin cancer. Job lost more than health; his appearance became repulsive. If ever Job had derived his self-esteem from the approval of other people, that source of strength was gone. But Job's view of himself was *spiritual* self-esteem, based not on the approbation of others but on his own confidence in God.

Lesions and swelling disfigured Job; incessant itching tormented him. Unable to rest and desperate for relief, he scraped at his sores with a shard from a broken pot, but his pain and ugliness only set the scene for Satan's *coup de main,* delivered by Job's wife.

> And his wife said to him, "Are you still holding on to your integrity? Curse God and die!" (Job 2:9, NIV)

Her bitter reaction to her husband's evidence testing displayed spiritual immaturity. She showed that she had not progressed in the plan of God. Certainly she did not share God's high opinion of her husband. Because she lacked the doctrinal frame of reference that was the most important dimension of her husband's life, she had no capacity to love him. She could not appreciate the integrity he had demonstrated in the adversities they both had suffered. Instead, she was vindictive, insensitive, and sarcastic.

Job's wife gave him bad advice which, however, he did not take. She proposed suicide, just as, centuries later, Satan would tempt Christ with suicide at the edge of Herod's Porch. The spiritual maturity of Job is expressed magnificently in the way he answered her.

> He replied, "You are talking like a foolish woman. Shall we accept good from God, and not trouble?" In all this Job did not sin in what he said. (Job 2:10, NIV)

Already suffering intensely, Job now was mocked by his wife. She, too, had suffered terrible losses, but by reacting to her circumstances she had lost control of her own life. Although she was insensitive to him, Job was sensitive to her. He did not snap back at her. In fact, Job presents a dramatic figure: here in an ashheap sits this aristocratic, formerly wealthy man, scraping at his dirty sores with a piece of trash, receiving abuse from the one he might have expected to stand by him. Yet despite crushing disappointments, Job maintained his divine perspective and refused to join his wife in reaction against God.

The reason Job's words were not sinful was that he made a significant distinction, indicated in a turn of phrase in his response to his wife. He did not call her a fool. Such a retort might have involved any number of mental and verbal sins. Instead, he told her that she was repeating the words a foolish woman would use. She was not a fool, he said, but she was talking *like* one. Job displayed a marvelous mental attitude at this point in his testing.

Any *personal* love that may have existed between Job and his wife was unable to sustain their relationship. *Impersonal* love was needed, not only for the relationship but for Job's own mental attitude. He did not let his thinking lapse into bitterness; he applied the doctrine he knew and treated his wife on the basis of the virtue in his own soul. Job had spiritual autonomy, characterized by impersonal love. He did not feel threatened by her wrath or her insults. He did not react with anger or self-pity. His impersonal love enabled him to pass this second increment of evidence testing.

Spiritually, Job was far in advance of his wife and much more mature than his three friends who arrived ostensibly to comfort him but who, in fact, would administer the third part of Job's evidence test.

THE THIRD EVIDENCE TEST OF JOB

The third increment of Job's evidence testing began with a seven-day period of silence in the company of three friends: Eliphaz, Bildad, and Zophar. Also present was a younger man, Elihu, who would observe the debate that was about to begin and would serve as a judge in the case of Job versus his three friends.

During the silence, each of Job's friends began to speculate about the reason for Job's sudden fall from wealth and prominence. Each concluded independently that Job must have committed a horrible secret sin that moved God to discipline him so strenuously. They became fascinated with sin in the life of someone else; they arrogantly assumed the role of helping God make Job see the error of his ways. The three were totally out of line. Rather than comfort their bereaved friend, they judged him. From this point on they must be considered Job's *former* friends. They did not grant him the benefit of the doubt, which they might have given a stranger.

Evidence testing, by definition, involves suffering "without any reason." Eliphaz, Bildad, and Zophar had absolutely no facts upon which to base their evaluation. They had less information than even Job possessed, but they were quick to condemn. Adversities similar to those Job suffered might have been divine discipline in the life of a negative, intractable believer. In the life of this mature believer, however, these same adversities constituted the honor of being presented as evidence for the prosecution in the appeal trial of Satan. Overt indications of suffering enable no one to distinguish spiritual losers from spiritual winners. The obvious and immediate lesson is to avoid judging *anyone* who is suffering.

The three friends knew a certain amount of doctrine. Indeed, Eliphaz and Bildad were theologians. Both correctly understood the doctrine of punitive suffering, but they erroneously applied it to Job, to whom it was not pertinent. In eloquent archaic Hebrew poetry, Eliphaz, Bildad, and Zophar embarked upon a series of debates seeking to prove Job's culpability.

The long period of silence also had a negative effect on Job. The pressures bore down on him until he began to react to his pain and become temporarily disoriented. The cruelty of his wife haunted him. He sensed a coldness in his three friends and realized what they were thinking. Misunderstanding, ostracism, and isolation caused him to become subjective, to feel sorry for himself. The intensity of his suffering drove his self-pity to the point of irrationality.

Can a mature believer become psychotic? Generally no, so long as he uses the divine resources provided through Bible doctrine. The inventory of metabolized truth in his soul protects him from neurosis and psychosis. But any believer at any stage of growth can allow his concentration to lapse. He can abandon the accumulated doctrine in his soul and revert to emotion as the sole controlling force in his life. Emotion tends to dominate the mentality in extreme pain. Emotion is nonrational, and when the believer is controlled by his emotions, he cannot think but can only retreat from reality. Job succumbed to self-pity and was incapable of lucid thought when finally he broke the silence and "cursed the day of his birth" (Job 3:1). His unreasonable desire was to go from spiritual maturity to oblivion.

Job's failure to pass the third test is recorded in Scripture to teach us a valuable lesson. No matter how far we advance in the spiritual life, our human resources cannot cope with extreme disaster. Only divine resources related to Bible doctrine can meet the problems of severe, prolonged pain and of the miserable circumstances of life. Job temporarily lost his ability to concentrate, but God remained faithful. True to His promise that He will never allow a believer to be tested beyond his ability, God permitted Job's evidence testing to proceed because He knew Job had not reached the limit of his endurance.

Success is never guaranteed in any stage of suffering for blessing, even though the pressure is within the believer's capacity to endure. Every believer always possesses free will and has the potential for success or failure. In Job's case, the Bible doctrine in his soul would yet prove sufficient to his suffering. He would recover from his state of irrationality. He would regain the divine viewpoint of his situation and go on to complete success in evidence testing.

Job was a mature believer, but even the greatest of believers can break under intense pressure. The solution was not in Job's inherent strength; the power was in the doctrine in his soul. The faithful intake, metabolization, and application of the Word of God builds up our inner resources, and we remain strong only as long as we think from the divine viewpoint and utilize divine problem-solving devices.

Although Job was surrounded by three men who knew doctrine, he would have to go it alone in recovering his spiritual poise and passing evidence testing. As "worthless physicians," they would only hinder him (Job 13:4). Job began to recover when he stated his case, appealing directly to God rather than attempting to justify himself to men.

> Keep silent and let me speak;
> then let come to me what may.

> Why do I put myself in jeopardy
>   and take my life in my hands?
> Though he slay me, yet will I hope in him;
>   I will surely defend my ways to his face.
> (Job 13:13-15, NIV)

In desiring to present his case to God, Job manifested his spiritual self-esteem. His personal love for God gave him confidence in God. Job realized his human resources were like "a windblown leaf" (Job 13:25), and as in the first two increments of evidence testing, he placed his trust in God.

Job had not entirely recovered. He periodically launched into false statements as he reacted to the pious arrogance of his comforters, who were neither lending comfort, providing solutions, nor giving answers.

> Though I cry, "I've been wronged," I get no response;
> Though I call for help, There is no justice.
> (Job 19:7, NIV)

This is the lament for which God would reprimand Job when the debate ended, but even as Job made false statements, he also showed signs of knowing the divine viewpoint.

> I know that my Redeemer lives
>   and that in the end he will stand upon the earth.
> And after my skin has been destroyed,
>   yet in my flesh I will see God. (Job 19:25-26, NIV)

Job anticipated the second advent of Christ and his own resurrection. He looked ahead to the final divine evaluation of his life as a believer on earth. Job found encouragement in the doctrine that the level of spiritual growth a believer achieves on earth will be the criterion for the distribution of blessings in eternity. There are eternal repercussions from the believer's use of divine provisions for handling suffering on earth.[73]

THE SILENCE OF GOD AND PASSING THE FINAL TEST

Job's doctrinal perspective, which had come into clear focus, was again obscured as he lowered himself to the level of his detractors, attempting to justify

---

73. See *Integrity of God*, pp. 147-54.

himself rather than glorify God. Job stopped vindicating God and began to complain that God was refusing to vindicate him.

> If only I knew where to find him;
>   if only I could go to his dwelling!
> I would state my case before him
>   and fill my mouth with arguments. (Job 23:3-4, NIV)

Job had no problem understanding his own blamelessness. He did have a problem with the silence of God. Why did God allow this debate to go on and on? Job was not guilty of bringing disaster upon himself. Why did God refuse to make Job's innocence clear to his critics?

God remained silent to allow Job to use the doctrine resident in his soul. All suffering for blessing requires the believer to utilize the inventory of Bible doctrine that he already possesses. Evidence testing is designed for the doctrine we have already learned, not for the doctrine we need to learn. God understood the pressure Job was enduring, but He would not intervene until Job had passed the test with his own knowledge and application of doctrine. Job understood the necessary doctrine. In fact, he had already used it to pass the first two evidence tests.

God also remained silent because under courtroom procedures, cross-examination was under way. He would not vindicate Job until Satan had finished his interrogation. Job did not realize that the silence of God that was troubling him so deeply was playing a key role in the glorification of God. Neither Job nor his three former friends realized how close Job was to reaching that exalted goal of the maximum glorification of God.

Job was dismayed and disturbed by the silence of God, but today the Church Age may be regarded as an entire dispensation of the silence of God. After having placed His message to man in the completed canon of Scripture, God speaks directly to no one. He communicates to the royal family only through His written Word. The test Job faced concerning the silence of God is the order of the day for us, the standard operating procedure for the royal family. Bible doctrine in the soul, not supernatural experience, is the greatest power in the world today, giving the mature believer the ability to think clearly and act with wisdom under any circumstances.

The long debate finally ended when his three critics "stopped answering Job because he was righteous in his own eyes" (Job 32:1). They ran out of words because Job adamantly opposed every suggestion that he was guilty of secret wrongdoing. Two judges conclude the debate, one human and one divine.

Job listened to the brilliant legal opinions of Elihu, the young judge who had been courteously observing Job's third evidence test. While showing respect for his elders, Elihu had become indignant about the confusion created by all parties involved. Elihu was a mature believer; Job was judged by his peer, who took the side of God in the debate and indicted Job and all three of his former friends.

> But Elihu...became very angry with Job for justifying himself rather than God. He was also angry with the three friends, because they had found no way to refute Job, and yet they had condemned him. (Job 32:2-3, NIV)

After Elihu, the human judge, condemned the arrogance of Job, then God, the divine judge, finally broke His silence. He privately dealt with His servant, reminding Job of divine omnipotence and faithfulness, which are constantly displayed in the wonders of nature (Job 38-41). Omnipotent God never needed Job's help or encouragement in any matter, least of all in the vindication of Job himself. Obviously, God knows how to deal with mature believers. At any moment God could have vindicated Job before his three petty antagonists, but a far greater issue was at stake: the vindication of God in the appeal trial of Satan.

> Would you discredit my [God's] justice?
> Would you condemn me to justify yourself? (Job 40:8, NIV)

Job finally understood the issue in his third-phase evidence testing. He admitted his sin of self-justification and used rebound to return to fellowship with God. The final two lines of Hebrew poetry express Job's application of rebound. He judged himself as having committed a sin (cf., 1 Cor. 11:31), and he changed his mind about attempting to justify himself to the three friends.

> Therefore, I condemn myself (self-judgment in rebound)
> and I have changed my mind in dust and ashes. (Job 42:6)

Job had now completely passed evidence testing. As in the first two increments of evidence testing, he now focused his attention on God, not on self or circumstances. Motivated by respect, awe, and personal love for God, true doctrinal thinking enables the believer to worship God regardless of adversity. Metabolized doctrine equates adversity with prosperity, living with dying, so that the mature believer's life is a testimony to the glory of God. Paul later would express this principle: "For me, living [is] Christ, and dying [is] profit" (Phil. 1:21).

The purpose of Job's suffering for blessing had been fulfilled and the suffering was removed. Not only was he relieved of suffering but his escrow blessings were restored and doubled (Job 42:10). Job's glorification of God through suffering was perpetuated as glorification of God through blessing.

NEW TESTAMENT COMMENTARY ON JOB

The application of Job's suffering to the Church Age believer is recorded in the epistle of James. There Job's tenacity is related to the essence of God. The focus of the doctrine of suffering is not suffering itself but the character of God.

> Remember, we consider blessed [happy] those who have endured [persevered in suffering for blessing]. You have heard of the perseverance of Job and you have seen the conclusion brought about by the Lord, because the Lord is full of compassion and mercy. (James 5:11)

Job had successfully passed numerous phases of suffering for blessing. In spiritual self-esteem, he had encountered providential preventive suffering in the four categories that serve as warm-ups for momentum testing. Having passed these tests, he gained spiritual autonomy and faced the four categories of momentum testing which propelled him into spiritual maturity. Then as a mature believer he suffered the sudden but temporary loss of escrow blessings in three increments of evidence testing.

Even if we do not consider self-induced misery or divine discipline, which undoubtedly afflicted Job in spiritual childhood, the profile of Job's life contains a tremendous amount of suffering. And yet he is identified as a happy man. The only explanation for Job's happiness and the only means of genuine, sustained happiness for anyone in the devil's world is the execution of God's plan. The Lord is the one who brought about the conclusion of happiness in Job's life, not just at the end of his life but with increasing strength at each step along the way.

Suffering is a fact of life in Satan's kingdom. Only by learning Bible doctrine and utilizing divine assets can the believer avoid becoming a victim of suffering. As members of the royal family of God living in the palace of the divine dynasphere, we possess assets that are unprecedented in all angelic and human history. At the moment of faith in Christ, God created us a new spiritual species, a new royal dynasty, capable of exercising the omnipotence made available to us for the advance to spiritual maturity. That forward momentum overcomes suffering at every step.

Prior to the Church Age, a few believers, like Job, utilized a limited availability of divine omnipotence and achieved marvelous results both in personal happiness and in evidence for the prosecution. Now every Christian has maximum divine power available for the execution of God's protocol plan. By fulfilling divine mandates, which are consolidated as a royal protocol in the palace of the divine dynasphere, we utilize His infinite power. As the Church Age believer advances in the divine dynasphere he increasingly shares the happiness of God and glorifies Him to the maximum in the angelic conflict.

...n outstanding example for us, but his terrible sufferings were not ...evere as the pain endured by the humanity of Christ. Nor were Job's ...dynamics as powerful as were our Lord's in the prototype divine dynasphere. The humanity of our Lord Jesus Christ is the supreme example and precedent for utilizing divine omnipotence under pressure. He established the pattern for the royal family. He endured the horror of the cross with perfect inner happiness. We now can utilize the same system of power that sustained the humanity of Christ. As we overcome the suffering in our lives, we can appreciate, to a degree that Job would never understand, that "the Lord is full of compassion and mercy."

Suffering, Happiness, and the Essence of God

SUFFERING POSES NO THREAT to the plan of God. The pain of adversity is real, but even the most horrible suffering loses its dread in the light of the grace of God. In fact, the protocol plan of God *incorporates* suffering and *uses* adversity for the purpose of blessing the advancing believer. Suffering tests his understanding and application of doctrine. As he passes each test, he confirms and deepens his love for the Lord Jesus Christ and hones his use of the problem-solving devices for spiritual adulthood.

God loves every believer with His infinite, personal love. *Nothing* "shall be able to separate us from the love of God, which is in Christ Jesus our Lord" (Rom. 8:39). God never desires any harm to come to any member of the royal family. Yet suffering exists; believers face severe pain of body and anguish of soul.

This study of suffering has explained from Scripture how and why Christian suffering coexists with God's love for the believer. Most Christian suffering is self-induced misery under the law of volitional responsibility. Believers defy God's desires and bring harm on themselves. They ignore the precise protocol of God's plan, and such ignorance and arrogance merely complicate the problems of living in the devil's world.

.sistent self-induced misery, all suffering in the Christian way
.ed by God for the believer's benefit. Even unbearable divine
...ne is a gracious attempt to restore the believer to the divine dynasphere.
Indeed, the fact that *ignoring* and *violating* the protocol plan of God cause self-induced misery demonstrates by contrast that *learning* and *executing* divine protocol bring blessing. No degree of suffering can destory the blessing of life in the palace of the divine dynasphere.

Through suffering God reveals His marvelous power to sustain and bless the believer who follows divine protocol and utilizes his royal assets. Suffering focuses the attention of the believer, who is imperfect and prone to distractions. Adversity compels him to remember, apply, and thus more fully understand the Bible doctrine in his soul. Suffering accelerates his spiritual growth. Suffering helps him see the essence of God.

Suffering is inevitable for the believer on earth. Every Christian must prepare himself to meet and conquer adversity as part of advancing to spiritual maturity. To be ready for suffering when it comes, he must give first priority to learning, metabolizing, and applying Bible doctrine, as consistently taught by a theologically orthodox pastor. Each believer must receive, retain, and recall the Word of God in the power of the Holy Spirit in the divine dynasphere.

The purpose of this book is to delineate systematically and comprehensively the divine viewpoint regarding Christian suffering. In the midst of adversity, the spiritually adult believer shares the happiness of God as a consequence of thinking divine viewpoint and consistently utilizing the omnipotence of God. We must think as God thinks and regard adversity in the light of His marvelous objectives for our lives. By perception of the doctrines pertinent to suffering, we gain access to the problem-solving devices that convert suffering into blessing. Each problem-solving device is efficacious because of its relationship to the essence of God.

REBOUND is based on divine *justice* and *faithfulness*. Because God judged all the sins of the human race at the cross, He is always consistent in forgiving our sins when we name them to Him (1 John 1:9).

The FAITH-REST DRILL depends upon God's *omnipotence, immutability, veracity,* and *faithfulness,* which stand behind all His promises. Furthermore, His *integrity* and *omniscience* guarantee that God is rational and that true conclusions can be reached logically from doctrinal premises.

HOPE as a problem-solving device also depends on divine *veracity.* Hope is our absolute confidence that God is true to His word. Divine veracity is manifested in pertinent biblical doctrines that cause us to anticipate future blessings that will glorify God to the maximum.

PERSONAL LOVE FOR GOD focuses on His absolute *righteousness,* which divine attribute is the object of His own *personal love.* Only when directed toward perfect God does our personal love become a virtue in itself.

IMPERSONAL LOVE FOR ALL MANKIND is modeled after God's *impersonal love* for the fallen, degenerate, spiritually dead human race. God never feels threatened by sinful man. He saved us because of His own *integrity,* not because we deserved salvation. Therefore, impersonal love for the entire human race on the basis of our Christian integrity follows the pattern of *divine self-esteem* and *divine love* as expressions of the integrity of God.

Finally, the believer's HAPPINESS as a problem-solving device is sharing the very *happiness* of God. The believer enjoys God's happiness as a consequence of learning, metabolizing, and applying Bible doctrine. He thinks God's thoughts and shares His viewpoint concerning Christian suffering.

By inculcating our souls with the thinking of God as revealed in the Scripture, by applying His truths to the circumstances of our lives, by executing divine protocol in the power of His omnipotence, we come to appreciate who and what God is. We grow in our respect for the one "worthy of praise and glorification." Our resultant contentment is the most powerful solution to the frustrations, the difficulties, and the heartaches that we cannot avoid. No suffering in life is too great for the plan of God.

Divine Judgment in Contrast to Divine Discipline

GOD'S DEALINGS WITH UNBELIEVERS IN TIME

AN ESSENTIAL DISTINCTION must be understood concerning God's punitive actions against man during the course of human history: divine *discipline* is not the same as divine *judgment*. Discipline is reserved for believers; judgment is for unbelievers but may affect all categories of the human race and fallen angels as well. The believer suffers only in time, never in eternity (Rev. 21:4). He is disciplined in time—individually and collectively—but his appointment with eternal judgment was canceled when he believed in Christ (Heb. 9:27; Rom. 8:1). The unbeliever suffers in time and in eternity. He may face individual and collective divine judgment in time; he will receive individual judgment throughout eternity.

Because God deals with unbelievers as well as with believers, the doctrine of divine judgment toward unbelievers on earth reveals God's justice and grace and also explains a tremendous amount of worldwide suffering. Like discipline to the believer, divine judgment in time to the unbeliever is administered in progressive stages:

1. JUDGMENT BY PAIN

2. JUDGMENT BY DEATH

3. JUDGMENT BY FINESSE

Judgment by pain and judgment by death are the progressive stages of divine judgment in time. Finesse judgment presents a principle by which Jesus Christ controls history despite Satan's rule over the world.

JUDGMENT BY PAIN

The first stage of divine judgment, judgment by pain, is an expression of God's grace to the unbeliever, just as warning discipline expresses God's grace to the believer. Evangelism is the objective of all judgment by pain. On the cross Jesus Christ paid for the salvation of every human being who will ever live, whether or not that person ever believes in Christ (1 John 2:2). Our Lord has accomplished completely all the work of salvation; nothing remains for an individual to do but to accept the work of Christ on his behalf. The way of salvation is simple and plain: "Believe in the Lord Jesus, and you shall be saved" (Acts 16:31).

Because God will never violate man's free will, He must wait for positive volition before He can actually apply salvation to any individual. In grace, God has already gone to the farthest extreme—the judgment of His own Son. With the work fully accomplished, God continues to do all that is possible to bring the unbeliever to eternal salvation.

Normal evangelism involves the presentation of the Gospel. God has an obligation to supply Gospel information to all who are receptive and desire to know Him when first they become aware of His existence. Their positive volition at the point of God-consciousness usually remains positive at Gospel hearing. They believe in Christ with no greater stimulus than a clear presentation of true Gospel information. But for others, who are indifferent or antagonistic to their first awareness of God—negative volition at God-consciousness—God still repeatedly extends the opportunity to be saved.

> The Lord is not slow about His promise [to judge unbelievers], as some count slowness, but is patient toward you, not wishing for any to perish but for all to come to repentance [change of mind about Christ]. (2 Pet. 3:9, NASB)

When normal evangelism fails, God shifts gears into crisis evangelism. Crisis evangelism involves judgment by pain. As with discipline to the recalcitrant believer, judgment by pain to the negative unbeliever is designed to shock him into temporary objectivity. The pain proves his inherent weakness, his need of a relationship with God, and provides a lucid moment in which the Gospel can be considered.

The salvation of the apostle Paul is a dramatic example of crisis evangelism. Saul of Tarsus, as Paul was known during his meteoric career as a Pharisee, was a zealous persecutor and murderer of Christians. Only when struck blind on the road to Damascus did he objectively consider the Gospel of Christ. Judgment by pain was responsible for the salvation of the greatest believer who has ever lived.

JUDGMENT BY DEATH

If repeated judgment by pain fails to bring the unbeliever to faith in Christ, judgment by death becomes the only alternative. Judgment by death against unbelievers who have hardened their volition against God is divine protection of the human race. The evils of cosmic influence must be restrained; therefore, following a period of grace before judgment, God removes the cancer from society in order to preserve believers and perpetuate mankind.

The Pharaoh of the Exodus, Amenhotep II, suffered increasingly intense pain in the plagues against Egypt. By persistently rejecting the message of Moses, Pharaoh "hardened his heart" (Ex. 8:32). His obstinance through the first five plagues locked him in the cosmic system beyond any possibility of escape so that he was incapable of right decisions. For him, faith in Christ, who is the God of Israel, had become impossible; he had shackled his own volition (Rom. 2:5; 2 Cor. 4:3-4).

When further grace becomes pointless, God normally removes the unbeliever from this life. However, God did not remove Pharaoh but "allowed [him] to stand . . . in order to proclaim [God's] name through all the earth" (Ex. 9:16). Following the fifth plague, "*God* hardened Pharaoh's heart" by allowing him to continue making negative decisions (Ex. 9:12; Rom. 9:17-18). Pharaoh's deceitful negative volition presented an opportunity for God to evangelize the world through further displays of divine power (Ex. 7:3; 11:9; Josh. 2:9-10). In the final divine exploitation of Pharaoh's stubbornness, God administered judgment by death as the tenth plague.

Pharaoh was not merely a private individual; he ruled an empire. His negative volition typified the obstinance of many of his subjects, who shared his rejection of salvation and applauded his decisions to retain the Jews as a race of slaves. The tenth plague killed the eldest son of every household in Egypt that joined Pharaoh in rejecting the message of Moses.

God's action was not indiscriminate genocide. Many Egyptian families believed in the God of Israel and survived that night of judgment, and many joined the Exodus as the "mixed multitude" of Gentiles (Ex. 11:3; 12:38). Furthermore, the Egyptian infants who died before reaching the point of God-consciousness, which is also the age of accountability, received automatic salvation (2 Sam. 12:23).[74] Pharaoh himself did not die in the tenth plague but was allowed to release the Jews and then precipitate yet another crisis, at the Red Sea, which again glorified God (Ex. 14:13-18).

Judgment by death was the extreme measure taken by God to remove individual negative unbelievers and in doing so to demolish hardened opposition to the Exodus. God's promises to Israel and to mankind hinged on the national freedom of the Jews through whom would eventually come all client nation concepts, the Mosaic Law, the written canon of Scripture, and above all the Messiah, the Lord Jesus Christ. God was protecting the human race, fulfilling His unconditional covenants, and advancing His plan of grace by administering judgment by death.

JUDGMENT BY FINESSE

The third category of divine judgment demonstrates the genius of Jesus Christ in controlling history despite the fact that Satan rules the world. In finesse judgment, our Lord uses evil to destroy evil.

Arrogance cannot tolerate arrogance; one form of evil despises another form of evil. An intense, human-good crusader cannot abide an insouciant rounder. The libertine regards the religious reformer with contempt. One form of prejudice despises another form of prejudice. The Nazi hates the Communist. Each is hostile toward the other. The very multiplicity of gates into the cosmic system, which successfully appeals to the weaknesses of so many different kinds of people, is the system's ultimate flaw. The greatest destroyer of evil is evil.

For the wraths of man shall praise Thee. (Ps. 76:10*a*, NASB)

The sons of Sceva were sorcerers who traveled throughout the region around Ephesus discrediting Paul and promoting themselves at his expense (Acts 19:13-20). Thoroughly evil men, they posed as exorcists, claiming to cast demons out of the possessed.[75] Although they were permanent residents of the

---

74. See *Integrity of God*, p. 67.
75. See *Demonism*.

cosmic system, these unbelievers tried to use the names of Christ and Paul in incantations aimed at exorcising a demon from a young man. The evil demon perfectly squelched the arrogance of these evil charlatans:

> I recognize Jesus and I know about Paul, but who are you?
> (Acts 19:15*b*)

The demon then attacked the Sons of Sceva so that they fled wounded from the house. As a result "the name of the Lord Jesus was being magnified" (Acts 19:17) in the vindicated doctrinal ministry of Paul.

The principle of finesse judgment applies to nations as well as to individuals. An evil nation is often permitted power in history for the sole purpose of being used by God to judge another evil nation. Israel is God's chosen nation, but in 721 B.C., again in 586 B.C., and again in A.D. 70, God's client nation had degenerated into evil as its citizens lived perpetually in the cosmic system. The pivot of mature believers had shrunk; the spin-off of cosmic believers was dragging down the entire nation. On each of these three occasions, God raised up an evil empire to punish Israel. Evil$_1$ destroyed Evil$_2$. In 721 B.C. the Assyrian Empire destroyed the Northern Kingdom of Israel. In 586 B.C. the Chaldean Empire destroyed the Southern Kingdom. In A.D. 70 the Roman Empire destroyed religious, pharisaical, rebellious Judea.

Finesse judgment of collective groups is not reserved strictly for degenerate client nations. As foretold in prophecy, God will destroy the worldwide religion of the Tribulation, which will be sponsored by Satan, with an attack by a rival political entity, also sponsored by Satan (Rev. 17:16-17). God's objective will be achieved by Satan when the devil betrays one part of his own cosmic system in a treacherous ploy to increase the power of another part.